ARK OF GOD

The Incredible Power of the Ark of the Covenant

David Hatcher Childress

Adventures Unlimited Press

ARK OF GOD

The Incredible Power of the Ark of the Covenant

Adventures Unlimited Press

Ark of God:
The Incredible Power of the Ark of the Covenant

ISBN 13: 978-1-939149-49-7

Published by:
Adventures Unlimited Press
One Adventure Place
Kempton, Illinois 60946 USA
auphq@frontiernet.net

AdventuresUnlimitedPress.com

10 9 8 7 6 5 4 3 2 1

An artist's conception of Solomon's temple with the Ark of the Covenant.

Thanks to the many people who have helped me in researching and finishing this book including Jennifer Bolm, Chas Berlin, Graham Hancock, Ann Madden Jones and many others.

ARK OF GOD

The Incredible Power of the Ark of the Covenant

David Hatcher Childress

TABLE OF CONTENTS

CHAPTER ONE

RAIDERS OF THE LOST ARK

"Jones, archeology is like a religion,
but you and I have fallen from the true faith."
—French archeologist Belloq to Indiana Jones,
Raiders of the Lost Ark

The World Explorers Club, of which I am the founder, took a trip to Ethiopia, and during the two weeks that our group was there we had the chance to visit the northern city of Axum in Tigray Province. It is here in a small church protected by a heavy iron fence that Ethiopians believe the biblical Ark of the Covenant is kept.

Upon returning to the United States from that trip in early November 2014, I was surprised to receive a message from a friend that linked to the following article on the website worldnewsdailyreport.com. The headline was "Ethiopia: Ark of Covenant Reported Stolen by Church Authorities" (my friend, knowing I had just been to Ethiopia, asked facetiously if I had anything to do with the strange heist):

> Axum: The Patriarch of the Ethiopian Orthodox Tewahedo Church, His Holiness Abune Mathias, announced this morning that the most prized biblical treasure in the world, the Ark of Covenant, was stolen last night from the catacombs of the Church of Our Lady Mary of Zion. The guardians of the artefact were allegedly put to sleep through the use of chemical weapons, before the robbers entered the crypt and stole the precious Holy item.

The criminal operation was reportedly executed by a team of 12 to 16 highly-trained professionals who travelled aboard two black military helicopters. They landed less than 500 meters away from their objective after allegedly arriving from the East. The men were dressed in black military-style uniforms and seemed to function as a well coordinated army unit. They were equipped with night-vision equipment and armed with high caliber weapons, giving them an incredible advantage over the local security forces.

The protection of the Ark was left to a group [of] untrained volunteers with AK-47s. The Church did not see any need for more security as the Ark was expected to protect itself from people with impure intentions.

The 11 guards and armed volunteers present on the site to defend the Ark were neutralized by the thieves, using some high technology grenades that released a rare opium-based soporific gas. The robbers then went into strenuous labor, using jackhammers and explosives to enlarge the corridors in various locations inside the catacombs leading to the Ark, in order to be able to remove the large chest from its underground vault.

The entire operation was over in less than an hour, an incredibly short time considering the number of obstacles that had to be overcome. This amazing efficiency suggests that the thieves had repeated the operation and had carefully prepared their crime.

Few signs of the crime were visible this morning on the site, but a lot of damage was reported inside the catacombs under the building.

The Ethiopian Orthodox Church claims to possess the Ark of the Covenant in a chapel in the small town of Axum, in their country's northern Highlands. It arrived nearly 3,000 years ago, they say, and has been guarded by a succession of virgin monks who, once anointed, are forbidden to set foot outside the chapel grounds until they die. No one except the Guardians are ever allowed to see the Ark, not even the Patriarch of the Church.

The story is told in the *Kebra Nagast* (in Ge'ez language, *Glory of the Kings*), Ethiopia's chronicle of its royal line: the Queen of Sheba, one of its first rulers, traveled to Jerusalem to benefit from King Solomon's wisdom; on her way home, she bore Solomon's son, Menelik. A few years later, Menelik went to visit his father, and on his return journey was accompanied by the firstborn sons of some Israelite nobles—who, unbeknown to him, stole the ark and carried it with them to Ethiopia.

When Menelik learned of the theft, he reasoned that since the ark's frightful powers hadn't destroyed his retinue, it must be God's will that it remain with him. It was then presumably kept in the islands of Lake Tana for about four hundred years and finally taken to Axum, where it was kept safe for more than two thousand years.

The disappearance of the Ark is certainly dramatic news for the Ethiopian Orthodox Church, as much of its prestige came from the possession of the relic and many of its rituals were centered on it. His Holiness Abune Mathias was visibly emotional when he made the announcement [and] many of the journalists and faithfuls present for the press conference, burst into tears when they heard the news.

This was a fascinating story, but having just been to this church, I could not picture it being real. Some details like the opium-based sleeping gas and general military assault on the church just didn't ring true, and indeed, it turns out that the worldnewsdailyreport website is in fact a hoax news website similar to *The Onion* humor website. The rather fantastic stories on the worldnewsdailyreport website are written in such a manner as to be believable, and its subtle humor is lost on many people who think that the stories are genuine news articles.

Many quite incredible stories are released by authentic news outlets daily and the only thing that is fabricated in this amazing

13

story is that an assault team stormed the church in Axum and stole the Ark. The Ethiopian Church does indeed claim that the famous Ark of the Covenant of the Bible is kept in that small church—a church that has a single priest as its caretaker. A tall and heavy iron bar fence surrounds the church and other priests occupy several larger churches nearby. No one, not even the Prime Minster of Ethiopia, may enter the church. All Ethiopians are aware of this church and its importance.

Indeed, because the Ark of the Covenant is kept in this small church in Axum the mayor of the town will not allow any mosques to be built inside the city limits. Mosque building is a relatively new activity in this part of northern Tigray province and mosques have recently been built in nearby towns. When asked about this prohibition, the mayor of Axum was reported to have said, "When they let us build a Christian church in Mecca we will allow them to build a mosque here."

Ethiopia is a rugged, fertile and mountainous country with a rich and mysterious history that includes the belief that they have the biblical relic. How did it get to Ethiopia anyway? But first, what is the Ark of Covenant?

Indiana Jones and the Ark of the Covenant

It has recently come out that the most re-watched actor is Harrison Ford and the most re-watched movie is *Raiders of the Lost Ark*. This movie, one of the most popular films ever made, is about an archaeologist, Indiana Jones, who is enlisted by the US Government just prior to World War II to find the Ark of the Covenant. It would be found inside an Egyptian temple at the lost city of Tanis in the Nile Delta. After many adventures, Indiana Jones and his friends discover the resting place of the Ark, but the Nazis who are also after the Ark take it away from them.

Indiana gets the Ark back, and attempts to take it via ship to the United States, but the ship is captured by the Nazis, and the Ark is taken to an island in the Mediterranean where it is opened after a Qabalistic ritual. The opening of the Ark unleashes an unholy power that proceeds to destroy all who look upon it—and then the Ark

A scene featuring the Ark from *Raiders of the Lost Ark*.

reseals itself. At the end of the movie, the Ark is taken to a gigantic warehouse in Washington D.C. where it is crated and stored at the Smithsonian Institution—presumably lost forever in a secret warehouse. Indiana Jones rediscovers this lost crate briefly at the beginning of the fourth movie, *Indiana Jones and the Kingdom of the Crystal Skull*.

So what was the Ark of the Covenant, anyway? The Ark of the Covenant first appears in the Old Testament story of the Exodus. This book says that after about a year of wandering in the Sinai desert, Yahweh (in the form of a thick cloud) communicated with Moses on Mount Sinai during his 40-day stay upon the mountain (Exodus 19:20; 24:18). Yahweh supposedly showed Moses the pattern for the tabernacle, a sort of mobile temple the people would use to worship in the wilderness. Yahweh also gave him the detailed instructions for the construction of the Ark of the Covenant to be made of shittim (acacia) wood to house the Tablets of Stone upon which were written the Ten Commandments.

The Book of Exodus says that the wooden Ark is to be 2½ cubits in length, 1½ in breadth, and 1½ in height (approximately 52×31×31 inches). It is to be plated entirely with gold, and a crown or molding of gold is to be put around it. Four rings of gold are to be attached to its four legs, and through these, two staves of shittim wood overlaid with gold for carrying the Ark are to be inserted— one on each side—and these are not to be removed. The box that is the Ark is therefore three boxes together: an inner box of gold, a

15

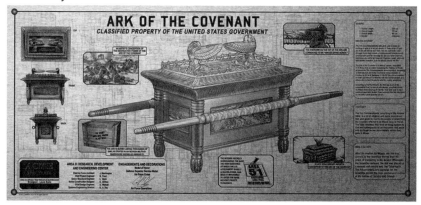

A poster for promoting *Raiders of the Lost Ark* products.

middle box of wood, and an outer box also made of gold.

On top of the gold and wood box is to be placed a large gold statue called a kapporet (traditionally known as the "Mercy Seat" in Christian translations). This gold statue was to be of two angels—cherubim—facing each other and holding a shallow golden bowl in the center of the lid. Upon this golden bowl supposedly dwelt a cloud of light known as the Shekinah Glory. The complete assembly of golden box and cherubim statue is finally to be placed behind a veil (Parochet) in the tabernacle—a series of tent-walls that mark off the priestly area around which the huge Israelite community of tens of thousands is encamped—a full description of which is given in Exodus 26.

When carried, the Ark was also hidden under a large veil made of skins and blue cloth, always carefully concealed, even from the eyes of the priests who carried it. The veiled Ark was carried about 2,000 cubits in advance of the larger group by the Levite priests when the people were on the move. Moses during this period began wearing a veil to cover his face, as it was strangely illuminated after his encounter with Yahweh on Mount Sinai.

During the early sojourns with the Ark it levitates and flies; it kills hundreds of people; it causes a skin disease on one of Aaron's wives; it parts rivers... it does many things—some credible, some not.

In Numbers 16 we are told the strange tale of a group of 250 Israelite noble sons of various tribes who have decided to rebel against Moses and his brother Aaron and their long, arduous trek to the Promised Land.

Moses and Aaron gather up these rebellious tribal leaders and tell them that they should let the holy Ark of the Covenant decide who should command the great host of Israelites. The 250 rebellious young leaders agree to this, and Moses and Aaron lead them inside the Holy of Holies tent that is within the very large tabernacle enclosure.

With each person holding an incense censer of brass, the group enters the Holy of Holies (Numbers 16:17-18). Yahweh tells Moses and Aaron to separate themselves from the rest of the group, which they do, and then fall flat upon their faces. Everyone else in the tent is consumed by fire from the Ark of the Covenant and killed. Later Moses tells their fathers and the elders of Israel, "touch nothing of theirs, lest ye be consumed in all their sins" (Numbers 16:26).

After the death of Moses, Joshua leads the Israelites down to the Jordan River. When the Ark was carried by the Levite priests into the bed of the Jordan River, the waters parted as God had parted the waters of the Red Sea, opening a pathway for the entire host to pass through (Joshua 3:15–16; 4:7–18).

Joshua then led the Israelites into Canaan where they laid siege to the city of Jericho. There, Joshua says that God spoke to him, telling him to march around the city once every day for six days with seven priests carrying ram horns in front of the Ark of the Covenant. On the seventh day Joshua told them to march around the city seven times and then the priests were to blow their horns. At this point Joshua ordered the people to shout, and the walls of the city collapsed so that the Israelites were able to charge directly into the center. The city was completely destroyed, with every adult, child and animal in it slaughtered by Joshua's army. Only a woman named Rahab and her family were spared and this was because she had hidden two spies sent by Joshua in her home. Afterward, Joshua had the remains of the city burned and cursed any man who would rebuild Jericho to do so at the cost of his firstborn son (Joshua 6:4–20).

After this the Ark was taken to an ancient city called Shiloh. Shiloh, north of Jerusalem, became the first capital of Israel and

17

An old print of the Israelites carrying the Ark of the Covenant.

held the Ark until the First Temple was built at Jerusalem by King Solomon. After that it was placed in a special room in the temple tabernacle known as the Holy of Holies, likened to a throne room, where one entered the divine presence of God. The Holy of Holies was located in the westernmost end of the temple building, being a perfect cube: 20 cubits by 20 cubits by 20 cubits. The inside was kept in total darkness and contained the Ark of the Covenant, in which was placed the Tablets of the Covenant. According to Hebrews 9:4 in the New Testament, Aaron's rod and a pot of manna were also placed inside the Ark.

Theoretically the Ark remained in the Holy of Holies inside the tabernacle at Jerusalem for about 350 years until 586 BC when the huge Babylonian army of Nebuchadnezzar attacked the city. The Babylonians were jealous of Israel's wealth and power, and had for many generations sought to destroy the country, which was at the crossroads of most of the major trade routes of the day, with ports on both the Mediterranean and the Red Sea.

Jerusalem could not withstand the siege, and finally the city fell. The temple was looted and destroyed, and the Israelites were taken into captivity in Babylon. Yet, where was the Ark? Was it destroyed or taken back to Babylon? This seems unlikely, as such an important artifact as the Ark would have been mentioned as part of the spoils, which it was not. In Jeremiah 52 the spoils taken from the temple in Jerusalem are enumerated, but the Ark of the Covenant is not listed. It would seem that such an important object would have been mentioned if the Babylonians were now in possession of the Ark and the gold statues of its lid.

Apparently the Ark of the Covenant was not in the temple at the time that the Babylonians sacked it. Had it been removed to a secret cave beneath the temple or to some other place outside of Jerusalem? Perhaps it had vanished from the Holy of Holies at some time between 950 BC and 600 BC. The Ethiopian book the *Kebra Nagast* makes this claim, as does the theory that the Ark was taken to Ireland and Scotland by the Jewish-Egyptian Queen Scota. Both of these stories will be examined carefully in later chapters.

So, what became of the Ark? When did it actually disappear from the temple? Was it destroyed or taken to some secret location yet to be found? What was this object and why was it so important anyway? Perhaps the whole story of the Ark of the Covenant is a mere myth—how could these events have occurred as described in the Bible?

But, for all of the biblical tales, movies, and strange adventures in search of the fabled object we are still led to wonder—what exactly is this Ark of the Covenant? What strange power—a power of the god Yahweh—did the wood and metal device have? How could the Ark fly through the air? Was there some other machine that was part of the Ark? In the next few chapters we will examine the stories and the power of the Ark of the Covenant.

The Ark of the Covenant with the tabernacle in the wilderness.

An artist's conception of the Ark of the Covenant.

CHAPTER TWO

THE HISTORY SURROUNDING THE ARK

Any sufficiently advanced technology is
indistinguishable from magic.
— *Arthur C. Clarke*

The Holy of Holies and the Tabernacle

There are two different tabernacles that are referred to in the Old Testament. One is the tabernacle in King Solomon's Temple, which was made of stone with a special room to house the Ark of the Covenant. Before this, while the Ark was on the move, it was kept in a series of tents and fabric walls that was known as the Tabernacle in the Wilderness.

The Holy of Holies was the inner sanctuary within the tabernacle and temple in Jerusalem where the Ark of the Covenant was kept. The Holy of Holies was located in the westernmost end of the temple building, which we will see later in the chapter was a pretty interesting location. The inside was in total darkness and contained the Ark of the Covenant, in which was placed the Tablets of the Covenant, otherwise known as the Ten Commandments, Aaron's rod and a pot of manna. The Mercy Seat was where the Divine Presence would manifest. At times the Divine Presence would speak to Moses, but at other times it would discharge some powerful energy and literally zap the people who stood around the Ark.

The Holy of Holies was entered once a year by the High Priest on the Day of Atonement (Yom Kippur), to sprinkle the blood of sacrificial animals — a bull offered as atonement for the priest and his household, and a goat offered as atonement for the people. The

An artist's conception of the pillar of smoke and fire.

priest also offered incense upon the Ark of the Covenant and the Mercy Seat which sat on top of the Ark in the First Temple. The Second Temple had no ark and the blood was sprinkled where the Ark would have been and the incense was left on the Foundation Stone. The animal was sacrificed on the Brazen Altar and the blood was carried into the most holy place. Golden censers were also found in the most holy place.

Visitors went into the tabernacle entering by way of the East Room. The room was without windows and was illuminated solely by light created by what was known as the Golden Candlestick. The Candlestick, also known as a menorah, had six branches and a shaft, upon which rested seven lamps. The purest olive oil was used in the lamps and they burned continuously.

Inside the East Room to the right stood a table upon which were arranged 12 loaves of shewbread. There were two piles, each containing six loaves of the unleavened bread. The bread was representative of the service of mankind, which culminated in the planting and harvesting of this grain, and symbolized the 12 tribes of Israel.

The tabernacle was to contain:

1) A wooden Ark, gilded inside and outside, for the Tablets of

An old print of the 12 tribes of the Israeliites in their camp around the tabernacle.

the Covenant, with a pure gold cover as the Mercy Seat for the Divine Presence;

2) A gilt table for the shewbread;

3) A golden menorah, a lampstand of seven oil lamps for a light never to be extinguished;

4) The dwelling, including the curtains for the roof, the walls made of boards resting on silver feet and held together by wooden bolts, the purple curtain veiling the Holy of Holies, and the outer curtain;

5) A sacrificial altar made of bronzed boards for its korban;

6) The outer court formed by pillars resting on bronze pedestals and connected by hooks and crossbars of silver, with embroidered curtains;

7) The recipe for preparation of the oil for the lampstand.

The Urim and Thummim and the Second Temple

In 586 BC, the Babylonians attacked Jerusalem and destroyed Solomon's Temple. A large portion of the inhabitants of Jerusalem and the surrounding area was taken into captivity in Babylon. They were released some years later and returned to Jerusalem circa 536 BC. However, there is no record of what became of the Ark in the biblical books of Kings and Chronicles.

The Second Temple was built around 516 BC and lasted until about 70 AD when it was mostly destroyed by the Romans. Since some of the original artifacts were lost after the destruction of the First Temple, the Second Temple lacked the following holy relics: the Ark of the Covenant containing the Tablets of Stone, the Urim and Thummim (divination objects contained in the High Priest's breastplate, or Hoshen); the holy oil; and the sacred fire. The golden censers may have been replaced and would be standing in the Holy of Holies, and the sacrificial blood was sprinkled where the Ark would have been and the incense was left on the Foundation Stone.

The mysterious Urim and Thummim are not well described in the Bible, and there has been much speculation as to exactly what they were. From the contexts in which they are mentioned,

A High Priest of Israel wearing the special garments with gold thread and gems.

it is implied that they are some kind of objects used in a yes-or-no prophecy game. The Jewish Encyclopedia describes them as:

> Objects connected with the breastplate of the high priest, and used as a kind of divine oracle. ...It is called a "breastplate of judgment" ("ḥoshen ha-mishpaṭ"); it is four-square and double; and the twelve stones were not put inside the ḥoshen, but on the outside. It is related in Lev. viii. 7-8 that when, in compliance with the command in Ex. xxix. 1-37, Moses consecrated Aaron and his sons as priests, "He [Moses] put upon him [Aaron] the coat, and girded him with the girdle, and clothed him with the robe, and put the ephod upon him, and he girded him with the cunningly woven band [A. V. "curious girdle"] of the ephod, and bound it unto him therewith. And he put the breastplate upon him: and in the breastplate he put the Urim and the Thummim." Deut. xxxiii. 8 (R. V.), in the blessing of Moses, reads: "And of Levi he said: Thy Thummim and thy Urim are with thy godly one, whom thou didst prove at Massah, with whom thou didst strive at the waters of Meribah."

Thummim is widely considered to mean innocent, while Urim comes from a root word meaning lights, so some kind of reference to "revelation and truth" might be inferred. Wikipedia says that most of the Talmudic rabbis, and the Jewish-Roman historian Josephus, follow the belief that divination by the Urim and Thummim involved questions being answered by great rays of light shining out of certain jewels on the breastplate. Some even believed that the 12 stones, which were inscribed with the names of the 12 tribes of Israel, each stood for certain letters, and words might be formed from the succession of lights displayed. Most people think it was a simpler affair than that, and as indicated above, was more of a yes-or-no proposition. In this sense, drawing out the Thummim from behind the breastplate might mean innocent, and the Urim guilty. Or one meant yes and one no.

The Urim and Thummim were kept inside the breastplate, so

some scholars think that they were relatively small items. I tend to think they could be somewhat sizeable, and were probably pieces of crystal. 1 Samuel 28:6 reads: "He inquired of the Lord, but the Lord did not answer him by dreams or Urim or prophets." This has been widely interpreted to mean there were three specific ways the Lord communicated with the people—through dreams, prophets and the Urim and Thummim. Crystals are well known for their electrical and optical properties, and are widely used in communications devices today. Maybe the high priests had an actual crystal communications device to learn the will of god.

The whole subject of what the priests wore, which was very strictly detailed in the Bible, is interesting. As referenced in the above quote from the Jewish Encyclopedia, Moses had minute instructions as to how to outfit the priests. The usual priestly vestments had eight components: linen trousers, a linen tunic, an intricate belt or sash (called in early Bible translations the "curious girdle"), a robe, an apron called an ephod, the breastplate, a turban, and a metal band attached to the turban with a blue sash.

As we have touched upon and will see in greater detail soon, the Ark had an unfortunate habit of harming people in its vicinity. Is the special garb the priests were to wear some kind of protective gear? We learn in Ezekiel 44:17-19 that the priests were to wear only linen garments into the inner court and temple, no wool, since "They must not wear anything that makes them perspire." When they leave the inner sanctuary and go to the outer courtyard where people are, they are to change clothes and leave the ones they were wearing inside, "so that the people are not consecrated through contact with their garments." By "consecrated" do they mean "contaminated"? Did the Ark emit some kind of radiation?

Something was certainly going on. Says Exodus 28:33-35:

> Make pomegranates of blue, purple and scarlet yarn around the hem of the robe, with gold bells between them. The gold bells and the pomegranates are to alternate around the hem of the robe. Aaron must wear it when he ministers. The sound of the bells will be heard when he enters the Holy

Place before the Lord and when he comes out, so that he will not die.

Exodus 28:42-43 instructs:

Make linen undergarments as a covering for the body, reaching from the waist to the thigh. Aaron and his sons must wear them whenever they enter the tent of meeting or approach the altar to minister in the Holy Place, so that they will not incur guilt and die.

What is so dangerous about entering the holy place of the Ark that being a priest was a deadly profession? We will explore a very interesting theory on that subject in chapter six. In that regard, it is important to note that many of the outer garments were to be interwoven with gold metallic thread. The metal strip attached to the turban was to be a gold plate that hung on the priest's forehead. Did these metals serve a purpose?

Later History

The Jewish Hasmonean Kingdom came into power ruling from Jerusalem circa 140 BC until it was conquered by the Romans in 63 BC. Salome Alexandra, the queen of the Hasmonean Kingdom,

A scene on the Arch of Titus in Rome showing loot from the Second Temple.

appointed her elder son Hyrcanus II as her heir but her younger son Aristobulus II was determined to have the throne. When Queen Salome Alexandra died, the younger brother grabbed the throne while his brother was out of town and a civil war began.

In 63 BC the Romans were fighting the Third Mithridatic War. The Roman general Pompey was in northern Syria fighting against the Armenians when he sent a lieutenant to investigate the conflict in Judea.

Both Hyrcanus and Aristobulus appealed to the Roman general for support. General Pompey returned to his tent for some days and began a march to Jerusalem. Aristobulus was tired of waiting and took his small army off to return to Jerusalem which his forces controlled. He was pursued by Pompey and the superior Roman army and therefore surrendered. Aristobulus's followers closed Jerusalem to Pompey's forces.

The Romans surrounded the city and then stormed it in 63 BC, making Jerusalem and Judea proper, Samaria and Idumea (biblical Edom) into the Roman province of Iudaea. The installation of Herod the Great (an Idumean) as king in 37 BC made Israel a Roman client state and marked the end of the Hasmonean dynasty.

The priests continued with the religious practices inside the temple during the siege. The temple was not looted or harmed by the Romans. Pompey himself went into the Holy of Holies and the next day ordered the priests to repurify the temple and resume the religious practices. Meanwhile King Herod began an expansion and restoration of the Second Temple. Religious worship there continued much as it had in the past.

In the Flavius Josephus book *The Jewish War* we are told that when the Roman emperor Caligula planned to place his own statue inside the temple, Herod's son Agrippa I was able to intervene and convince him not to do this.

Because of a Jewish rebellion against Rome in 66 AD the general Titus and his legions retook the city in 70 AD (74 years after Herod died) and destroyed much of the Second Temple, now called Herod's Temple by historians.

Many of the treasures of the Second Temple, including huge

menorah candelabra, were taken back to Rome and used to fund the building of the Colosseum and the Arch of Titus. The Arch of Titus is a famous monument today and features a Roman victory procession with soldiers carrying spoils from the temple, including a large menorah.

Although Jews were allowed to inhabit the destroyed city after 70 AD, Jerusalem and the remains of the Second Temple were dismantled by the Roman Emperor Hadrian at the end of the Bar Kokhba revolt in 135 AD. At this time he established a new city that he called Aelia Capitolina and Jews were banned from living there. A pagan Roman temple was set up on the former site of the Second Temple, known as Herod's Temple.

Herod's Temple and the Western Stone

As Muslim influence increased in the region, a small prayer house was built on the temple site by the Rashidun caliph Umar, but the first al-Aqsa Mosque was a large structure begun by the Umayyad caliph Abd al-Malik and finished by his son al-Walid in 705 AD. In 746 AD an earthquake destroyed the mosque and it was rebuilt by the Abbasid caliph al-Mansur in 754 AD. Another earthquake destroyed most of al-Aqsa Mosque in 1033, but two years later a new mosque was built by the Fatimid caliph Ali az-Zahir. This is basically the mosque which stands on Solomon's Temple Mount to the present day.

At present it is conjectured that the sanctified place once known as the Holy of Holies is located under the Dome of the Rock shrine which stands next to the al-Aqsa Mosque on the Temple Mount in Jerusalem. Most Orthodox Jews today completely avoid climbing up the Temple Mount, to prevent them from accidentally stepping on the Most Holy Place or any sanctified areas. Some ark hunters believe that the Ark of the Covenant may be hidden in a secret tunnel somewhere beneath the Dome of the Rock or the Wailing (Western) Wall of the temple, a scene of devotional Jewish worship.

In this Western Wall of the former Second Temple is one of the largest megalithic building stones ever used, the gigantic Western Stone. The Western Stone is a monolithic granite block that forms

The gigantic Western Stone at the base of Solomon's Temple. (*Wikipedia*)

part of the lower level of the Western Wall in Jerusalem. To see it a visitor needs to enter a tunnel along the northwestern side of the Western Wall on a guided tour.

Says Wikipedia:

> This largest stone in the Western Wall is visible within the Western Wall Tunnel and ranks as one of the heaviest objects ever lifted by human beings without powered

machinery.

It ranks as the fifth heaviest stone ever quarried and moved on Wikipedia. It has an estimated weight of 570 tons, making it smaller than the gigantic stones at Baalbek (at 600 to 1,000 tons) and slightly larger than the Great Stele at Axum (at 520 to 540 tons). The stone is 13.6 meters (44.6 feet) long and 3 meters (9.8 feet) high and has an estimated width of 3.3 meters (10.8 feet).

Wilson's Arch is the modern name for an ancient stone arch whose top is visible today in the northwest corner of the Western Wall. It once spanned 42 feet supporting a road and aqueduct that continued for 75 feet and allowed access to a gate that was level with the surface of the Temple Mount. It was first identified in 1864 by Charles William Wilson, for whom it is now named. Wilson had joined the British Ordnance Survey of Jerusalem in 1864, and then the surveying project to improve the city's water system.

What concerns us here is the gigantic cut-stone block so big and important that it is called by name, a mysterious block of stone that is baffling to archeologists of all types, and is perhaps the most controversial object at the Temple Mount. Who could have quarried this massive block of stone and placed it here at the northwestern corner of the foundation stones of the Temple Mount? Mainstream archeologists currently credit Herod and his Roman engineers (working mainly after his death) with erecting this gigantic, smooth stone as well as all the other smaller stone blocks around it.

It would seem that archeologists are making the same mistake at the Temple Mount in Jerusalem as they are with the even larger blocks at Baalbek in Lebanon. Both sites have similar gigantic blocks on the lower level of what became Roman reconstruction efforts on earlier megalithic temples. Baalbek is a mysterious prehistoric megalithic platform that has a Roman Temple of Jupiter built on top of it. The Roman construction is impressive enough, but some of the gigantic blocks, including some still at the nearby quarry, would seem to have been impossible to move, not only by the Romans, but even by modern machinery.

Did the Romans really cut and erect the largest stones at

Baalbek? Probably not—and similarly with the Western Stone—it is likely these blocks come from an earlier period, perhaps around 1000 BC or earlier. The Western Stone is apparently, like the ashlars at Baalbek, left over from some gigantic stone platform that was part of some unknown structure that has almost entirely vanished—stones that could not be relocated by the Romans, or even King Solomon, in their efforts to make a new structure out of the blocks of an earlier structure.

One would think that modern archeologists would have begun to realize that the Western Stone, and much of the lower part of the wall, predates any Roman attempts to expand and rebuild the Second Temple. In my opinion it is clear that the Western Stone is very old and part of the earliest phase of any building on the Temple Mount, even predating King David and King Solomon. While it seems possible that King Solomon, in possession of the Ark of the Covenant at the time, was able to levitate—or otherwise move—this 570 ton stone into place, it seems more likely that this block and ones below it are the work of the Nephilim, whom the Israelites regarded as giants.

When looking at the photo of the Western Stone and the blocks around it, a number of things strike me as being important. First, the smaller square and rectangular blocks above the Western Stone are clearly not the original stones meant to be interlocked with this huge block and are probably the work of Roman engineers.

Secondly, the Western Stone is very smooth and highly articulated, as are the stones beneath it. All of these stones are very well cut and they are fitted together perfectly. There are at least eight smaller stones beneath the gigantic Western Stone, of which we can see neither end.

Thirdly, there is a large notch at the top of the Western Stone. This notch was probably originally meant to have another megalith with a similar notche fitted into it, beginning a pattern that was probably repeated. This megalithic stonework would have consisted of finely-cut blocks that were locked into each other with occasional notches and even a jigsaw pattern.

There may have been keystone cuts and metal clamps in some

of these walls, but none are visible. Perhaps it was the sight of such imposing architecture—huge building blocks like at Baalbek—that convinced the Israelites, like the Greeks and their "cyclopean" construction, that it could only be attributed to men who were of giant stature and therefore capable of lifting such great stones. The cutting, articulation and polishing of these fine feats of construction are amazing enough, but it is the moving of such huge blocks that is the most incredible. Why would anyone ever want to cut and move such an enormous block of stone? Did they want to do something that was the most difficult thing that they could imagine?

In short, the spot that held the Ark of the Covenant in the First Temple is somewhere near the megalithic construction that is the Western Stone and the stones beneath it. The box-like notches that we see on the Western Stone and some of the stones beneath it may have been part of the original, though probably not. They seem to be of a later time, perhaps that of King Solomon, when iron tools were used to make these notches so that wooden beams could be inserted to create ceiling beams and floor joists. Or, more intriguingly, perhaps some sort of large machine was mounted to them in the distant past.

Ethiopian priests believe that the Ark of the Covenant was used to move large stones like the obelisks at Axum. Had the Ark helped in levitating the 570-ton block known as the Western Stone? The Holy of Holies, the Western Stone and the entire Temple Mount area have a bizarre history that goes back many thousands of years. As we will explore later, this portion of the Temple Mount is probably the area excavated by the Knights Templar.

The Legend of Buraq and the Night Flight

The Temple Mount is a location of many mysteries and great mystique. It has the mysterious megalithic blocks, similar to those at Baalbek, and the larger megalithic walls in Peru and Bolivia. This site was also a locale in one of the most curious episodes in the Quran: Mohammed's much debated Night Flight.

The Quran, and more so the Hadith (writings after Mohammed's death), give a fractured and incredible story of Mohammed going

An artist's conception of the flying horse Buraq.

out for an evening stroll from his cousin's house to the Kaaba in Mecca, about 10 years after he had conquered Mecca and Medina, circa 621 AD, and suddenly meeting the Archangel Gabriel. Gabriel whisked him away in a flying machine — the Buraq, said to be a type of flying horse — to "the mosque at the furthest place," presumed to be the Masjid al-Aqsa in Jerusalem. After praying, Mohammed once again mounted the Buraq and was taken by Gabriel to the various heavens, to meet first the earlier prophets and then God (Allah). Mohammed was instructed to tell his followers that they were to offer prayers 50 times per day. However, at the urging of Moses (Musa), Mohammed returns to God and it was eventually reduced to 10 times, and then five times per day. The Buraq then transported Mohammed back to Mecca and the long night was over.

It is a curious story and one that would cause some to doubt its authenticity. How could this story be true? Are there really flying horses? Or is the Buraq really some sort of vimana flying machine that is featured so heavily in the epics of ancient India and Ethiopia's *Kebra Nagast*?

It would seem that the Quran and the Hadith are talking about a flying machine of some sort, which in ancient times were often depicted as a flying horse, a flying cart or a flying carpet. In ancient India aerial flight was usually depicted as a chariot being drawn through the air by swans or other large birds. However, in Tibet, Mongolia and throughout Central Asia, flying vehicles were usually depicted as flying horses. Tibetan flags to this day often depict the Chintamani horse that flies through the sky and has a box, or ark, on its back.

The Quran does not actually give us very much information about the Night Flight, but it is mentioned in sura 17. The strange flying vehicle called the Buraq is not mentioned at all in the Quran but is mentioned in a lengthy discussion in the Hadith. Here it is said that Mohammed mounted the Buraq, and in the company of Gabriel, they traveled to the "farthest mosque."

It is difficult to find good definitions of the Buraq and the best source seems to be Wikipedia:

> Buraq was a mythical flying animal, similar to the Greek flying horse called Pegasus and similar flying horses in Persian Zoroastrian literature. While the Buraq is almost always portrayed with a human face in far-eastern and Persian art, no Hadiths or other early Islamic references allude to it having a humanoid face. This human face on the flying horse may have been influenced by a misrepresentation or translation from Arabic to Persian of texts and stories describing the winged steed as a "… beautiful faced creature."

The Buraq could take a step the entire length of the distance that he was able to see, thereby covering vast expanses of land in a few hours. Wikipedia give us this excerpt from a translation of *Sahih al-Bukhari* that describes Al-Buraq:

> Then a white animal which was smaller than a mule and bigger than a donkey was brought to me. …The animal's step (was so wide that it) reached the farthest point within

35

the reach of the animal's sight.
—Muhammad al-Bukhari, *Sahih al-Bukhari*

Another description on Wikipedia is this Islamic Hadith:

> Then he [Gabriel] brought the Buraq, handsome-faced and bridled, a tall, white beast, bigger than the donkey but smaller than the mule. He could place his hooves at the farthest boundary of his gaze. He had long ears. Whenever he faced a mountain his hind legs would extend, and whenever he went downhill his front legs would extend. He had two wings on his thighs which lent strength to his legs.

Wikipedia states that other legends say that the Buraq was said to be the transport for the prophet Abraham (Ibrahim) when he visited his wife Hajera or Hagar and son Ishmael in Mecca. According to tradition, Abraham lived with one wife, Sarah, in Syria (Haran), but the Buraq would transport him in the morning to Mecca to see his family there, and take him back in the evening to Syria.

A clearly related Islamic tradition is that the angel Gabriel has a flying horse named Haizum. Haizum is a white, flaming, spiritual horse which has a pair of wings like Pegasus and can fly swiftly from one cosmic plane to another in a second. In Islamic tradition Haizum was a gift to Gabriel from God-Allah for pleasing Him.

The Buraq-Haizum was some sort of flying machine, it would seem, being described as a winged horse. The *Kebra Nagast,* as we shall see in later chapters, also refers to flying through the air on carts and this earlier text was well known in Arabia, Nubia and Ethiopia. Mohammed's daughter took refuge in the Coptic Christian kingdom of Ethiopia for some years and the Quran refers in a positive way to the "blameless Ethiopians." Therefore, Mohammed may have been familiar with the flying vehicle stories of Ethiopian epics. The main verse in the Quran is sura 17:

> Exalted is He [the Buraq] who took His Servant [Mohammed] by night from al-Masjid al-Haram to al-

Masjid al-Aqsa [furthest mosque], whose surroundings We have blessed, to show him of Our signs. Indeed, He is the Hearing, the Seeing.

What were the signs—the "Our signs"—that the Quran is referring to? Perhaps one sign that is being referred to is the Western Stone, part of the First Temple and also part of the Second Temple—and any temple to come? The sign that Mohammed saw was this wall of colossal stone blocks that was a sign of the Nephilim, the sign of the gods who could move great stone blocks and also fly in the sky.

Rather than a journey on a flying horse, was it a journey by some sort of airship? Did Mohammed make a flying saucer journey from Mecca to Jerusalem, then up into space to see "Yahweh" or "Allah" and then return at dawn to a sleepy Mecca just awakening to a new day?

It would seem that the Buraq was some small flying machine, a vehicle that held two people: Mohammed and Gabriel. The two left Mecca in the late evening and then flew to the Temple Mount at Jerusalem which was then a garbage dump. No mosque or prayer room existed there. There were the giant blocks of the Western Wall, and perhaps this is what they looked at.

Then Gabriel and Mohammed, flying on al-Buraq—the white flying machine—went up in the sky to look at Earth as a ball in space and experience the awe that such a view gives any observer. Perhaps he was taken to some land of the immortals or seventh heaven where Moses, Abraham and the other prophets (including Jesus) supposedly conversed with Mohammed. Or, perhaps this portion of the story is indeed fiction—but at any rate, they return to Mecca where Mohammed is dropped off by the Kaaba and Gabriel takes off again with the flying machine called Buraq. Muslims all over the world believe that something like this happened, or perhaps it was an extended dream that has been immortalized, as some Islamic scholars believe.

Either way it is a strange story and it has important points that affect all Muslims to this day. It is said that Mohammed used to pray toward Jerusalem but during the Night Flight he was told to pray toward Mecca, and all Muslims today therefore pray toward Mecca, rather than Jerusalem.

Also, it was on the Night Flight that Mohammed was told that praying five times a day would be sufficient, whereas constant prayer is an important part of Islam. It has been pointed out that the Sabians of southern Arabia had a tradition of praying five times a day; this may have influenced Mohammed.

A problem that Islamic scholars often comment on concerning the Night Flight is that not only is the whole story quite fantastic by normal standards but it is a story about going to a mosque that did not exist. It would exist in the future, however. At the time of the Night Flight Herod's Temple was a pile of rubble used as a garbage dump and had been for hundreds of years. Probably the odd pilgrim or traveler had a look at the Western Wall and the gigantic Western Stone and then passed on.

Islamic scholars point out the term used for mosque, "masjid," literally means "place of prostration," and includes monotheistic places of worship such as Solomon's Temple or Herod's Temple. Today the al-Aqsa Mosque does sit on the Temple Mount and was finished in 705 AD. Today it is the third holiest place in Islam, after Mecca and Medina.

Was Mohammed on some sort of time travel trip in Gabriel's flying saucer? Certainly the trip to Jerusalem has the familiarity of a vimana story from the Hindu epics. Just as in the Old Testament, stories in the Quran really have no word for airship or vimana, so the authors do the next best thing, which is bring in something that the reader might understand like a flying horse or a flying carpet. The *Kebra Nagast*, as we shall see later, uses the allegory of a flying wagon.

Was the Ark of the Covenant a Device from Egypt?

The Ark of the Covenant, the Holy of Holies and the power of the Ark have only just been touched upon. We will look at all this more carefully and examine the awesome power of the Ark shortly. But first let us sum up some of the evidence.

Moses was raised as a high priest in Egypt and then led hundreds of thousands of people and their animals out of Egypt into the Sinai and Arabian Deserts and eventually to the lands around the Dead Sea and Jerusalem. Along the way he made or revealed a powerful energy source that was a glowing light, a flying scout vehicle, a weapon against enemies and something to part rivers and destroy walls. It was a device that was clearly physical in nature and it seemed to have some sort of electrical function that made it do the various things it was alledged to have done. Had this device possibly come from Egypt, a land of various electrical devices and power tool technology?

Indeed, the power source used with the Ark was probably a device already constructed in Egypt. Electricity was used by the Egyptians, as evidenced by electroplated gold objects, electrical lighting reportedly being used in the temples, the Dendera glyphs of electrical apparati, and the depiction of the djed column as some sort of electrical generator.

It has been suggested that the dimensions of the Ark of the Covenant would fit conveniently into the box that is in the King's Chamber of the Great Pyramid. Was there some kind of technology tin use in that structure? Given that the he was a High Priest, it seems highly likely that Moses would be familiar with the secret electrical devices that the priests used in temples in Egypt.

But before we look more carefully into what sort of device the Ark of the Covenant was let us look at some of the strange stories surrounding the Ark of the Covenant in the Bible and flying vehicles and destructive weapons that are described. They say that truth is stranger than fiction—because fiction has to make sense. How do we sort out the truth in ancient stories that don't seem to make sense, at least in the way we see currently see the ancient world and its level of technology.

The special ephod worn by a High Priest of Israel.

CHAPTER THREE

TALES FROM THE BIBLE

Behold, the Lord rideth upon a swift cloud, and shall come into
Egypt: and the idols of Egypt shall be moved at his presence, and
the heart of Egypt shall melt in the midst of it.
—*Isaiah* 19:1

Our main source for information on the Ark of the Covenant is the
Old Testament of the Bible. The story of the Ark of the Covenant
begins at the end of the Book of Exodus. The lethal powers of the
Ark are mentioned in Leviticus, and much of Numbers deals with
the preparations and journey from Sinai to the land of Moab, which,
of course, involved the Ark. The Kingdom of Moab stretched along
the east side of the Dead Sea, with the kingdoms of Edom to the
south and Ammon to the northeast. The Promised Land of Canaan
stretched to the west of Ammon, encompassing the northern tip of
the Dead Sea, and straddling the River Jordan, which flowed from
the north into the Sea.

The fabulous and mysterious city of Petra was in Edom. Other
cities that seem to have been located there are the infamous towns
of Sodom and Gomorrah. According to the Torah, Sodom and
Gomorrah were allied with the cities of Admah, Zeboim and Zoar.
These five cities were known as the "cities of the plain" and this
plain seems to be the Plain of Siddim extending from the Dead Sea
to the south.

The boundary between Edom, which controlled the ports of
Eilat and, later, Ezion-Geber—Solomon's specially-built port for
the journeys to the gold-laden land of Ophir—and Moab was the
Wadi Zered. This extensive wadi runs east-west and is situated

today in Jordan and ends at the southeastern end of the Dead Sea.

Though there is some confusion as to where the "cities of the plain" were located (Wikipedia says that it was at the northern end of the Dead Sea) general tradition places them at the southern end. The cities of Sodom, Gomorrah, Admah and Zeboim were all destroyed in a spectacular hail of fire and brimstone, but the town of Zoar was spared because, as we shall see, it was the place Lot and his family were to take refuge. Zoar existed for many centuries hence, and biblical references to the town are found in Isaiah 15:5 and Jeremiah 48:34. The town is also mentioned in other sources dating from the Hellenistic Age to the Middle Ages. Most important in locating it is the mosaic map found on a church floor in Madaba, Jordan created around 560 AD; it shows Zoar slightly southeast of the Dead Sea.

The location of the cave where Lot and his daughters are said to have lived after fleeing to Zoar has also been a known quantity for quite some time. A Byzantine (5th to 7th centuries AD) monastic center was built outside a natural cave where Bronze Age artifacts have, in fact, been found. A museum of Lot's cave artifacts has recently opened at the site, near the modern town of Safi, dubbed the "Museum at the Lowest Place on Earth" due to the area's extreme elevation of 1,329 feet below sea level.

So there is pretty clear evidence of where Zoar was located. Could its sister cities have been far away? We will discuss the awesome destruction of those cities in a moment. But first we must mention that the area round the Dead Sea was also the home of giants.

The Land of the Rephaim

Also in the area lived the Rephaim (also known as Anakites or Anakim), giants who had inhabited areas around the Dead Sea since ancient times. The Israelites were instructed to exterminate all of the previous inhabitants of the area around Cannan and the Rephaim are listed among the tribes to be destroyed.

The Bible mentions the Rephaim in: Gen 14:5, 15:20; Numbers 13; Deut 2:10-11, 2:18-21, 3:11; Josh 12:4, 13:12, 15:8, 17:15,

18:16; 2 Sam 5:18, 5:22, 23:13; and 1 Chron 11:15, 14:9, 20:4. In Deuteronomy 3:11, it is implied that Og, the King of Bashan, was one of the last of the Rephaim. His bed was said to be nine cubits long in ordinary cubits. With an ordinary cubit being about 18 inches long, this would make his bed about 13 feet long. We might surmise that King Og was about 10 feet tall. He may have had an elongated cranium—as many royal persons did in those days—and this could give an extra foot to an already very tall person.

As we have seen, most of the area on the eastern side of the Dead Sea was known as Moab, and this was known as one of the lands of Rephaim. They also became known as Zamzummim by the Ammonites further north (Deuteronomy 2:18-2), which is a derivative of a Hebrew word that means "buzzing." This apparently means that the Rephaim had an element of speech that evoked a buzzing sound. Southern Africa has a click speech, and the Rephaim may have had some sort of odd buzzing and clicking speech.

The Rephaim and the Anakim apparently lived on both the northern side of the Dead Sea (Canaan), and along the eastern side of that large body of water, the largest lake in the Levant by far. An area of northern Moab was called Ar, a region on the east side of the Jordan before the time of Moses, which was also considered the land of the giants. According to Deuteronomy 2:10:

> A race of giants called the Emites had once lived in the
> area of Ar. They were as strong and numerous and tall as the
> Amorites, another race of giants.

The cities of Sodom and Gomorrah, plus Admah and Zeboim, were apparently inhabited by the Rephaim until they were suddenly destroyed.

According to Deuteronomy 2:11, Anak was a patriarch or king of the Rephaim. In Numbers 13 we are told about giants who are the sons of Anak. These giants are then referred as the Anakim. Moses sends 12 spies—one from each of the 12 tribes—to scout out the land of Canaan, north of the Dead Sea, and give a full report upon their return. The spies enter from the Negev desert and journey

43

northward through the Judaean hills until they arrive at the brook of Eshcol near Hebron, where reside Sheshai, Ahiman, and Talmai, the sons of Anak.

After the scouts have explored the entire land, they bring back samples of the fruit of the land, most notably a gigantic cluster of grapes which requires two men to carry it on a pole between them. The scouts then report to Moses and the congregation that "the land indeed is a land flowing with milk and honey," but 10 of the 12 spies discourage the Israelites from even attempting to possess the land, for they report that the men were taller and stronger than the Israelites. Moreover, the sons of Anak dwell in the land, and they felt like grasshoppers in their presence. The Anakites are later mentioned briefly in the books of Deuteronomy, Joshua, and Judges. In Joshua, Caleb, one of the 12 spies sent by Moses into Canaan, later drove out the descendants of Anak—his three sons—from Hebron, also called Kiriath Arba. It is thought that some of the giants found refuge with the Philistines where they survived up till the time of David. Goliath was a Philistine.

The Destruction of Sodom and Gomorrah

The Rephaim giants lived around the Dead Sea and were probably present when the four "cities of the plain" were utterly destroyed. Other strange and tall men also lived north of the Sea of Galilee and into Syria and Iraq. Possibly all of these "giants" and "angels" were tall men (some possibly with elongated heads). In Genesis 19:1-22 we read about two strange men who come up to the gate of Sodom where a man called Lot happens to be sitting on a bench nearby. Lot immediately recognizes these strange men as "angels" or perhaps more correctly, as servants of the Lord. He invites them to his house to spend the night but then local men, drunk, come to Lot's house to demand to see the men—and have sex with them. Lot offers them his virgin daughters instead. Says Genesis 19:1-22:

> The two angels came to Sodom in the evening, and Lot was sitting in the gate of Sodom. When Lot saw them, he

rose to meet them and bowed himself with his face to the earth and said, "My lords, please turn aside to your servant's house and spend the night and wash your feet. Then you may rise up early and go on your way." They said, "No; we will spend the night in the town square." But he pressed them strongly; so they turned aside to him and entered his house. And he made them a feast and baked unleavened bread, and they ate.

But before they lay down, the men of the city, the men of Sodom, both young and old, all the people to the last man, surrounded the house. And they called to Lot, "Where are the men who came to you tonight? Bring them out to us, that we may know them." Lot went out to the men at the entrance, shut the door after him, and said, "I beg you, my brothers, do not act so wickedly. Behold, I have two daughters who have not known any man. Let me bring them out to you, and do to them as you please. Only do nothing to these men, for they have come under the shelter of my roof." But they said, "Stand back!" And they said, "This fellow came to sojourn, and he has become the judge! Now we will deal worse with you than with them." Then they pressed hard against the man Lot, and drew near to break the door down. But the men reached out their hands and brought Lot into the house with them and shut the door. And they struck with blindness the men who were at the entrance of the house, both small and great, so that they wore themselves out groping for the door.

Then the men said to Lot, "Have you anyone else here? Sons-in-law, sons, daughters, or anyone you have in the city, bring them out of the place. For we are about to destroy this place, because the outcry against its people has become great before the Lord, and the Lord has sent us to destroy it." So Lot went out and said to his sons-in-law, who were to marry his daughters, "Up! Get out of this place, for the Lord is about to destroy the city." But he seemed to his sons-in-law to be jesting.

As morning dawned, the angels urged Lot, saying, "Up! Take your wife and your two daughters who are here, lest you be swept away in the punishment of the city." But he lingered. So the men seized him and his wife and his two daughters by the hand, the Lord being merciful to him, and they brought him out and set him outside the city. And as they brought them out, one said, "Escape for your life. Do not look back or stop anywhere in the valley. Escape to the hills, lest you be swept away." And Lot said to them, "Oh, no, my lords. Behold, your servant has found favor in your sight, and you have shown me great kindness in saving my life. But I cannot escape to the hills, lest the disaster overtake me and I die. Behold, this city is near enough to flee to, and it is a little one. Let me escape there—is it not a little one?—and my life will be saved!" He said to him, "Behold, I grant you this favor also, that I will not overthrow the city of which you have spoken. Escape there quickly, for I can do nothing till you arrive there." Therefore the name of the city was called Zoar.

Sodom is Destroyed in Sulfur and Fire from Above

Genesis 19:23-29 tells the rest of the story: that Lot travels overnight with his family to the small town of Zoar that is to be spared, and then the Lord, perhaps through his mysterious servants or "angels," destroys the other four cities with brimstone and fire:

> The sun had risen on the earth when Lot came to Zoar. Then the Lord rained on Sodom and Gomorrah sulfur and fire from the Lord out of heaven. And he overthrew those cities, and all the valley, and all the inhabitants of the cities, and what grew on the ground. But Lot's wife, behind him, looked back, and she became a pillar of salt.
>
> And Abraham went early in the morning to the place where he had stood before the Lord. And he looked down toward Sodom and Gomorrah and toward all the land of the valley, and he looked and, behold, the smoke of the land

went up like the smoke of a furnace.

So it was that, when God destroyed the cities of the valley, God remembered Abraham and sent Lot out of the midst of the overthrow when he overthrew the cities in which Lot had lived.

While the Ark of the Covenant had tremendous power (it was said to have killed hundreds people at a time and was partly responsible for the destruction of the walls of Jericho), the torrent unleashed on upon these four cities was far more extraordinary than the power of the Ark of the Covenant. Yet, we might ask ourselves if there is not some possible relation here.

The sort of angels that visit Lot and his family do not seem like normal angels as we would ordinarily view them. They walk up to the gates of the city of Sodom, perhaps having come from the southern port of Eilat which was one of the major cities of Edom, a kingdom that bordered upon Moab at the southern end of the Dead Sea. Or perhaps they arrived outside the city by some sort of aircraft, a vimana perhaps, as mentioned in the Indian epics such as the *Ramayana* and the *Mahabharata*. Indeed, these books are replete with stories of flying vehicles and of devastating weapons that destroy complete cities, just as the Bible describes the destruction of Sodom and Gomorrah.

Were some sort of ancient astronauts or high tech humans with advanced weapons and airships there to check out the wicked towns of Sodom and Gomorrah? Perhaps they knew of an impending natural catastrophe and were coming to check on the area before the event. And when they discovered, as perhaps they previously suspected, that travelers and strangers were not treated very well in these cities, they decided to destroy them—or allow them to be destroyed? It is like the cities were nuked with atomic weapons, or each hit with some very large conventional bomb similar to the large bombs in use today.

While the book of Genesis does not mention any flying vehicles, aerial ships are mentioned at other times in the Bible, such as in Ezekiel's vision of a craft coming down from the sky. The *Kebra*

47

The destruction of Sodom and Gomorrah. (Chas Berlin)

Nagast also features the Ark of the Covenant in association with flying vehicles—as if the Ark was some sort of energy machine that could either power an aircraft or create some sort of anti-gravity effects.

Indeed, it seems that the advanced cultures in India, China, Sumeria and Egypt apparently had electricity, geared machines, and power tools with diamond-tipped saws, grinders and drills. They had many metals, including bronze and iron, and they had a basic knowledge of electricity. With metal machines and electrical devices, a culture can create heavy machinery such as steashovels, as well as powered flight. The kind of advanced culture that can quarry 200-ton obelisks, move them many miles to other sites, and then erect them—as the Egyptians and Axumites were known to have done—would have knowledge of electricity, moving saws and even of explosives and other chemical reactions. Modern historians have still not figured out what chemicals were used in the Greek Fire spoken of in ancient texts over two thousand years ago. Greek Fire could burn underwater and was hurled at enemy ships from catapults as fireballs of burning pitch and secret chemicals.

So, was the Ark of the Covenant some sort of electrical device that did more than just accumulate some static energy to occasionally shock those nearby? Some sort of battery and accumulator that charged over time and was capable of being turned on to "giant stun-gun mode" at the flip of a switch? Perhaps the cloud of energy was the signal to show that the device was sufficiently charged for a deadly discharge of volts, like a huge stun-gun, to be unleashed with the flick of a switch. Imagine a large Tesla coil arcing volts across two metallic rods.

The Ancient Book called the Pentateuch

To understand the basic information we have on the Ark of the Covenant we need to understand the first five books of the Bible: the Pentateuch. These books are: Genesis, Exodus, Leviticus, Numbers, and Deuteronomy. The Ark of the Covenant is first mentioned in Exodus and most of the early strange tales of the Ark are told in Numbers.

Genesis begins with the story of Creation (Genesis 1–3) and the story of the Garden of Eden, and gives an account of Adam and Eve, as well as their descendants. We then have the story of Noah and the great flood (Genesis 3–9). Following this is an account of the Tower of Babel and the tale of Abraham's covenant with God (Genesis 10–11). We are then told of the Patriarchs, Abraham, Isaac, and Jacob,

49

and the life of Joseph (Genesis 12–50). The destruction of Sodom and Gomorrah occurs and God gives the Patriarchs a promise that the land of Canaan shall be their land, but at the end of Genesis the sons of Jacob, because of famine, end up leaving the area north of the Dead Sea—Canaan—for Egypt.

Exodus is the story of Moses, raised as an Egyptian priest, who then leads the Israelites out of captivity in Egypt (Exodus 1–18) and tells them he will take them to the Promised Land. On the way, they camp at Mount Horeb (Sinai) where Moses meets with Yahweh and receives the Ten Commandments. Moses communicates Yahweh's laws and covenant (Exodus 19–24) to the people of Israel. Then there is the violation of the commandment against idolatry as his brother Aaron took part in the construction of the Golden Calf (Exodus 32–34). Exodus concludes with the instructions for building the Ark of the Covenant and the tabernacle (Exodus 25–31; 35–40).

Leviticus is all about rituals and how they should be performed. It begins with instructions to the Israelites on the proper use of the tabernacle, which they had just built (Leviticus 1–10). This is followed by rules concerning who is clean and unclean, and when (Leviticus 11–15), the Day of Atonement (Leviticus 16), and various moral and ritual laws (Leviticus 17–26).

Numbers starts with a census where the number of Israelites are counted (Numbers 1–3). The narratives tell how Israel consolidated itself as a community at Sinai (Numbers 1–9), set out from Sinai to move towards Canaan, and spied out the land (Numbers 10–13). Because of the people's unbelief at various points (Numbers 14), the Israelites were condemned to wander for 40 years in the desert instead of immediately entering the Promised Land. Moses is even told by the glowing cloud that was Yahweh that he would not live to enter the Promised Land because of his many sins (Numbers 20). At the end of Numbers (Numbers 21–35) the host of Israel leaves the Sinai Desert and go around Edom and through Moab on the eastern side of the Dead Sea. Here two tribes, the Balak and Balaam oppose the Israelites (Numbers 22–24; 31:8, 15–16). They defeat two kings, Og and Sihon (Numbers 21), and so come to occupy some territory on the eastern side of the Jordan, within sight of the

Promised Land, Canaan. The town of Jericho is within their sight.

Deuteronomy consists mainly of a series of speeches by Moses on the eastern side of the Jordan River opposite Jericho, exhorting Israel to obey Yahweh's laws. At the very end (Deuteronomy 34), Moses climbs Mount Nebo and is allowed to see a vista of the Promised Land. However, he never makes it there, as he had been forewarned by the Lord. He died in Moab and was buried there, but the writer Deuteronomy notes that no one knew exactly where. Soon afterwards, Israel begins the conquest of Canaan.

Moses the Magician

We just don't know who Moses was and what knowledge he had. He was raised in the pharaoh's household, we are told, and he would therefore be a magician and presumably know about electric devices and other technology that may have been used in Egyptian temples of the time. He may have spent many of his missing years in Ethiopia, visiting Axum with its gigantic obelisks and going to Lake Tana, the source of the Blue Nile. He probably got married there as well, as one of his wives was an Ethiopian. This may be significant as we will see in later chapters.

Moses may also have been a "conehead." Various royal Egyptians during the period of his lifetime, circa 1000 to 1500 BC, were coneheads in the sense that they had elongated skulls, known in science as a "dolichocephalic" head. It is known that many members of the eighteenth Egyptian dynasty possessed such skulls, including Nefertiti and her famous husband Akhenaten, plus Tutankhamun, Meritaten, Meketaten and others. Egyptologists have largely ignored this feature of some royal Egyptians, at first because some thought that depicting the head with this unusual shape was just a feature of stylized art. Others suggested that it was a rare disease brought on by incest among the royal families (although Nefertiti was not an Egyptian, but from Mittani, which was in central Turkey). We now know that the practice of cranial deformation was widespread around the planet (an enigma in itself) and was practiced in Egypt, Hungary, Malta, Turkey, Kurdistan, China, Korea, Mexico, Peru, Vanuatu and other places. See my book, coauthored by Brien

Foerster, *The Enigma of Cranial Deformation.*[22]

So the question we are asking here is, was Moses possibly a person with a misshapen and elongated skull? It is not particularly important to the story, but it is very much a possibility, which is fascinating! In Exodus 34:35 we learn that Moses wore a veil over his face after his initial meeting with Yaweh on Mount Sinai. Why did he have to hide his face? Was it burned or misshapen after getting the Tablets of the Law, "inscribed by the finger of God" and seeing the Lord's incredible power? According to Exodus 34:29, "And it came to pass, when Moses came down from mount Sinai with the two tablets of the testimony in Moses' hand, when he came down from the mount, that Moses knew not that the skin of his face shone by reason of his speaking with him."

He was disfigured at this time and therefore wore a veil to cover his face for the rest of his life. So, remember this bit of oddity whenever you read about Moses in this book or others, and see how Moses is depicted in movies and television. In reality, no one saw his face after he came down from Mount Sinai. He did have several wives, though we do not know much about their personal relationships.

The story of Moses begins in Exodus, a book that is arguably the most important book of the collection of books known as the Bible. Exodus lays the foundation for the books that are to come and it contains epic history — a history that includes a deadly weapon that the Israelites call the Ark of the Covenant.

According to Exodus, Moses was born around the month of February/March circa 1391 BC (or some think 1593 BC) and lived to be about 120 years old. He was the youngest of three children, a brother, Aaron, being three years older and a sister, Miriam, being about three to six years older than Aaron. The Hebrews were slaves in Egypt at this time and the pharaoh had ordered that all newborn Hebrew males be drowned in the Nile, fearing that they were growing in population. Moses' mother, Jochebed, hid him in a basket by the side of the River Nile for three months. When she cold no longer hide the child she cast the basket into the waters of the Nile, abandoning the baby Moses to God's protection.

52

The basket was not observed until it reached the place where a daughter of the pharaoh was bathing. While not named in the Bible, Josephus says her name was Thermuthis, while others think that her name may have been Bithiah. A daughter named Bithiah is mentioned in 1 Chronicles 4:18, but it is unclear whether she is a later pharaoh's daughter. There are a number of them, including a wife of King Solomon, and the Egyptian-Hebrew princess Scota who brought the Ark to Ireland and Scotland according to Celtic legend (to be discussed later).

The princess saw the basket and asked her maidens to fetch it for her, and so acquired the baby Moses and raised him as her own son.

The word "mose(s)" derives from the Egyptian meaning "born of" so therefore Tutmoses was "born of the god Tut or Thoth." Other pharaohs of this time include Ahmose I and Kamose, who disappeared from history after a three-year reign. The biblical Moses must have had a pre-name such as Tut, Ah, or Ka, but this was dropped after the Exodus. We are never told what his full name was. However, he was trained as an Egyptian military general and a powerful Egyptian priest-magician.

While a powerful Egyptian prince at the age of 40, on a trip in the countryside, he saw an Egyptian slave master killing a Hebrew and lost his temper—killing the Egyptian slave master. Knowing that he would be punished severely for his actions Moses fled to the land of Midian, generally thought to be located along the northern coast of the Red Sea, south of Eilat and Aqaba. Today this area is part of Saudi Arabia.

This area also contains the mysterious Jabal al-Lawz, a mountain located in northwest Saudi Arabia near the Jordan border, whose name means mountain of almonds. This is the tallest mountain in the area and has been proposed as an alternative to Mount Sinai in the Sinai penninsula because it is the only partially active volcano around. In his book *The Gold of Exodus*, Howard Blum asserts the Mount Sinai described in Exodus would seem to be a volcano.[11]

Rather, the mountain of the burning bush, Mount Horeb, may have been Jabal al-Lawz, located in the northern part of Midian.

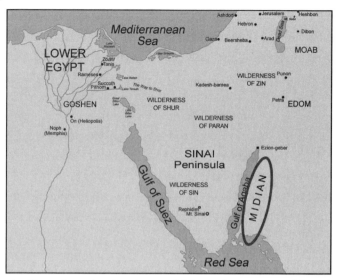

Theoretically, a burning bush would have been something that one might conceivably find near its summit during one of its frequent eruptions.

While in Midian Moses saved seven beautiful daughters of a Midian priest named Jethro (also Reuel or Hobab) from a group of shepherds who would like to have had their way with them. Jethro adopted Moses as his son and married him off to his daughter, Zipporah. Moses stayed in Midian for 40 years as the head shepherd for Hobab. Reuel-Hobab is the spiritual and ancestral founder of the mysterious Druze sect.

It would seem that during this time Moses made a journey across the Red Sea to the Axumite port of Adulis and then to Axum in Ethiopia. The great obelisk at Axum was probably standing at the time, and Moses could well have visited Lake Tana and other areas of the country. During this time he probably married an Ethiopian woman, though while she is mentioned in Genesis she is not named. The best we can learn is that he has a wife named Zipporah (of Midian), another wife who is Ethiopian, and two sons by Zipporah named Gershom and Eliezer.

The Roman historian Josephus says that Moses married a woman named Tharbis as a general in his early adult life. Moses had led the Egyptians in a campaign against invading Nubians and defeated them. Moses then besieged the Nubian city of Meru, where from the ramparts Tharbis watched him lead the Egyptian army. She fell in love with him and agreed to marry Moses and deliver the city into his power. She and Moses married, but Moses eventually returned to Egypt and exile. The Ethiopian woman mentioned in Numbers 12:1 would be another woman entirely it would seem.

One day when he was around the age of 80 in Midian, Moses was leading his flock to Mount Horeb (Jabal al-Lawz?), and he came across a burning bush. Coming closer to it, Moses realized a voice was coming from it. Moses believed that God spoke to him from the burning bush and the voice identified itself as Yahweh.

Moses said that Yahweh instructed him to return to Egypt and free the Hebrews from their bondage. Moses, with his brother Aaron, had learned certain tricks of sorcery, such as how to transform a staff into a serpent (hypnotism?) and also to inflict—and heal—the sores of leprosy. Yahweh also gifted Moses with the power to change river water to blood and other forms of sorcery. Moses went back to the pharaoh's court, where much time had passed and the pharaoh of the oppression was now dead, as were many of the royal court of that time. A new pharaoh had come to power and he challenged Moses to defeat his magicians. Moses and Aaron had their staffs turned into snakes and fought against the staffs-turned-snakes of the Egyptian priests.

Moses and Aaron then saw that ten plagues were visited on Egypt: 1) the fish and other water life were killed off; 2) frogs from the Nile overran the countryside; 3) Egypt was invaded by lice; 4) Egypt was invaded by flies; 5) disease infected the livestock; 6) incurable boils broke out among the people; 7) thunderstorms and hail destroyed crops and buildings; 8) locusts covered the countryside; 9) the land was enveloped by total darkness; and 10) the firstborn male of every Egyptian family died.

When the pharaoh lost his firstborn son he told the Hebrews to leave Egypt. All the ten plagues affected only the Egyptians and passed over the Hebrews, and they now celebrate these events in a seven-day holiday known as Passover.

The Hebrew host left in haste; instead of letting the bread they

55

would need for sustenance rise, they took unleavened bread (as is served at Passover). As the Israelites neared the northern part of the Red Sea, an area of marshes, the pharaoh had changed his mind and ordered his army to give chase. With the Egyptian army bearing down upon them the Israelites reached the sea, and Moses lifted up his rod and the water parted, allowing the Hebrews to pass. Once they had reached the other side, Moses lifted up his staff again and the path closed, drowning the pharaoh's army.

Some biblical scholars suggest that a strong wind had been blowing in the marshy area of the northern Red Sea which pushed the water back into a wind-driven low tide that came flooding back into the marshes when the wind suddenly stopped. A number of historians have suggested that the entire set of plagues may have been a series of ecological disasters caused by the volcanic explosion of Thera in the Aegean Sea circa 1500 BC.

The Creation of the Ark of the Covenant

And so we have a prelude to the building of the Ark of the Covenant, the tabernacle, the Urim, Thummin and other artifacts. The Israelites continued into the deserts of Sinai and apparently western Saudi Arabia, as Moses was familiar with that area. When they reached a place called Marah, people complained that the water was very bitter so Moses cast a tree into the water, making it turn sweet.

After several days, they complained that they were running short of food and started cursing Moses that they had been better off in Egypt. At this point Moses was told that Yahweh would solve the problem by providing manna as food in the morning and flocks of quail in the evening.

The Israelites arrived at the mountain of God, where Moses' father-in-law Jethro visited the host. At Jethro's suggestion Moses appointed judges over Israel.

Then in Exodus 19 it says that Yahweh would come to the mountain and show himself to the Israelites if they agree to be his people. The people accept this and then gather at the foot of the mountain. They are told not to touch anything or advance any further

up the mountain or they will be harmed by the power of Yahweh.
In Exodus 19:12-13 Moses is warned:

> And thou shalt set bounds unto the people round about,
> saying, Take heed to yourselves, that ye go not up into the
> mount, or touch the border of it: whosoever toucheth the
> mount shall be surely put to death: There shall not an hand
> touch it, but he shall surely be stoned, or shot through;
> whether it be beast or man, it shall not live: when the trumpet
> soundeth long, they shall come up to the mount.

Moses then goes down to the Israelites to prepare them for
the meeting with Yahweh, who descends onto the mountain like a
spaceship landing at a spaceport. We are told in Exodus 19:16-22:

> And it came to pass on the third day in the morning,
> that there were thunders and lightnings, and a thick cloud
> upon the mount, and the voice of the trumpet exceeding
> loud; so that all the people that was in the camp trembled.
> And Moses brought forth the people out of the camp to meet
> with God; and they stood at the nether part of the mount.
> And mount Sinai was altogether on a smoke, because the
> Lord descended upon it in fire: and the smoke thereof
> ascended as the smoke of a furnace, and the whole mount
> quaked greatly. And when the voice of the trumpet sounded
> long, and waxed louder and louder, Moses spake, and God
> answered him by a voice. And the Lord came down upon
> mount Sinai, on the top of the mount: and the Lord called
> Moses up to the top of the mount; and Moses went up. And
> the Lord said unto Moses, Go down, charge the people, lest
> they break through unto the Lord to gaze, and many of them
> perish. And let the priests also, which come near to the Lord,
> sanctify themselves, lest the Lord break forth upon them.

After this, Moses and Aaron are told by a voice to ascend
the mountain. Yahweh gives them the Ten Commandments and

An old print of the Israeliites watching the display of lights on Mount Sinai.

supposedly the entire host of Israelites can hear it. Moses goes up the mountain alone into the presence of Yahweh, who pronounces the Covenant Code (a detailed code of ritual and civil law), and promises Canaan to them if they obey. Moses comes down the mountain and writes down Yahweh's words and the people agree to keep them.

Yahweh calls Moses up the mountain with Aaron and the elders of Israel, and they feast in the presence of Yahweh, though only Moses can approach Yahweh and speak with him. Finally, Yahweh calls Moses up the mountain to receive a set of stone tablets containing the law, and he and Joshua go up, leaving Aaron below. Aaron unfortunately allows an idolatrous golden calf statue to be made which infuriates Moses, and he breaks the tablets written by the finger of Yahweh. Moses returns to the summit of the mountain and makes a new set of tablets with the Ten Commandments on them.

From this time on Moses wears a veil because his face is radiant.

Shortly after that he returns to the mountain and is told to build the Ark of the Covenant, which he does.

So the stage is set for our investigation into the Ark of the Covenant. Yahweh and his angels seem to be very active all over the Middle East around this time, sending emissaries to Sodom to see what sort of people are living there—and then deciding to allow the cities to be destroyed.

These "angels" of the Old Testament seem to be a lot like

An old print of Moses with the Ten Commandments, his face hidden by a veil.

normal people. Though Lot recognizes them as angels, or "servants of the Lord," others in the town do not recognize them as some sort of beings different from them, but rather as attractive humans whom they want to have sex with. The homosexual rape of these visitors was not something that Yahweh or his servants were willing to tolerate.

Now, a renegade Egyptian priest named Moses was starting a new religion, perhaps based on the Atonist religion of Egypt. Did he bring some high tech artifacts with him from Egypt? Did his god have an airship, flying saucer or vimana that he flew around in? Perhaps with some clever prior arrangement Moses met up with group of people who had an airship and would meet him at Mount Sinai or anyplace they chose. With the flash and fanfare of an airship landing, Moses and Aaron would talk with the occupants of the airship—probably people they had already met—and then convey their messages to the Israeli host of thousands of people as if God was speaking to them and giving them commandments, which were essentially Eastern concepts of karma and harmless living.

With great sound and fury the airship comes and goes, and as we shall see, returns to fly through the air and guide the people through the night, similar to the Star of Bethlehem.

And why did Moses wear a veil after his encounters with Yahweh? His face was radiant—perhaps partially burnt from being around the flash and thunder of this noisy craft of Yahweh and his friends.

It would seem that this craft was probably a real nuts-and-bolts machine that had more than one occupant. It may have been a full-blown ancient alien space craft capable of going to other planets, or perhaps it was just a primitive ancient airship made by humans with the best of the technology available in 3000 BC or even 15,000 BC—perhaps a primitive gas-filled zeppelin-balloon or an advanced propeller or gyro craft with a full electric control room. Perhaps they were airships of the Anunnaki, or from the Rama Empire of ancient India. We can only guess.

But for now, let us go back to the future—back to a time of giants, electric death rays and wars of extermination and conquest.

A time when great civilizations were collapsing and the Earth was wracked by earthquakes, volcanoes and tsunamis. Later, more large armies such as the Babylonians would attack Jerusalem and Egypt in even larger conflicts.

But that was hundreds of years away. For now, Moses and the Israelites needed to move all of their people to the plains of Moab and then to the land of Canaan where they would destroy the city of Jericho. They brought the Ark before them in their conquests—a terrible and destructive weapon.

An artist's conception of the Ark of the Covenant in the temple.

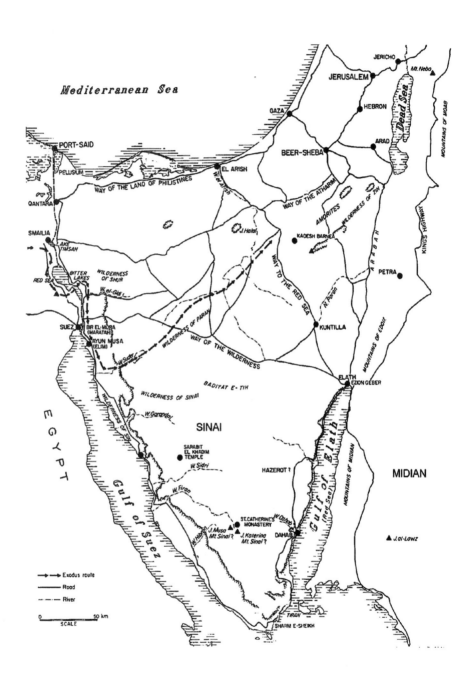

CHAPTER FOUR

A FEARSOME WEAPON

The Ark of the Cov
enant was the thing that brought me out of mainstream
journalism. I thought, "What could this thing be?"
—*Graham Hancock*

The Ark of the Covenant must be thought of as two or even three separate things. First of all it is a box with a cavity in the middle of it that can contain a medium-sized object, such as an electrical device of some kind. Secondly, the "Ark" can be that object inside of the box, something powerful and destructive. Thirdly, there is the Mercy Seat and Shekinah Glory that rest between the golden statues of two angels facing each other on a slab of gold, which is also the lid of the box. All three of these things have their function but each is separate from the other. There is a further description of the Ark as a flying vehicle, which seems to be something completely different again.

The other famous "ark" of the Bible is Noah's ark, which was a gigantic ship with a closed top and many levels or decks to accommodate people, animals and supplies. This ark is a different kind of wooden box, in this case a very large vessel in which to ride out the catastrophic biblical flood.

Normally an ark was a chest of wood and metal that held a statue of a god, or other sacred objects, and was carried by four to six men in front of a marching army. The Egyptian army was well known to have an ark containing a statue of the god Amun which was carried in front a troop of Egyptian soldiers to the many forts at the edges of the Egyptian realm.

One such fort was the military garrison of Megiddo in northern

Israel. This fortress, while physically in Israel, was manned by Egyptian soldiers for hundreds of years because of the special relationship between the two countries. This arrangement would be similar to joint military bases today, such as the NATO bases in Turkey.

So, typically an ark was a chest that contained an important object. What object did the Ark of the Covenant contain? A similar wood and metal box was discovered in the tomb of Tutankhamun in 1922. This chest is described as his hunting chest and is decorated with scenes of the young king hunting from a chariot. The lid is not hinged and simply lifts off. This chest apparently contained about a dozen boomerangs. The chest and boomerangs are on display at the Egyptian Museum in Cairo. It is a known fact, though little-discussed, that ancient Egyptians hunted with boomerangs that are identical to those used by Australian Aboriginals.

Exodus describes the Ark of the Covenant as a vehicle for Yahweh to communicate with Moses. As a vehicle for Yaweh, we know this about the Ark of the Covenant:

1. Yahweh is a talking cloud of energy on Mount Sinai.
2. Yahweh is also a cloud of energy between the golden angels on the Ark lid.
3. Moses (and others) can hear this cloud talk to him.
4. This cloud of energy can light up the room.
5. This cloud of energy can zap people with energy and cause skin problems.
6. This cloud of energy can zap people and kill them.
7. The Ark can levitate and fly through the air.
8. The Ark can part rivers and make thick city walls fall down.
9. The Ark is the power and will of Yaweh, the Lord.

Given the construction of the Ark, layered with gold and carried on gilded poles, it is possible that it could act as a simple electrical capacitor that would, over time, generate static electricity and focus it in a ball of light similar to St. Elmo's fire in the central gold dish area between the two golden cherubim statues. As we are about to see, the Ark has more powers than a normal electrical capacitor. Remember, gold is a very good conductor of electricity. A soft metallic element, gold is indestructible and all gold from ancient times still exists today. It will not rust or oxidize like most other metals. However, gold is too soft to make machines with moving parts but is used instead for the highest quality electrical devices.

As for the voice of Yahweh coming through the Ark, we might theorize that some sort of radio or cell phone transmission was being received, and this was therefore part of the electrical device carried inside the chest. On the other hand, the supposed communication between Moses and Yahweh through the Ark may well have been fabricated by Moses to impose the will of "YHWH" on the great host of the Israelites, a de facto army marching around the Sinai and northwestern Arabia for decades. It would seem that the Ark was more of an energy device than a communication device, so we will focus on this aspect of the puzzle that is the Ark of the Covenant.

St. Elmo's Fire and Ball Lightning

St. Elmo's Fire is the phenomenon that occurs when ionized air, a plasma—or electrically charged gas—emits a coronal discharge or glow. We get a good definition of the electrical science behind St. Elmo's fire from Wikipedia:

> St. Elmo's fire is a form of matter called plasma, which is also produced in stars, high temperature flame, and by lightning. The electric field around the object in question causes ionization of the air molecules, producing a faint glow easily visible in low-light conditions. Roughly 1000 volts per centimeter induces St. Elmo's fire; the number depends greatly on the geometry of the object. Sharp points lower the required voltage because electric fields are more concentrated in areas of high curvature, so discharges are more intense at the ends of pointed objects.
>
> Conditions that can generate St. Elmo's fire are present during thunderstorms, when high voltage differentials are present between clouds and the ground underneath.

An old print of St. Elmo's Fire emanating from a ship's masts during a storm.

Air molecules glow owing to the effects of such voltage, producing St. Elmo's fire. The nitrogen and oxygen in the Earth's atmosphere cause St. Elmo's fire to fluoresce with blue or violet light; this is similar to the mechanism that causes neon lights to glow.

It was a phenomenon noticed primarily by sailors, and such figures as Columbus, Magellan, Caesar and Pliny the Elder wrote about St. Elmo's Fire. Pliny the Elder documented in the first century AD the blue flames that appeared out of nowhere during or just after thunderstorms. Sailors attributed the glow to the patron saint of Mediterranean seamen, "St. Elmo," a mispronunciation of St. Ermo or St. Erasmus. They were not afraid of the bluish glow and believed it was a sign of salvation from the saint, as the phenomenon typically occurred toward the end of a storm.

For St. Elmo's Fire there need only be atmospheric conditions of a certain kind to generate the fire, but with the Ark of the Covenant there was another source of electrical buildup and that was the box itself with its sandwiched layers of conductor walls and nonconductor walls (the wood).

A similar, but more mysterious phenomenon is ball lightning. The scientific community can't agree on what ball lightning is, but it's definitely not St. Elmo's Fire. Ball lightning can float around in the air, while St. Elmo's Fire stays put, glowing around a ship's mast, mountain peak, tower, etc.

Ball lightning is an as yet unexplained electrical atmospheric phenomenon. Because of the many reports of various-sized

An old print of ball ligntning coming through a window.

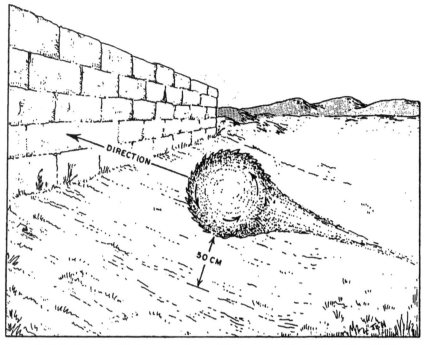

Ball lightning suddenly appearing and hitting a wall in South Africa, 1920.

luminous, spherical balls coming inside of houses, like down a chimney or even through a window, this phenomenon began to be studied by scientists. Sometimes the ball just dissipates, while at other times the ball explodes—sometimes with fatal consequences. Reports often associate ball lightning with thunderstorms, however a flash of lightning lasts but a few seconds while ball lightning can go on for a considerable time.

Archivist William Corliss has a large section on ball lightning in his book *Remarkable Luminous Phenomena in Nature*.[32] Among the chapters are: "Ordinary" Ball Lightning; Ball Lightning with Projections or Spikes; Ball Lightning with Divergent Rays; Rod-Shaped Ball Lightning; Double and Triple Ball Lightning; Miniature Ball Lightning; Giant Ball Lightning; Black Ball Lightning; Ball Lightning's Electromagnetic Effects; Artificial Ball Lightning; Repeating Ball Lightning; and a dozen more. His book leaves no doubt that ball lightning is an extremely variable phenomenon. It is a relatively common but little-understood marvel that has piqued

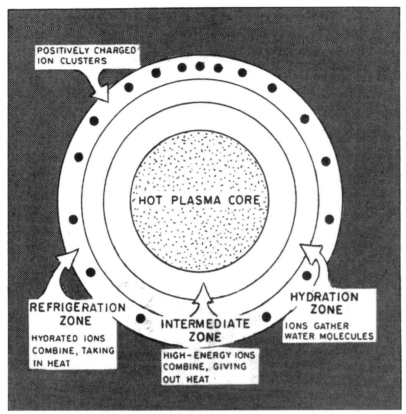

A theoretical diagram of ball lightning by D.J. Turner.

the interest of many top scientists.

In his book *Ball Lightning Explanation Leading to Clean Energy*,[34] Clint Seward proposes that ball lightning is a spinning plasma ring or toroid. He built a lab to produce lightning arcs and by modifying the conditions he produced small, bright, electrical balls that mimic ball lightning and persist in the atmosphere after the arc ends. By using a high speed camera he was able to show that the bright balls were spinning plasma toroids.

Seward published images of the results of his experiments, along with his method. Included is a report by a farmer of observing a ball lightning event forming in a kitchen, and the effects it caused as it moved around the kitchen. This is the only eyewitness account of ball lightning forming, then staying in one area, then ending, that the author had heard of.[34]

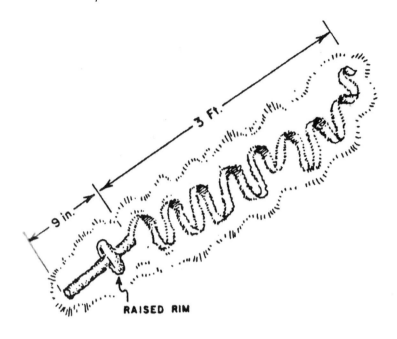

Ball lightning witnessed as having a glowing ribbon tail. (Corliss)

American Tesla researchers James and Kenneth Corum produced and photographed a form of ball lightning using a Tesla coil that they had specially built. This Tesla coil produced intermodulation effects and spewed out electric fireballs that varied in diameter between the size of a ping pong ball and a tennis ball. These fireballs could also explode when hitting an object, producing a sudden shock.[34]

Was the Ark of the Covenant a modified Tesla coil that spewed out deadly fireballs in every direction around the device? It is an interesting thought and it would explain why falling face-first onto the ground, as Moses and Aaron did, could save a person's life, as the fireballs would be flying over their heads.

Another possible device would be a Van de Graaff generator that uses a moving belt to accumulate electric charge on a hollow metal globe on the top of an insulated column. This creates very high electric potentials and a visible spark can be seen to jump to other objects. Invented in 1929 by American physicist Robert Van de Graaff, the potential difference achieved in modern Van de Graaff generators can reach five megavolts.

Electric fireballs generated with a Tesla coil at the James & Kenneth Corum laboratory.

A simple Van de Graaff generator consists of a belt of silk, or a similar flexible dielectric material, running over two metal pulleys, one of which is surrounded by a hollow metal sphere. Two electrodes in the form of comb-shaped rows of sharp metal points, are positioned respectively near the bottom of the lower pulley and inside the sphere, over the upper pulley. As the belt passes in front of the lower comb, it receives a negative charge which escapes from the points that are now ionized. As the belt touches the lower roller, it transfers some electrons, leaving the roller with a negative charge.

Electrons then leak from the belt to the upper comb and to the terminal, leaving the belt positively charged as it returns down and the terminal negatively charged. The sphere accumulates charge at the outer surface until there is a an electrical discharge and a change of polarity of the belt. These generators do not have a high voltage but are easy to make and work surprising well.

Was a simple machine similar to a Tesla coil or Van de Graaff generator kept inside the box and used to send out showers of electric fireballs in every direction, causing panic and shocking deaths to those in the vicinity of the fearsome device? Many of the descriptions of the Ark in action sound a lot like this scenario. There are also the curious electrical devices depicted on temple walls in Egypt (to be discussed in the next chapter).

So the golden statue could have easily had a glowing St. Elmo's Fire in its center dish, but this golden dish probably couldn't shoot fireballs at people. This would be a separate device kept inside the box.

However, another device is indicated in the Bible and this device is something that flies through the air. It is described essentially as an airship with smoke and lights.

Death and Destruction Ark of the Covenant Style

After building the Ark Moses reminds the people of their covenant and shows them Yahweh himself who has become a pillar of fire guiding the people at night and a pillar of smoke (cloud) in the day. It is something like an airship with smoke and lights, which are either integral parts of the airship's operation or perhaps for special effects.

When the Lord threatens to strike down the Israelites because they do not believe in him "despite all the signs I have performed in their midst," Moses pleads for them, saying it has been well noticed what the Lord has done. According to Numbers 14:13-14:

> But Moses said to the Lord, "Then the Egyptians will hear of it, for by Your strength You brought this people from their midst, and they will tell it to the inhabitants of this land: for they have heard that thou Yahweh art among this people, that thou Yahweh art seen face to face, and that thy cloud standeth over them, and that thou goest before them, by day time in a pillar of a cloud, and in a pillar of fire by night."

Just before this (Numbers 12: 1-16) there is a drama over Moses' Ethiopian wife, where Aaron's wife Miriam (both Moses and Aaron had a number of wives) "speaks against her." Then Yahweh comes down as a pillar of cloud to the tabernacle to set things straight (Numbers 12: 5-10):

> And the Yahweh came down in the pillar of the cloud, and stood in the door of the tabernacle, and called Aaron and Miriam: and they both came forth. And he said, Hear now my words: If there be a prophet among you, I the Yahweh will make myself known unto him in a vision, and will speak unto him in a dream. My servant Moses is not so, who is faithful in all mine house. With him will I speak mouth to mouth, even apparently, and not in dark speeches; and the similitude of the Yahweh shall he behold: wherefore then were ye not afraid to speak against my servant Moses? And the anger of the Yahweh was kindled against them; and he departed. And the cloud departed from off the tabernacle; and, behold, Miriam became leprous, white as snow: and Aaron looked upon Miriam, and, behold, she was leprous.

Aaron pleads with Moses to cure her and after speaking with Yahweh Moses says that she will be healed. Miriam goes into her tent for seven days and then emerges healed. The Israelites then left the spot where they had been camped, a place named Hazeroth, and moved into the wilderness of Paran.

Aaron's family was further afflicted when his two eldest sons, born of his wife Elisheba, were consumed by fire emanating from the presence of the Lord. These sons, Nadab and Alihu, had been part of the select retinue who were allowed to climb Mount Sinai and have a feast in the presence of the Lord. They emerged unscathed from that, but were to eventually commit a fatal error.

In Leviticus 8, Aaron and his sons are ordained as the first priests. In a ceremony conducted by Moses following orders given him by Yahweh, Aaron is clothed in the full priestly regalia, including the breastplate containing the Urim and Thummim. The men are anointed with oil, perform sacrifices, are fed offerings and told to stay at the entrance to the tent of meeting for seven days and "…do what the Lord requires, so you will not die."

On the eighth day, Aaron and his sons performed sacrifices, placing them on the altar. Says Leviticus 9:23-24:

> Moses and Aaron then went into the tent of meeting. When they came out, they blessed the people; and the glory of the Lord appeared to all the people. Fire came out from the presence of the Lord and consumed the burnt offering and the fat portions on the altar. And when all the people saw it, they shouted for joy and fell facedown.

In the very next verses, Leviticus 10:1-4, we are told:

> Aaron's sons Nadab and Abihu took their censers, put fire in them and added incense; and they offered unauthorized fire before the Lord, contrary to his command. So fire came out from the presence of the Lord and consumed them, and they died before the Lord. Moses then said to Aaron, "This is what the Lord spoke of when he said: 'Among those who approach me I will be proved holy; in the sight of all the people I will be honored.'"

This seems a little harsh. Two newly-minted priests go up in flames because they fail to take the fire to light their censers from the altar, and use "profane" fire instead. The religious take on this is that the priests were willful and presumptive in taking the step to light the censers at all, because Yahweh was commanding (in a very detailed way) what they should have been doing, and he hadn't told them to do this yet. This "presence of the Lord" is not to be taken lightly!

The Lord may have felt bad about this incident, because Leviticus 16:1-2 reports:

> The Lord spoke to Moses after the death of the two sons

of Aaron, when they drew near before the Lord and died, and the Lord said to Moses, "Tell Aaron your brother not to come at any time into the Holy Place inside the veil, before the mercy seat that is on the ark, so that he may not die. For I will appear in the cloud over the mercy seat."

After these verses, the Lord sets out the rules for the Day of Atonement, which would involve Aaron going into the Holy of Holies only once per year.

It is hard to tell in these stories whether the presence of the Lord that is burning things up is always coming from the Mercy Seat of Ark of the Covenant. In fact, the presence seems to move about, showing itself to the people, marching ahead as a pillar of cloud, etc. It is odd that "strange fire," as the old King James version of the Bible called it, would upset Yahweh so much that he could not control himself, killing innocents who were only trying to do his bidding and please him.

Did something in the incense burners, like the hot coals, react with the electrical device that was standing in the Ark and cause fire to come out and consume them? Perhaps it was just one of many discharges from the Ark that came from time to time; the Ark just happened to discharge at this time and Yahweh didn't really care about strange fire from the incense. The perception at the time was that this was the obvious cause of the sudden fiery discharge from the Ark, when it was merely a coincidence. The Ark was clearly a powerful device and was not to be messed with.

Chapter 16 in the book of Numbers is chock full of danger and doom from the volatile forces of the Lord. Korah, a descendent of Levi, and Dathan and Abiram, sons of Eliab, lead a revolt against Moses and Aaron, unhappy about the way things are going on the long and arduous trek to the Promised Land. They want to know why those two leaders should have all the decision-making power when the Lord is among the entire congregation, which is full of good people. Indeed, they bring 250 "princes of the assembly, famous in the congregation, men of renown" with them to protest. Says Numbers 16:4-7:

And when Moses heard it, he fell upon his face; and he spoke unto Korah and unto all his company, saying, "Even tomorrow the Lord will show who are His and who is holy, and will cause him to come near unto Him. Even him whom He hath chosen will He cause to come near unto Him.

This do: Take you censers, Korah and all his company, and put fire therein and put incense in them before the Lord tomorrow. And it shall be that the man whom the Lord doth choose, he shall be holy. Ye take too much upon you, ye sons of Levi."

Moses points out to the Levites that God had given them the honor of being the guardians of the tabernacle and ministers to the congregation, so they shouldn't also covet the role of Aaron and the priesthood. He exhorts Dathan and Abiram to stand with him, but they are bitter about being taken from a land of milk and honey and made to wander in the wilderness. Angry, Moses tells the Lord not to honor any of their offerings, as he has never hurt any of them. Says Numbers 16:16-21:

And Moses said unto Korah, "Be thou and all thy company before the Lord, thou and they and Aaron, tomorrow. And take every man his censer and put incense in them, and bring ye before the Lord every man his censer, two hundred and fifty censers, thou also and Aaron, each of you his censer."

And they took every man his censer and put fire in them and laid incense thereon, and stood in the door of the tabernacle of the congregation with Moses and Aaron. And Korah gathered all the congregation against them unto the door of the tabernacle of the congregation; and the glory of Yahweh appeared unto all the congregation.

And Yahweh spoke unto Moses and unto Aaron, saying, "Separate yourselves from among this congregation, that I may consume them in a moment."

Aaron and Moses prostrate themselves and entreat the Lord not to punish everyone for one man's sins. So the Lord tells Moses to go tell the people to get away from the tents of Korah, Dathan and Abiram. Moses, followed by the Elders, goes to their tents, where they meet him at the doors with their wives and children. Moses warns the others to get away and touch nothing of theirs, "lest ye be consumed in all their sins." Many people clear the tents. Numbers 16:28-35 relates:

> Then Moses said, "This is how you will know that the Lord has sent me to do all these things and that it was not my idea: If these men die a natural death and suffer the fate of all mankind, then the Lord has not sent me. But if the Lord brings about something totally new, and the earth opens its mouth and swallows them, with everything that belongs to them, and they go down alive into the realm of the dead, then you will know that these men have treated the Lord with contempt."
>
> As soon as he finished saying all this, the ground under them split apart and the earth opened its mouth and swallowed them and their households, and all those associated with Korah, together with their possessions. They went down alive into the realm of the dead, with everything they owned; the earth closed over them, and they perished and were gone from the community. At their cries, all the Israelites around them fled, shouting, "The earth is going to swallow us too!"
>
> And fire came out from the Lord and consumed the 250 men who were offering the incense.

The Lord then instructs Moses to have Aaron's son extract the censers from the charred remains and scatter the coals away from camp. The censers are to be hammered into an overlay for the altar.

The next day, the whole congregation is upset, accusing Moses and Aaron of killing the Lord's people. The end of Numbers 16 goes like this (verses 42 to 50):

> But when the assembly gathered in opposition to Moses and Aaron and turned toward the tent of meeting, suddenly the cloud covered it and the glory of the Lord appeared. Then Moses and Aaron went to the front of the tent of meeting, and the Lord said to Moses, "Get away from this assembly so I can put an end to them at once." And they fell facedown.
>
> Then Moses said to Aaron, "Take your censer and put incense in it, along with burning coals from the altar, and hurry to the assembly to make atonement for them. Wrath has come out from the Lord; the plague has started." So Aaron did as Moses said, and ran into the midst of the assembly. The plague had already started among the people, but Aaron offered the incense and made atonement for them. He stood between the living and the dead, and the plague stopped. But 14,700 people died from the plague, in addition to those who had died because of Korah. Then Aaron returned to Moses at the entrance to the tent of meeting, for the plague had stopped.

So here we have the Ark killing people with a sudden flash of light plus with the plague or some radiation sickness. The Bible also indicates that it caused an earthquake. We might think that this earthquake (if it ever happened at all) may just have been a coincidence and was probably a large exaggeration of the actual event—we just have no way of really knowing.

Still, it seems clear that there is some sort of energy machine in the box that can build up a powerful charge of electricity. That there is some hint of radiation coming from the device is indicated by Moses telling the people, "...and touch nothing of theirs, lest ye be consumed in all their sins." Perhaps there was some harmful residue—like radiation—still lingering on their clothes and jewelry. While all of their property became taboo, only the things they were wearing at the time of their death really mattered.

There is also the curious incident of the creation of manna to feed the Israelites during a time of famine. This was credited to the

Ark of the Covenant, and if the manna was created by the machine, this would make the device very multi-functional. It would have to have been some sort of super 3D printing device and at this point probably controlled by ancient aliens or some other ultra-high tech source.

In the *Ancient Aliens* television show it was suggested that this "Manna Machine" had atomic power and the ability to create manna and destroy people as well, depending on where you turned the dial, so to speak.

It seems unlikely that the high-tech device inside the Ark was using atomic power—but some sort of sophisticated battery? Yes. This battery was possibly being charged by the slow accumulation of static power by the condenser gold and wood box.

The Power of Yahweh and the Battle of Jericho

The Israelites continued through the deserts of Sinai and eastern Arabia (Midian) and at the end of the book of Deuteronomy we learn how Moses and his huge troop of men, women, children and animals arrived at Mount Pisgah on the east side of the Dead Sea and the Jordan River. Most Bible historians think Mount Pisgah is a portion of the range of Abarim, and that Mount Nebo was the highest peak of Mount Pisgah; it was this that Moses climbed. Here he saw the Promised Land and the walled city of Jericho in the distance but he was not to cross over the Jordan. Says Deuteronomy 34:

> Then Moses climbed Mount Nebo from the plains of Moab to the top of Pisgah, across from Jericho. There the Lord showed him the whole land—from Gilead to Dan, all of Naphtali, the territory of Ephraim and Manasseh, all the land of Judah as far as the Mediterranean Sea, the Negev and the whole region from the Valley of Jericho, the City of Palms, as far as Zoar. Then the Lord said to him, "This is the land I promised on oath to Abraham, Isaac and Jacob when I said, 'I will give it to your descendants.' I have let you see it with your eyes, but you will not cross over into it." And Moses the servant of the Lord died there in Moab,

An old print of the destruction of Jericho.

as the Lord had said. He buried him in Moab, in the valley opposite Beth Peor, but to this day no one knows where his grave is. Moses was a hundred and twenty years old when he died, yet his eyes were not weak nor his strength gone. The Israelites grieved for Moses in the plains of Moab thirty days, until the time of weeping and mourning was over. Now Joshua son of Nun was filled with the spirit of wisdom because Moses had laid his hands on him. So the Israelites listened to him and did what the Lord had commanded Moses.

Moses, at 120 years old, was now dead. Joshua was in control of the great host of Hebrews and he would need the power of the Ark to cross the River Jordan and then attack and destroy the ancient

80

walled city of Jericho. In Joshua chapter 2 we are told how Joshua sent spies across the Jordan to Jericho to check on the defenses of the city. They are given the name of a prostitute named Rahab who shelters them. In a sense, she runs an inn and brothel in Jericho, and probably knows that the Israelites desired to destroy the city and kill everyone, but she doesn't seem to care. She tells the spies that everyone in the neighborhood is afraid of the great host of Israel—literally a gigantic army—on the eastern side of the Jordan.

In Joshua 3 we are told how the Ark of the Covenant is capable of parting the waters of the Jordan River which are at flood stage:

> Early in the morning Joshua and all the Israelites set out from a place called Shittim and went to the Jordan River, where they camped for some days before crossing over. After three days the officers went throughout the camp, giving orders to the people: "When you see the ark of the covenant of the Lord your God, and the Levitical priests carrying it, you are to move out from your positions and follow it. Then you will know which way to go, since you have never been this way before. But keep a distance of about two thousand cubits between you and the ark; do not go near it." Joshua told the people, "Consecrate yourselves, for tomorrow the Lord will do amazing things among you." Joshua said to the priests, "Take up the ark of the covenant and pass on ahead of the people." So they took it up and went ahead of them.
>
> And the Lord said to Joshua, "Today I will begin to exalt you in the eyes of all Israel, so they may know that I am with you as I was with Moses. Tell the priests who carry the ark of the covenant: 'When you reach the edge of the Jordan's waters, go and stand in the river.'"
>
> ...Now then, choose twelve men from the tribes of Israel, one from each tribe. And as soon as the priests who carry the ark of the Lord—the Lord of all the earth—set foot in the Jordan, its waters flowing downstream will be cut off and stand up in a heap."
>
> So when the people broke camp to cross the Jordan, the

81

priests carrying the ark of the covenant went ahead of them. Now the Jordan is at flood stage all during harvest. Yet as soon as the priests who carried the ark reached the Jordan and their feet touched the water's edge, the water from upstream stopped flowing. It piled up in a heap a great distance away, at a town called Adam in the vicinity of Zarethan, while the water flowing down to the Sea of the Arabah [Dead Sea] was completely cut off. So the people crossed over opposite Jericho. The priests who carried the ark of the covenant of the Lord stopped in the middle of the Jordan and stood on dry ground, while all Israel passed by until the whole nation had completed the crossing on dry ground.

Having now crossed the Jordan, we learn in Joshua 4 that Yahweh supposedly instructs Joshua to have one man from each of the 12 tribes collect a stone each from the dry riverbed and bring it to the camp as a sign of the power of God. At the end of Joshua 4 the new leader commands the priests to come out of the Jordan with the Ark, and when they do so the water rushes back and the normal flow of the river is restored. The Israelites camp at a place called Gilgal on the eastern border of the land of Jericho.

In the next chapter, Joshua 5, we learn that Amorite kings on the western side of the Jordan and the Canaanite kings on the coast hear about this event and they no longer have the courage to fight the Israelites and are afraid of them. They have essentially given up Jericho to the Israelites. The Israelites camp at Gilgal for some time and observe Passover. Also, since the Israelites had left Egypt they had not performed circumcision on the young men, so these men are all circumcised and remain in the camp. Circumcision was a common practice in ancient Egypt and one of Yahweh's commands.

Then at the end of Joshua 5 a strange encounter takes place between Joshua and a man with a sword in the vicinity of Jericho. The encounter carries on into Joshua 6. In Joshua 5:13-15 we are told:

Now when Joshua was near Jericho, he looked up and

saw a man standing in front of him with a drawn sword in his hand. Joshua went up to him and asked, "Are you for us or for our enemies?" "Neither," he replied, "but as commander of the army of the Lord I have now come." Then Joshua fell facedown to the ground in reverence, and asked him, "What message does my Lord have for his servant?" The commander of the Lord's army replied, "Take off your sandals, for the place where you are standing is holy." And Joshua did so.

Who is this strange man, some kind of angel, such as those described in the story of Sodom and Gomorrah, who is waiting for Joshua on the outskirts of Jericho? Then we are told that the city of Jericho has simply sealed itself up and locked its gates because of the huge army of Israelites camped nearby:

> Now the gates of Jericho were securely barred because of the Israelites. No one went out and no one came in. Then the Lord said to Joshua, "See, I have delivered Jericho into your hands, along with its king and its fighting men. March around the city once with all the armed men. Do this for six days. Have seven priests carry trumpets of rams' horns in front of the ark. On the seventh day, march around the city seven times, with the priests blowing the trumpets. When you hear them sound a long blast on the trumpets, have the whole army give a loud shout; then the wall of the city will collapse and the army will go up, everyone straight in." (Joshua 6:1-5)

Joshua takes the advice of the man with the sword—the Lord (Yahweh) he is called later—and instructs his army to do as the man has told him. Says Joshua 6:11-21:

> So Joshua son of Nun called the priests and said to them, "Take up So he had the ark of the Lord carried around the city, circling it once. Then the army returned to camp and

spent the night there. Joshua got up early the next morning and the priests took up the ark of the Lord. The seven priests carrying the seven trumpets went forward, marching before the ark of the Lord and blowing the trumpets. The armed men went ahead of them and the rear guard followed the ark of the Lord, while the trumpets kept sounding. So on the second day they marched around the city once and returned to the camp. They did this for six days.

On the seventh day, they got up at daybreak and marched around the city in the same manner, except that on that day they circled the city seven times. The seventh time around, when the priests sounded the trumpet blast, Joshua commanded the army,

"Shout! For the Lord has given you the city! The city and all that is in it are to be devoted to the Lord. Only Rahab the prostitute and all who are with her in her house shall be spared, because she hid the spies we sent. But keep away from the devoted things, so that you will not bring about your own destruction by taking any of them. Otherwise you will make the camp of Israel liable to destruction and bring trouble on it. All the silver and gold and the articles of bronze and iron are sacred to the Lord and must go into his treasury."

When the trumpets sounded, the army shouted, and at the sound of the trumpet, when the men gave a loud shout, the wall collapsed; so everyone charged straight in, and they took the city. They devoted the city to the Lord and destroyed with the sword every living thing in it—men and women, young and old, cattle, sheep and donkeys.

After the destruction of Jericho, Joshua had the remains of the city burned and cursed any man who would rebuild the city that he would do so at the cost of his firstborn son. Large ruins of the outer walls still exist today. It was once thought to have been the oldest city in the world.

The destruction of Jericho is a famous story from Bible, yet it is

An old print of the destruction of Jericho.

not really clear just how the walls of Jericho came tumbling down. The Ark seems to have something to do with it, and the blowing of the trumpets and shouting give the impression of some sort of sonic weapon—a sound canon type device—that would shake the walls of Jericho like an earthquake and make them crumble. Indeed, it almost sounds like the destruction of the walls happened in an earthquake, perhaps one that was artificially created or was predicted to occur at a specific time.

And who was the man with a sword, commander of the army of Yahweh, that Joshua met? He seemed to know something about the power of the Ark of the Covenant that Joshua did not know. Had he also assisted in some way in the destruction of the walls of Jericho? Perhaps he and his holy army had the sonic canons that needed to be used to breach the thick walls.

Indeed, was this mysterious man perhaps someone in possession of a vimana airship and various technology and weapons that a vimana might have? As I describe in my book *Vimana: Flying*

Machines of the Ancients[37] ancient texts in India and elsewhere describe flying vehicles that are used by kings and princes to travel great distances and to wage war on their neighbors and enemies.

Might this mysterious stranger with advice on how to take a fortified city have been from ancient India, Tibet, or elsewhere and be in possession of some fairly sophisticated equipment, including an airship? Or similarly, perhaps he was some sort of ancient astronaut who wanted to guide the Israelites to victory, as ancient astronaut theorists would easily suggest.

It is quite possible that the marching and blowing of horns around the city of Jericho was a signal for a larger power, such as a vimana or two, to unleash a devastating sonic wave against the city walls that would cause portions of the walls to crack and break similar to a localized earthquake—this one artificially created by man, as the Bible states. These airships would not even have to have been in sight of the people, using long-range weapons to accomplish their objectives.

I conclude that the Ark was not completely responsible for the collapse of the walls of Jericho, but rather a second destructive energy source, more powerful than the energy machine inside the Ark, was used. That weapon was probably unleashed from some sort of airship, the same one that was guiding Moses and the Israelites through the desert and landing on Mount Sinai with a great deal of fire and light.

The Ark is Moved to Shiloh

After the destruction of Jericho, Joshua takes the Israelite host to a location called Shiloh in the hills west of Jericho. Though archeologists are not completely certain, Shiloh is thought to have been located near modern Khirbet Seilun in the West Bank. Shiloh became the first capital of Israel; here Joshua set up the ancient wilderness tent shrine called the tent of meeting, or tabernacle, and inside this enclosure Joshua divided the land among the 12 tribes.

The Holy of Holies was also set up at Shiloh and the Ark of the Covenant was placed inside it. Supposedly it remained in this enclosure for 369 years ("Talmudic sources"—Wikipedia) until it was taken into the battle camp at Eben-ezer when the Israelites went to war with the Philistines (1 Samuel 4:3–5).

Subsequently, Shiloh became one of the leading religious shrines in ancient Israel, a status it held until shortly before David's elevation of Jerusalem.

After the defeat at the hands of the Philistines at Ai (to be discussed shortly), Joshua lamented before the Ark (Joshua 7:6-9). When Joshua read the Law to the people between Mount Gerizim and Mount Ebal, they stood on each side of the Ark. The Ark was again set up by Joshua at Shiloh, but when the Israelites fought against Benjamin at Gibeah, they had the Ark with them and consulted it after their defeat.

Capture of the Ark and Mass Destruction

In the two books of Samuel we are told more tales of the fearsome power of the Ark. In 1 Samuel we learn that a childless woman, Hannah, vows to Yahweh that if she has a son, he will be dedicated to him and the Ark. Eli, the priest of the tabernacle at Shiloh, blesses her, and a child named Samuel is born. Samuel is dedicated to the Lord and becomes a servant of Eli at the tabernacle.

Samuel becomes the second-in-charge priest of the tabernacle, after Eli, who is custodian of the Ark. We are then told at the beginning of 1 Samuel 4 that the Israelites are going to war with the Philistines who live just north of Israel:

> And Samuel's word came to all Israel. Now the Israelites went out to fight against the Philistines. The Israelites camped at Ebenezer, and the Philistines at Aphek. The Philistines deployed their forces to meet Israel, and as the battle spread, Israel was defeated by the Philistines, who killed about four thousand of them on the battlefield. When the soldiers returned to camp, the elders of Israel asked, "Why did the Lord bring defeat on us today before the Philistines? Let us bring the ark of the Lord's covenant from Shiloh, so that he may go with us and save us from the hand of our enemies." So the people sent men to Shiloh, and they brought back the

ark of the covenant of the Lord Almighty, who is enthroned between the cherubim. And Eli's two sons, Hophni and Phinehas, were there with the ark of the covenant of God. When the ark of the Lord's covenant came into the camp, all Israel raised such a great shout that the ground shook.

Hearing the uproar, the Philistines asked, "What's all this shouting in the Hebrew camp?" When they learned that the ark of the Lord had come into the camp, the Philistines were afraid. "A god has come into the camp," they said. "Oh no! Nothing like this has happened before. We're doomed! Who will deliver us from the hand of these mighty gods? They are the gods who struck the Egyptians with all kinds of plagues in the wilderness. Be strong, Philistines! Be men, or you will be subject to the Hebrews, as they have been to you. Be men, and fight!" So the Philistines fought, and the Israelites were defeated and every man fled to his tent. The slaughter was very great; Israel lost thirty thousand foot soldiers. The ark of God was captured, and Eli's two sons, Hophni and Phinehas, died. (1 Samuel 4:1-11)

The news of the capture of the Ark and the death of Eli's sons is immediately taken to Shiloh by a messenger "with his clothes rent, and with earth upon his head." The old priest, Eli, falls off his chair and dies when he hears the news.

The Philistines take the Ark back to the temple of their god Dagon, who recognizes the supremacy of Yahweh. The Philistines are afflicted with plagues and decide to return the Ark to the Israelites. Says 1 Samuel 5:1-8:

After the Philistines had captured the ark of God, they took it from Ebenezer to Ashdod. Then they carried the ark into Dagon's temple and set it beside Dagon. When the people of Ashdod rose early the next day, there was Dagon, fallen on his face on the ground before the ark of the Lord! They took Dagon and put him back in his place. But the following morning when they rose, there was Dagon, fallen on his face on the ground before the ark of the Lord! His head and hands had been broken off and were lying on the threshold; only his body remained. That is why to this day neither the priests of Dagon nor any others who enter Dagon's temple at Ashdod step on the threshold.

The Lord's hand was heavy on the people of Ashdod and its vicinity; he brought devastation on them and afflicted them with tumors. When the people of Ashdod saw what was happening, they said, "The ark of the god of Israel must not stay here with us, because his hand is heavy on us and on Dagon our god." So they called together all the rulers of the Philistines and asked them, "What shall we do with the ark of the god of Israel?"

At this point, another incident of mass destruction occurs when the Ark is returned to Israel on an oxcart. When it gets to the small village of Beth-shemesh it kills, by some sort of flash of energy, 70 of the village's men. The bizarre story is told in 1 Samuel 6:1-16:

The ark of the Lord was in the country of the Philistines seven months. And the Philistines called for the priests and the diviners and said, "What shall we do with the ark of the Lord? Tell us with what we shall send it to its place." They said, "If you send away the ark of the God of Israel, do not send it empty, but by all means return him a guilt offering. Then you will be healed, and it will be known to you why his hand does not turn away from you." And they said, "What is the guilt offering that we shall return to him?"

They answered, "Five golden tumors and five golden mice, according to the number of the lords of the Philistines, for the same plague was on all of you and on your lords. So you must make images of your tumors and images of your mice that ravage the land, and give glory to the God of Israel. Perhaps he will lighten his hand from off you and your gods and your land. Why should you harden your hearts as the Egyptians and Pharaoh hardened their hearts? After he had dealt severely with them, did they not send the people away, and they departed? Now then, take and prepare a new cart and two milk cows on which there has never come a yoke, and yoke the cows to the cart, but take their calves home, away from them. And take the ark of the Lord and place it on the cart and put in a box at its side the figures of gold, which you are returning to him as a guilt offering. Then send it off and let it go its way and watch. If it goes up on the way to its own land, to Beth-shemesh, then it is he who has done us this great harm, but if not, then we shall know that it is not his hand that struck us; it happened to us by coincidence."

The men did so, and took two milk cows and yoked them to the cart and shut up their calves at home. And they put the ark of the Lord on the cart and the box with the golden mice and the images of their tumors. And the cows went straight in the direction of Beth-shemesh along one highway, lowing as they went. They turned neither to the right nor to the left, and the lords of the Philistines went after them as far as the border of Beth-shemesh. Now the people of Beth-shemesh were reaping their wheat harvest in the valley. And when they lifted up their eyes and saw the ark, they rejoiced to see it. The cart came into the field of Joshua of Beth-shemesh and stopped there. A great stone was there. And they split up the wood of the cart and offered the cows as a burnt offering to the Lord. And the Levites took down the ark of the Lord and the box that was beside it, in which were the golden figures, and set them upon the great stone. And the men of Beth-shemesh offered burnt offerings and sacrificed sacrifices on that day to the Lord. And when the five lords of the Philistines saw it, they returned that day to Ekron.

But suddenly things go horribly wrong for the people in the village when the Ark of the Covenant lets loose a giant flash of energy that instantly kills a group of people gathered around it. 1 Samuel 6:17 begins:

90

These are the golden tumors that the Philistines returned as a guilt offering to the Lord: one for Ashdod, one for Gaza, one for Ashkelon, one for Gath, one for Ekron and the golden mice, according to the number of all the cities of the Philistines belonging to the five lords, both fortified cities and unwalled villages. The great stone beside which they set down the ark of the Lord is a witness to this day in the field of Joshua of Beth-shemesh.

And he struck some of the men of Beth-shemesh, because they looked upon the ark of the Lord. He struck seventy men of them, and the people mourned because the Lord had struck the people with a great blow. Then the men of Beth-shemesh said, "Who is able to stand before the Lord, this holy God? And to whom shall he go up away from us?" So they sent messengers to the inhabitants of Kiriath-jearim, saying, "The Philistines have returned the ark of the Lord. Come down and take it up to you."

Since the Ark had discharged its energy in what might be called a gigantic friendly-fire action that decimated an entire platoon of Israelites, it was now safe to be handled. The Ark would now be taken to a place called Kiriath-jearim, apparently on the outskirts of Shiloh, where it would remain for twenty years without being shown. We learn in 1 Samuel 7:1:

And the men of Kiriath-jearim came and took up the ark of the Lord and brought it to the house of Abinadab on the hill. And they consecrated his son Eleazar to have charge of the ark of the Lord. From the day that the ark was lodged at Kiriath-jearim, a long time passed, some twenty years, and all the house of Israel lamented after the Lord.

This terrible destruction at Beth-shemesh seems to be the last time that the Ark of the Covenant kills a large number of people with "a great blow." What is this great blow? This would be more

91

than just the static accumulation of electricity on the lid of the Ark. The lid was probably lifted and perhaps a button pushed and whoosh! A sudden discharge of awesome power and 70 men were incinerated. Perhaps the whole event is grossly exaggerated in the Bible, but why include this tale if it were not largely true? The Ark is essentially killing innocent people and the Israelites clearly think of it as a dangerous object.

Essentially the people had lost control of the power of the Ark and it was allowed to go into disuse for decades at Kiriath-jearim-Shiloh until it was finally moved to Solomon's Temple in Jerusalem. It was occasionally taken into battle, however the Bible does not speak of any more instances of the Ark itself killing anyone or discharging onto a crowd. The faint light in the center of the gold cherubim—the Shekina Glory—would have continued to function, since it needed no battery and had no moving parts.

An Electrical Device from Egypt?

As I have said, I think that the Ark of the Covenant is several objects written about as one object. There is a device kept inside the box and another device that is also electrical in nature—a simple electrical condenser.

The construction of the boxes of the Ark of the Covenant made it a simple electrical condenser, though an expensive one with all of the gold used in the powerful device. The three boxes that made up the Ark of the Covenant were a sandwiching of gold, a conducting metal, and acacia wood, a non-conductor. The chafing of these layers would build up static electricity in certain dry atmospheric conditions.

The golden statue at the top may have acted as a focus for this static DC electricity—similar to a powerful static electricity shock—that could have discharged at times onto people who were standing near it. If these people were wearing metal objects like bracelets, necklaces, earrings, and even armor, the Ark may have been easily disposed to discharge upon them.

If the Ark had not been grounded for some long period of time, the electrical charge built up in it could give a very nasty, even fatal, shock to someone who touched it. If the shock itself was not fatal, then the surprise of the shock could well be. After the Ark had been discharged, however, it would be quite safe to touch as some of the temple priests did.

One might conclude that a powerful static electric charge discharged from the Ark onto a crowd could cause a large number of heart attacks out of sheer terror of the tingling sensation of the wrath of God.

But in some of these cases, it is almost like some neutron-flash grenade is detonated in the air above the Ark when it is activated. This would seem to be a second, more powerful electrical device than the simple condenser of the chest and gold statue. Unless it is all some super-exaggeration, we seem to have a high-voltage death ray device that probably discharged from a battery.

But what was the powerful electric device inside the Ark? Was it an electrical device taken from Egypt, something similar to devices depicted in temples such as djed pillars with globes on top of them? It seems to be that it was the object inside the box that was killing dozens of people in a single super-flash of electrical power. The men of Beth-shemesh may have lifted the lid of the Ark and unleashed (perhaps after pushing some buttons) the tremendous power of God in a scene similar to the ending of *Raiders of the Lost Ark*.

As we have seen, the Ark was credited with many things, including flying, mass killing, causing disease, parting water, creating manna, and making the walls of cities fall down. It also shone as a brilliant bright light when "turned on." Perhaps the Ark did not do all of these things, and it would be safe to say that a considerable amount of myth and legend has grown up around this ancient artifact of great power.

That the Ark could also fly or levitate is spoken of in the Bible. Ancient tales of flight are always of interest and the Ark of the Covenant plays into this subject. Let us now examine the stories of flight surrounding the Ark of God.

Van de Graaff Generator

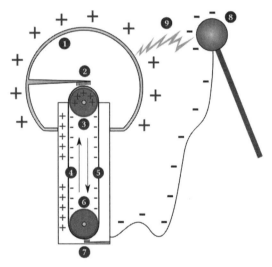

1. hollow metal sphere
2. upper electrode
3. upper roller (for example an acrylic glass)
4. side of the belt with positive charges
5. opposite side of belt, with negative charges
6. lower roller (metal)
7. lower electrode (ground)
8. spherical device with negative charges
9. spark produced by the difference of potentials

CHAPTER FIVE
A FLYING MACHINE

...and the Ark of the Covenant of the Lord went
before them in the three days' journey to search out
a resting place for them.

—Numbers 10:29-36

The Ark of the Covenant is not just an electrical device of some sort, it is also said to have the power to fly. At one point after the Ark has been unveiled to the great Israelite host, it flies through the air for three days through the air so that Israelites can find their way through the desert.

There is no doubt that when the Ark was moved it was typically carried by four men via the poles and metal rings, and sometimes in a cart. However, there are stories of the Ark being able to levitate and even lift up the people carrying it with the poles. Sort of like the Ark becoming weightless, a form of anti-gravity.

There are other stories of flight surrounding the Ark that make us think that there is another object that is an actual airship. A column of smoke and fire led the Israelites, hovering above them, driven by "the Lord." The Lord also appeared to be present in other clouds that interacted with the people, even actively smiting enemies. Where these mechanical vehicles, emitting exhaust, or cloaked by some weird invisibility device?

The *Kebra Nagast* indicates that Solomon owns a flying vehicle, a vimana of some sort. It also features flying wagons, wherein entire caravans, including the Ark of the Covenant, soar for days. Let's look closer at these intriguing tales.

A Flying Machine

The Ark that Flies

The book of Exodus ends with Moses bringing the Ten Commandments down from Mount Sinai with instructions on building the tabernacle, the Ark, and other things. Then, in Numbers 1 and 2, we learn that the Ark can fly as it literally leads the Israelites forward through the desert.

In Numbers 10:29-36 the Ark glows and flies in front of an advance party seeking out a new long-term campsite for the hundreds of thousands of people and animals that are the Israelite host:

> And Moses said unto Hobab, the son of Reuel the Midianite, Moses' father-in-law: "We are journeying unto the place of which the Lord said, 'I will give it to you.' Come thou with us, and we will do thee good; for the Lord hath spoken good concerning Israel."
>
> And he said unto him, "I will not go, but I will depart to mine own land and to my kindred."
>
> And he said, "Leave us not, I pray thee, inasmuch as thou knowest how we are to encamp in the wilderness, and thou mayest be to us instead of eyes.
>
> And it shall be, if thou go with us, yea, it shall be that what goodness the Lord shall do unto us, the same will we do unto thee."
>
> And they departed from the mount of the Lord three days' journey, and the ark of the covenant of the Lord went before them in the three days' journey to search out a resting place for them.
>
> And the cloud of the Lord was upon them by day when they went out of the camp.
>
> And it came to pass, when the ark moved forward, that Moses said, "Rise up, Lord, and let Thine enemies be scattered; and let them that hate Thee flee before Thee."
>
> And when it rested he said, "Return, O Lord, unto the many thousands of Israel."

The last quotes in the last two paragraphs are lines of ancient

Indiana Jones moves the Ark of the Covenant in the film *Raiders of the Lost Ark*.

Moses and Joshua in the tabernacle before the Ark of the Covenant. (*Tissot*)

An artist's conception of the Ark of the Covenant.

Replicas of the Ark of the Covenant like this one are available over the Internet.

A gold coin featuring the Ark of the Covenant was issued by the Pacific island nation of Niue.

Joshua crossing the River Jordan with the Ark of the Covenant by Benjamin West.

Moses with a veil over his face.

The pillar of smoke and fire over the tabernacle.

An artist's conception of the pillar of smoke and fire over the tabernacle.

The gigantic Western Stone of Solomon's temple and the perfectly fitted stones beneath it. (David Shankbone)

A photo of the southern side of the Temple Mount as it looks today.

An aerial photo of the Temple Mount with the al-Aqsa mosque and its golden dome.

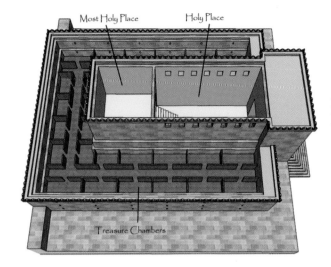

Left: Close-up of the Holy of Holies room with the ceiling removed.

Most Holy Place

Holy Place

Treasure Chambers

Above: An artist's concept of the interior of the temple. *Left*: The ark found in Tutankhamun's tomb with an inlaid design of a hunting scene.

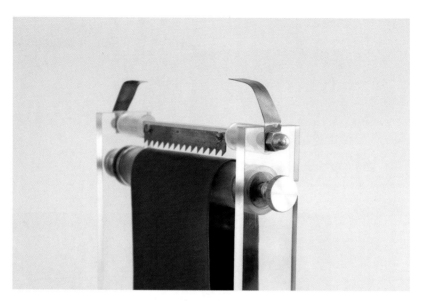

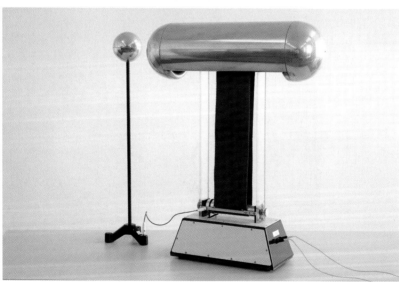

Above: Two views of a Van de Graaff generator showing the belt and comb. *Right*: A spark discharges from a Van de Graaff generator.

poetry called the "song to the ark," and reflect the belief that the Ark served as a throne of the Divine Warrior, where an invisible God sat during holy war. Here we get the impression that Moses was commanding and controlling the Ark, and having it fly through the air before them and then rest.

That the Ark was believed to be a seat for the Divine Warrior can be seen in 1 Samuel 4, where we learn that when the Israelites faced the Philistines, they were defeated and lost 4,000 in the first battle. Says 1 Samuel 4:3-4:

> When the soldiers returned to camp, the elders of Israel asked, "Why did the Lord bring defeat on us today before the Philistines? Let us bring the ark of the Lord's covenant from Shiloh, so that he may go with us and save us from the hand of our enemies."
>
> So the people sent men to Shiloh, and they brought back the ark of the covenant of the Lord Almighty, who is enthroned between the cherubim. And Eli's two sons, Hophni and Phinehas, were there with the ark of the covenant of God.

As we saw in the last chapter, when the Philistines learned that the Ark had been brought into the Israeli camp they lamented that they were doomed, and asked who would save them from the hands of the mighty god.

As it happened, even though it struck terror into the hearts of their foes, the presence of the Ark did not bring victory for the Israelites. They lost 30,000 in the battle the next day, and it was then that the Ark was captured by the Philistines.

In his 1992 book *The Sign and the Seal: The Quest for the Ark of the Covenant*,[4] Graham Hancock uses an important reference, *Legends of the Jews*,[9] (1911) by Louis Ginzberg for the assertion that the Ark could levitate and fly:

> The Ark gave the signal for breaking camp by soaring high and then swiftly moving before the camp at a distance of three days march.

97

Ginzberg here interprets the wording of Numbers 10 quoted above as saying that the Ark flew far ahead of the Israelites, "at a distance of three days march," but most modern interpretations say simply that the Ark went before the travelers during the three day journey through the Sinai.

In researching his book, Graham Hancock found other tales of the Ark performing strange feats and defying gravity. These are found mostly in Jewish sources wherein scholars debate the meaning of different parts of the Torah. They took the Torah to be the actual word of God, so no part of it could be meaningless. In delving for meaning in certain difficult to understand passages or odd nuances, different theories sprang up as to what was really going on. Midrash, in particular, is a category of rabbinic writings that derive either sermonic or legal implications from biblical text. Says Hancock:

> Travelling at the head of the Israelite column, the sacred relic was borne on the shoulders of "the Kohathites" (or 'sons of Kohath') a sub-clan of the tribe of Levi to which both Moses and Aaron also belonged. According to several legends, and to rabbinical commentaries on the Old Testament, these bearers were occasionally killed by "sparks" which the Ark emitted and, in addition, were lifted bodily off the ground from time to time because "the Ark [was] able to carry its carriers as well as itself." Nor is this the only Jewish tradition to suggest that the Ark might have been able to exert a mysterious force that in some way was able to counteract gravity. Several other pieces of learned Midrashic exegesis also testify that it sometimes lifted its bearers off the ground (thus temporarily relieving them of what would otherwise have been a considerable burden). In a similar vein a particularly striking Jewish legend reports an incident during which the priests attempted to carry the Ark were "tossed by an invisible agency into the air and flung to the ground again and again." Another tradition describes an

occasion when "the Ark leaped of itself into the air."[4]

Hancock's sources for these anecdotes are the Jewish Encyclopedia and the Ginsberg book cited above. The website jewishvirtuallibrary.org has this to say on the subject:

> The Ark was used in the desert and in Israel proper for a number of spiritual and pragmatic purposes. Practically, God used the Ark as an indicator of when he wanted the nation to travel, and when to stop. In the traveling formation in the desert, the Ark was carried 2000 cubits ahead of the nation (Num. R. 2:9). According to one midrash, it would clear the path for the nation by burning snakes, scorpions, and thorns with two jets of flame that shot from its underside (T. VaYakhel, 7); another midrash says that rather than being carried by its bearers, the Ark in fact carried its bearers inches above the ground (Sotah 35a). When the Israelites went to war in the desert and during the conquering of Canaan, the Ark accompanied them; whether its presence was symbolic, to provide motivation for the Jews, or whether it actually aided them in fighting, is debated by commentators.

As noted by Hancock, the people designated to carry the Ark were a sub-clan of the priestly Levites. Some have drawn an association between the word "levitate" and the name of the tribe tasked with transporting the Ark. Most dictionaries date the word levitate only back to the 1600s, however, and make no mention of the Levites in its derivation. Hancock mentions that one reason for the Ark to levitate would be to take its great weight off the shoulders of its bearers. A surprising number of people have looked into the question of how much the Ark weighed; it does seem that a gilded chest with a golden statue atop it could be pretty unwieldy. The results of the studies are extremely varied, with a Bar-Ilan University article coming up with the cover alone weighing 1,207 kilograms (over a ton), and an article by Elihu A. Schatz on jewishbible.org coming up with a much more manageable 83 kilograms (183 pounds) for the whole assembly. This would put a mere 46 pounds on the shoulders of each carrier, assuming there were four.

Whether the Ark really flew on its own accord remains a question in my mind, but there is no question that something was flying around the Israelites.

The Cloud of the Lord

In Exodus 13:21-22 we learn that God accompanied the people of Israel on their journey, leading the way:

> By day the Lord went ahead of them in a pillar of cloud to guide them on their way and by night in a pillar of fire to give them light, so that they could travel by day or night. Neither the pillar of cloud by day nor the pillar of fire by night left its place in front of the people.

It was a glowing cloud, and enemies ran away in fear of the eerie, flying mass. Says Exodus 14:24-25:

> During the last watch of the night the Lord looked down from the pillar of fire and cloud at the Egyptian army and threw it into confusion. He jammed the wheels of their chariots so that they had difficulty driving. And the Egyptians said, "Let's get away from the Israelites! The Lord is fighting for them against Egypt."

This is a pretty hands-on approach, with the Lord hovering over the people, looking down from the fire and cloud and joining the fight against the pursuers. There is a hint here that the cloud/fire was an actual flying craft, like a small flying saucer manned by the Lord. Perhaps it was flying a small group of Israelite scouts forward as the people journeyed into northern Sinai at the northern end of the Gulf of Aqaba. This area is in the southern part of Edom, which then led north to the plains of Moab and Mount Nebo on the northeastern side of the Dead Sea.

In Numbers 10, quoted above, we are told that "the cloud of the

Lord was upon them by day when they went out of the camp." While the people were encamped, the cloud rested over the tabernacle — was this some sort of parking place for the vimana-type craft?

In Numbers 11:25, the cloud of the Lord visits with the elders of Israel to put some of the "spirit" that has been given to Moses on them, so that they can share in the burden of leadership.

The Lord comes down again in a pillar of fire in Numbers 12, when the kerfuffle over Aaron and Miriam complaining about Moses' Ethiopian wife occurred, and Miriam ended up with leprosy. This seems to be a description of a person arriving in an aerial vehicle, conversing with Moses and a few others to give them some instruction and then departing. It is a clear divergence from the burning bush that spoke to Moses earlier. A pillar of fire seems a lot like an airship-rocket or flying saucer type of machine.

In this story, we have the Lord coming down to a central tent in the middle of hundreds of thousands of people and their animals encamped near Mount Sinai. This sounds a lot like a small flying craft landing vertically onto a large plaza. Radiation from the craft may have afflicted Aaron's wife as she gazed at the craft. Moses

The pillar of smoke and fire hovering over the tabernacle.

at this time was always wearing a veil that covered his face—was this veil perhaps of metal, or cloth with metal fibers woven into it, something that protected Moses from the burning radiation that came when standing in front of the Ark of the Covenant or the vimana craft that was apparently also in use?

As I have mentioned, we seem to have two different high-tech devices here that get intermingled in the text: one is a wooden and gold chest with a gold statue on top of it and the other is a glowing craft that is like a flying saucer or a helicopter.

Ethiopians believe that the Ark eventually was brought to Ethiopia, and that the journey included flight in a "Wagon of the Lord." Biblical scholars and historians tend to discount Ethiopia's claims to the Ark, and even say that the ancient city of Axum—which features prominently in the *Kebra Nagast*—was not even in existence at the time. I think these historians are wrong, and the *Kebra Nagast* has at least some truth to it. Also, as we have seen, one of Moses' wives was an Ethiopian. Ethiopia is a neglected but important cog in the giant wheel of ancient civilizations. Let us look at King Solomon, Ethiopia and ancient flight.

The Airships of King Solomon

Throughout history certain kings or magicians were said to have possessed airships or flying chariots. Various Hindu figures such as Rama, Ravana, and Krishna were said to have possessed flying vehicles called vimanas in Sanskrit. Legend has it that King Solomon the Wise, the son of David, was also in possession of an airship. Solomon was the last ruler of a united Israel and ruled circa 970-931 BC. After his death Israel split into Judah in the south and Israel in the north. His descendants ruled Judah.

He was known for being very worldly, and having many wives, many from far-off countries. 1 Kings 11:1-3 tells us:

> King Solomon, however, loved many foreign women besides Pharaoh's daughter—Moabites, Ammonites, Edomites, Sidonians and Hittites. They were from nations about which the Lord had told the Israelites, "You must not

intermarry with them, because they will surely turn your hearts after their gods." Nevertheless, Solomon held fast to them in love. He had seven hundred wives of royal birth and three hundred concubines, and his wives led him astray.

In Deuteronomy 17:14-20, God had set forth how a king was to deport himself, and cautioned that he should not amass horses, wives, silver or gold. Solomon failed in all of these areas, creating a huge chariot army, marrying 1,000 women and gathering immense physical wealth.

Solomon was known for sending Phoenician ships on a mysterious three-year journey to a land of plentiful gold: Ophir. During a three-year journey from the Red Sea port of Ezion-Geber —an important port city to ancient Israel as it is to modern Israel—a fleet of ships would have had a year to make the long journey, a year to stay in Ophir and grow a crop of food if they needed to, and a year to return. They could have gone quite a distance in one year, and would certainly have traveled beyond the near countries

An aerial photo of the round and flat-topped mountain in Iran called Takht-i-Suleiman.

in the Indian Ocean during that time. They were probably going to Australia, Indonesia and even Peru in their search for shiploads of gold. The Bible says such treasure was collected, along with valuable spices, feathers and even exotic animals such as apes. Some of these products probably came from India, but the source of the gold is unknown.

Solomon is said to have used this fabulous gold treasure to build the famous temple in Jerusalem with a special inner temple to hold the Ark of the Covenant. Solomon built his temple on top of a gigantic wall of granite ashlars that formed a super-megalithic platform that was nearly identical to the one at Baalbek in nearby Lebanon. These gigantic cut stones are incredibly old, and at Baalbek a Roman temple has been built on top of the older platform. These giant blocks weigh in excess of 1,000 tons making some sort of anti-gravity the most likely method of moving the huge stones. The giant blocks at Jerusalem cannot be clearly seen because Solomon's Temple Wall is on top of them. Other structures were built up next to the wall so that a tunnel actually had to be dug around the wall in order to excavate its base and reveal the stones.

Solomon had a romantic affair with the Ethiopian Queen of Sheba who had come to visit him in about 940 BC. According to ancient Ethiopian tradition, recorded in the *Kebra Nagast*[13] ("Glory of Kings"—a sort of Ethiopian Old Testament that is the most important document to all Ethiopians), the reigning Queen, Makeda, left Axum, then the capital of Saba, and journeyed to Jerusalem. Her route probably took her across the Red Sea to present day Yemen and up the Hijaz Mountains of Saudi Arabia. Seeing the important Ark of the Covenant was a key goal of her visit.

After living with Solomon for some months, she returned to her own kingdom, where she bore King Solomon's son. He was named Menelik, and it was with this child, later to become the king of Saba, that the Solomonic line of rulership over Ethiopia was begun. This line was supposedly unbroken for three thousand years until the death of Haile Selassie (born Ras Tafari, 225th Solomonic ruler) in August of 1975.

Solomon was known as someone who was very wise and it

seems that he had been to remote lands and possessed a vimana of some sort. Perhaps he had several vimanas, and even a small air force. It seems incredible to us today, but aircraft may well have been relatively common in ancient times. Not in the way we have today with hundreds of airports and different airlines, but with a small number of craft that were produced in one or two locations, perhaps India and China. Others would suggest the craft came from Atlantis or perhaps ancient astronauts.

We have here a portrait of king who literally had everything, including his own Air Force One to take on special trips throughout Asia and Africa. Had Solomon ever flown across the Pacific to Tonga, Easter Island and Peru?

There are legends in Asia that Solomon did make visits to Central Asia and Tibet. Throughout the Middle East, as far as Kashmir, are mountains known as "thrones of Solomon," including one in northwestern Iran, a flat-topped mountain called Takht-i-Suleiman (which translates literally as Throne of Solomon). It has been conjectured that these may have been landing bases for Solomon's airship.

The Russian-American explorer, mystic and painter Nicholas Roerich testified that throughout Central Asia it is widely believed that Solomon flew about in an airship:

> Up to now, in the people's conception, King Solomon soars on his miraculous flying device over the vast spaces of Asia. Many mountains in Asia are either with ruins or stones bearing the imprint of his foot or of his knees, as evidence of his long-enduring prayers. These are the so-called thrones of Solomon. The Great King flew to these mountains, he reached all heights, he left behind him the cares of rulership and here refreshed his spirit.[41]

Roerich and his wife Helena collected very large quartz crystals on their journeys, plus they were the authors of a number of mystical books that included discussions of vimanas and the great Buddhist-Hindu past of Masters who possessed vimanas, magical machines and hidden fortresses deep in the remotest parts of the Altai Himalaya, Gobi Desert and Tibet.

Did King Solomon have some flying vehicle with which he flew to Persia, India and Tibet? With whom did he meet there? Given the many stories of flying vehicles from the ancient Indian epics, this is not so outlandish. Mountains with ruins on their summits that include large grassy areas do indeed exist all over the world. Were these mountaintop landing pads, built for the parking of flying vehicles that could take off vertically? We live on a strange planet—one full of impressive megalithic cities along these lines such as Machu Picchu, the mountaintop city in Peru. Similar huge airship fields are found directly in front of the megalithic walls of Sacsayhuaman above Cuzco.

Solomon's son also had an airship, as is told in the *Kebra Nagast*. In this story, known to every Ethiopian, Solomon's son Menelik ends up with the Ark and a flying wagon after a trip to Jerusalem and flies from Jerusalem to Gaza and Egypt and then to Axum.

The Story of the Ark in the Kebra Nagast

The full story of how the Ark came to be in Ethiopia—a controversial belief—is told in the ancient book known as the *Kebra Nagast*, or *The Glory of the Kings*. It is written in the coptic Ge'ez script and gives an account of the origins of the regal Solomonic line of the Ethiopian Kings. This lineage is said to begin in Axum circa 900 BC. However, mainstream scholars do not believe that Axum was a city in existence then. I think they are wrong.

It is not known when the original *Kebra Nagast* was written but even conservative scholars thinks that it is at least seven hundred years old. It gives detailed accounts of events that took place during the time of King Solomon so we might infer that the original text of the *Kebra Nagast* was nearly 3,000 years old! There is no reason why this cannot be the case. There are many texts that are over 3,000 years old from Egypt, Turkey, Iran, India, China and other areas of the world.

The *Kebra Nagast* tells the story of the Queen of Sheba—called Makeda in the text—and her visit to King Solomon, a story also in the Bible. However, the *Kebra Nagast* gives us more information about the Queen of Sheba and of the son that she had from her affair with King Solomon. This boy was named Menelik (often referred to as Menelik I, as there was a second Menelik in the late 1800s of modern Ethiopia's history). This boy grew up in Axum as a prince of the royal family. The *Kebra Nagast* then tells the story of how the Ark of the Convenant was brought to Ethiopia by Menelik. This part of the book contains descriptions of flying over the Red Sea and is similar to Hindu epics such as the *Ramayana*. The book finishes with a discussion of the conversion of the Ethiopians from the Sabean worship of the Sun, Moon, stars and planets to that of the "Lord God of Israel."

The *Kebra Nagast* seems to be a composite work from older

A series of stamps of Ethiopian queens issued in 1965 with Makeda on the top left.

books and is divided into 117 chapters. The book is presented in the form of a debate by the 318 "orthodox fathers" of the First Council of Nicea (325 AD). This council produced the first Christian doctrine, the Nicene Creed. In the book these fathers pose the question, "Of what doth the Glory of Kings consist?"

From chapter 3 through 17 a bishop named Gregory answers this question with a speech that ends with the statement that a copy of the Glory of God was made by Moses and kept in the Ark of the Covenant.

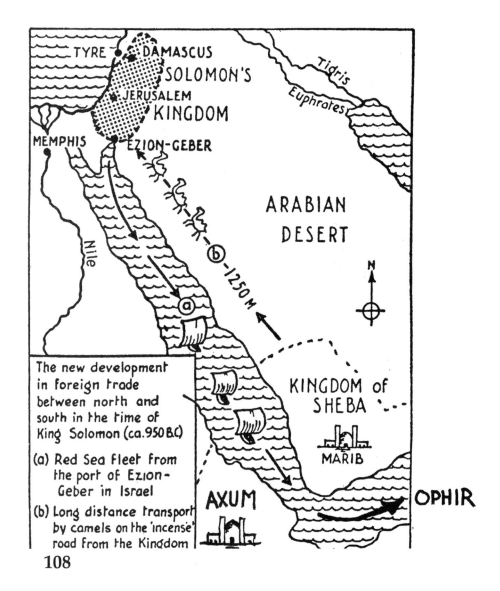

TYRE — DAMASCUS

SOLOMON'S

JERUSALEM

KINGDOM

MEMPHIS — EZION-GEBER

Nile

Tigris

Euphrates

ARABIAN DESERT

N

(b) 1250 M

(a)

KINGDOM of SHEBA

MARIB

AXUM

OPHIR

The new development in foreign trade between north and south in the time of King Solomon (ca. 950 BC)

(a) Red Sea fleet from the port of Ezion-Geber in Israel

(b) Long distance transport by camels on the 'incense' road from the Kingdom

Then starting with chapter 19 and going through chapter 94, the archbishop Domitius reads from a manuscript he had found in the church of "Sophia," which introduces the story of Makeda and her visit to King Solomon, their son Menelik, and how the Ark was transported to Ethiopia.

The *Kebra Nagast* narrates that Makeda, Queen of Saba (a country with a capital in Axum which also included parts of Yemen), learns from a merchant named Tamrin about the wisdom of King Solomon. Although the book does not tell us the route she takes, she leaves Axum for the coast and travels to Jerusalem to visit him. Says the book at the end of chapter 24:

> Then the Queen made ready to set out on her journey with great pomp and majesty, and with great equipment and many preparations. For, by the Will of God, her heart desired to go to Jerusalem so that she might hear the Wisdom of Solomon; for she had hearkened eagerly. So she made ready to set out. And 797 camels were loaded, and mules and asses innumerable were loaded, and she set out on her journey and followed her road without pause, and her heart had confidence in God.

Makeda probably journeyed from the mountains of Axum to the Axumite port of Adulis, south of present-day Masawa in Eritrea, and crossed the Red Sea by ships to a port near Jizan on the Arabian coast. This sea crossing would have included the animals as well. This apparently included the thousands of donkeys (asses)—Ethiopia is where these animals originated. Donkeys are used throughout northern Africa and the Middle East and even in China. The Egyptians used donkeys as well and would have gotten them from Ethiopia.

On the Arabian side of the Red Sea, a land which was also part of the kingdom of Saba, the huge expedition began to move north: 797 camels, thousands of donkeys and probably over a thousand people including camel drivers, donkey drivers, cooks, soldiers, nobility and servants. After probably several months journeying they made it to Jerusalem.

Makeda and her retinue stayed in Jerusalem for many months and she learned many things from Solomon. She is impressed by his knowledge and declares in chapter 28: "From this moment I will not worship the sun, but will worship the Creator of the sun, the God of Israel."

The night before she begins her journey home, Solomon tricks her into sleeping with him. That he tricked her somewhat preserves her purity in the whole affair, which is important because the Sabaen ruling monarch is supposed to be a virgin. After their tryst, Solomon has a dream in which the sun leaves Israel and goes to shine brightly over Ethiopia.

The next day, Makeda says she wants to leave, and Solomon showers her with parting gifts, including a flying machine! The end of chapter 30 states:

> And he went into his house and gave unto her whatsoever she wished for of splendid things and riches, and beautiful apparel which bewitched the eyes, and everything on which great store was set in the country of Ethiopia, and camels and wagons, six thousand in number, which were laden with beautiful things of the most desirable kind, and wagons wherein loads were carried over the desert, and a vessel wherein one could travel over the sea, and a vessel wherein one could traverse the air (or winds), which Solomon had made by the wisdom that God had given unto him.

Interestingly, earlier in chapter 30 it sounds like Solomon, in his wisdom, also created electric lights:

> Now the house of Solomon the King was illumined as by day, for in his wisdom he had made shining pearls which were like unto the sun, and moon, and stars [and had set them] in the roof of his house.

In chapter 31, Solomon takes his leave of Sheba. Believing that she is now with his child he gives her a special ring so that their child may identify himself to Solomon when he should return to Jerusalem.

On the journey home to Axum Makeda stops nine months and five days after leaving Jerusalem in a country called Bala Zadisareya (presumably along the Arabian coast of the Red Sea but possibly in Oman or elsewhere) where she gives birth to Menelik. The group continues back to Axum and the boy grows up to be strong and curious, learning the ways of the hunter and warrior. He then asks his mother who his father is. At the end of chapter 32 he says: "I will go and look upon the face of my father, and I will come back here by the Will of God, the Lord of Israel."

The Stealing of the Ark of the Covenant

In the next chapter, at the age of 22, Menelik prepares for the journey and his mother tells the officers of his retinue to present him to Solomon and then bring him safely back to Axum. She also tells them that henceforth the Sabaen custom of having a virgin queen as their ruler would end and a male dynasty of Solomon's seed starting with Menelik, would be created when the young man returned from Jerusalem. The queen then gives Menelik the special ring which Solomon had given her to identify his son.

At the end of chapter 33 Menelik travels to Jerusalem by way of Gaza, which we are informed Solomon had given to Sheba as a gift. The *Kebra Nagast* does not say how they traveled to Gaza but apparently it was through Egypt. It may have been via caravan, or they may have taken ships to Suez in the Egyptian Sinai and then gone overland to the Mediterranean and reached Gaza this way. Either journey would include a large number of donkeys and probably some camels as well.

In Gaza, Menelik is seen by the people as the identical image of King Solomon, and they wonder if he might actually be the king. They send spies to Jerusalem to find out if Solomon is there, and not with them in Gaza. Solomon hears about this and becomes curious about Menelik.

Finally in chapter 34 Menelik meets with Solomon and seeks

his blessing. He identifies himself to Solomon by showing him the ring. Overjoyed by this encounter, Solomon tries to convince Menelik to stay and succeed him as king, but Menelik insists on returning to his mother in Ethiopia. Menelik is taught many things by Solomon and his priests, including an extended version of the Ten Commandments.

King Solomon settles for sending Menelik back to Axum with a company formed from the first-born sons of the elders of his kingdom. This large group of Jewish nobility was to rule with Menelik and bring the customs of Israel to Ethiopia.

However, the young men of Israel are not that happy about having to go to this faraway land, and devise a plan to smuggle the Ark of the Covenant from the temple when they go. One of the young men is named Azaryas and he is the son of a temple priest named Zadok. Azaryas even has a dream wherein an angel comes to him and tells him he should take the Ark of the Covenant. Later an angel of the Lord appears in front of him as a pillar of fire and takes a very hands-on approach to the stealing of the Ark:

> And behold, the Angel of the Lord appeared again to Azaryas and he stood up above him like a pillar of fire, and he filled the house with his light. And he raised up Azaryas and said unto him, "Stand up, be strong, and rouse up thy brother Elmeyas, and 'Abesa, and Makari, and take the pieces of wood and I will open for thee the doors of the sanctuary. And take thou the Tabernacle of the Law of God, and thou shalt carry it without trouble and discomfort. And I, inasmuch as I have been commanded by God to be with it for ever, will be thy guide when thou shalt carry it away."

The conspirators had made a fake box to put in the Ark's place, hence the reference to the pieces of wood. The golden statue is not mentioned. At the end of chapter 52 they depart from Jerusalem in a great procession with the true Ark, instead of a replica which everyone else, including Menelik, believes they have.

However, the *Kebra Nagast* says that the wagons were given the

112

power to levitate and fly through the air.

At the end of chapter 52 we are told of their departure from Jerusalem to Gaza:

> And they loaded the wagons, and the horses and the mules in order to depart, and they set out on their journey prosperously, and they continued to travel on. And Michael the [Arch] Angel marched in front... And as for their wagons, no man hauled his wagon, but he himself [Michael] marched with the wagons, and whether it was men, or horses, or mules, or loaded camels, each was raised above the ground to the height of a cubit... And every one traveled in the wagons like a ship on the sea when the wind bloweth, and like a bat through the air when the desire of his belly urgeth him to devour his companions, and like an eagle when his body glideth above the wind. Thus did they travel; there was none in front and none behind, and they were disturbed neither on the right hand nor on the left.

At the beginning of chapter 53 they arrive in Gaza "which Solomon the king had given to the Queen of Ethiopia when she came to him." In chapter 54 Menelik discovers that he has the real Ark of the Covenant and not a copy. He worships the Ark and dances in front of it as did King David in the Bible. The *Kebra Nagast* started calling Menelik "David" in chapter 39, when Solomon had him annointed a king. The Ark is referred to as Zion and given the feminine form. The gleaming, bright-as-the-sun flying craft that holds the Ark is called variously Zion or the wagon of Zion. It seems to be a levitating airship which gives off a brilliant radiance, much as some UFOs have been described to do. In chapter 55 we are told of the final journey from Egypt to Axum:

> Then the wagons rose up as before and they set out early in the morning, and people sang songs to Zion, and they were all raised up the space of a cubit, and as the people of the country of Egypt bade them farewell, they passed before

them like shadows, and the people of the country of Egypt worshipped, for they saw Zion moving in the heavens like the sun, and they all ran with the wagon of Zion, some in front of her and some behind her. And they came to the sea of Al-Ahmar, which is the Sea of Eritrea [Red Sea], which was divided by the hand of Moses, and the children of Israel marched in the depths thereof, going up and down. …And when the holy Zion crossed over [the Red Sea] with those who were in attendance on her, and who sang songs to the accompaniment of harps and flutes, the sea received them and its waves leaped as do the high mountains when they are spit asunder, and it roared even as a lion roareth when he is enraged, and it thundered as doth the winter thunder of Damascus and Ethiopia when the lightning smiteth the clouds, and the sound thereof mingled with the sounds of the musical instruments. And the sea worshipped Zion. And whilst its billows were tossing about like the mountains their wagons were raised above the waves for a space of three cubits, and among the sound of the songs the [noise of the] breaking of the waves of the sea was wonderful…

And then they loaded their wagons, and they rose up, and departed, and journeyed on to the land of Medyam, and they came to the country of Belontos, which is a country of Ethiopia. And they rejoiced there, and they encamped there, because they had reached the border of their country with glory and joy, without tribulation on the road, in a wagon of the spirit, by the might of heaven, and of Michael the Archangel. And all the provinces of Ethiopia rejoiced, for Zion sent forth a light like that of the sun into the darkness wheresover she came.

In chapter 57, Solomon discovers that the Ark is gone from his kingdom. He goes in hot pursuit of the Ethiopian caravan. Incredibly, Solomon and his men are told a story of flying wagons when they question some Egyptians, and when they get to Gaza at the end of chapter 58:

114

And the King and his soldiers marched quickly, and they came to Gaza. And the King asked the people, saying "When did my son leave you?" And they answered and said unto him, "He left us three days ago. And having loaded their wagons none of them traveled on the ground, but in wagons that were suspended in the air; and they were swifter than the eagles that are in the sky, and all their baggage traveled with them in wagons above the winds. As for us, we thought that thou hadst, in thy wisdom, made them to travel in wagons above the winds." And the king said unto them, "Was Zion, the Tabernacle of the Law of God, with them?" And they said unto him, "We did not see anything."

Solomon is thrown into despair over the loss of the Ark, and weeps biterly with the elders of Israel. Then he decides that no outsiders need to know that the magical Ark, symbolic of God's might and power, is no longer among them. He orders the fake Ark to be gilded and decorated like the real Ark.

Ultimately, King Solomon turns for solace to his wife, the daughter of the pharaoh of Egypt, and she seduces him into worshiping the idols of her land (chapter 64).

The Ark in Axum

After a question from the 318 bishops of the Council, Domitius continues in the *Kebra Nagast* with a paraphrase of biblical history (chapters 66-83) then describes Menelik's arrival at Axum, where he is feted and Makeda abdicates the throne in his favor.

Menelik then engages in a series of military campaigns with the Ark, and "no man conquered him, on the contrary, whosoever attacked him was conquered" according to chapter 94, which is entitled "The First War of the King of Ethiopia." During these wars the flying wagons reappear. In a long and confusing paragraph at the end of chapter 94 the wars are summed up, and a war with ancient India is mentioned with vimanas that the *Kebra Nagast* calls wagons. As we have seen, Menelik has been crowned the king the Ethiopia and is now called David (which means "beloved by god"). Says the *Kebra Negast* in a long paragraph which I will break up for easier reading:

> And [Makeda] returned and encamped in the city of Zion [Axum] and they remained therein three months, then their wagons moved on and came to the city of the Government. And in one day they came to the city of Saba, and they laid waste Noba; and from there they camped round about Saba, and they laid it waste as far as the border of Egypt. And the majesty of the King of Ethiopia was

so great that the King of Medyam and the King of Egypt caused gifts to be brought unto him, and they came into the city of the Government, and from there they encamped in Ab'at, and they waged war on the country of India, and the King of India brought a gift and a tribute and himself did homage to the King of Ethiopia.

He [David/Menelik] waged war wheresoever he pleased; no man conquered him, on the contrary. Whosoever attacked him was conquered. And as for those who would have played the spy in his camp, in order to hear some story and relate it in their city, they were unable to run by the wagons, for Zion herself made the strength of the enemy to be exhausted.

But King David, with his soldiers, and the armies of his soldiers, and all those who obeyed his word, flew on the wagons without pain or suffering, and without hunger or thirst, and without sweat or exhaustion, and traveled in one day a distance which [usually] took three months to traverse [on foot].

And they lacked nothing whatsoever of the things which they asked God through Zion the Tabernacle of the Law of God to give them, for he dwelt with her, and His Angel directed her, and she was His habitation. And as for the king who ministered to His pavilion—if he were traveling on any journey, and wished something to be done, everything that he wished for and thought about in his heart, and indicated with his finger, everything [I say] was performed at this word, and everyone feared him. But he feared no one, for the hand of God was with him, and it worked for him and protected him from all evil forever and ever. Amen.

So, once again in the *Kebra Nagast* we have the mention of flying wagons that are able to travel in one day what would take three weeks to travel by foot.

That a war with India is mentioned is curious. Flying machines, known in Sanskrit as vimanas, are mentioned in many of the epic

117

books of India. In the popular epic the *Ramayana* much of the book takes place across an ocean to the west of India on an island called Lanka ruled by a dark-skinned king named Ravana. Is it possible that Ethiopia is the Lanka of the *Ramayana*? The links between Ethiopia and ancient India are strong. Apparently they once fought a war, one that historians seem to know nothing about!

The *Kebra Nagast* continues with the original council of Nicea where the bishop Domitius praises the book he has found (which is the *Kebra Nagast*), and says that the book establishes not only Ethiopia's possession of the true Ark of the Covenant but that a Solomonic dynasty was created from the firstborn son of Solomon, namely Menelik.

Then the bishop called Gregory delivers an extended speech with prophetic elements (chapters 95-112) that prove the messianic purpose of Jesus, the validity of the Ethiopian forms of worship, and the spiritual supremacy of Ethiopia over Israel. Ethiopia is the new Zion. This is also the core of Rastafarianism, made popular by Jamaican musicians such as Bob Marley, who is widely revered in Ethiopia. Zion, a place for all people, the 12 tribes of Israel—the 12 tribes of mankind, as described in 250 BC by the Greek philosopher Plato—was originally in the Levant of the Eastern Mediterranean but had moved to Ethiopia.

The *Kebra Nagast* concludes with a final prophecy that the power of the Roman church will be eclipsed by the power of the Ethiopian Orthodox church which followed the teachings of the Bishop Nestorius, who taught reincarnation among other things. It describes how King Kaleb of Axum met with Justinian of Byzantium, and it was decided he would subdue the Jews living in Najran (part of his kingdom in western Saudi Arabia, along the Red Sea, just north of Yemen). He would make his younger son Gabre Meskel his heir in order to accomplish this, and retire to a monastery (chapter 117).

The main action of the Kebra Nagast takes place in two time periods, the time of Solomon and Menelik (around 920 BC) and at the First Council of Nicea (325 AD). The final chapter, however, references Justinian of Rome, and Kings Kaleb and Gebre Meskel

An Assyrian seal showing a bearded man in a flying disk. (British Museum)

of Ethiopia, who are historical kings who lived in the 6th century AD. This shows clearly that the book as we know it today was compiled from earlier stories, and was probably put together much later than when the main events it describes took place. These were all important times in the history of Ethiopia, however.

It was at the Council of Nicea that the early church was split, creating the Roman Catholic Church with its special doctrines; other factions such as Nestorian Christians, Greek Orthodox and the Ethiopian Orthodox Church were split off from the Catholic Church. These churches continued to teach a doctrine that Christ and Jesus were different egos, and Masters and reincarnation were part of their doctrine. Jesus was called "Master" by his disciples, a familiar Hindu and Buddhist title. Baptism in the Christian church originated with Hindus in India.

The Roman Catholic Church removed all references to reincarnation from the books allowed to be in the collected work known as the Bible. Other books became the Apocrypha or were left out of the canon entirely. Because the Council had decided against them, bishops such as Nestorius were sent into exile. He went to Baghdad and started the Nestorian Christian Church.

119

An Assyrian seal showing three men in a flying disk. (British Museum)

Ancient Flight

So what are we to make of the stories of the Ark flying up into the air versus the tales of flying wagons in the *Kebra Nagast*? Throughout history there have been tales of flight—from flying carpets to Ezekiel's fiery wheels within wheels. Within the legends of ancient history there are countless stories of flying people, flying chariots, flying horses, and other airborne items usually dismissed as fantasy and myth. I detail many of these stories in my books *Technology of the Gods*[30] and *Vimana*,[37] among others.

Circa 300 BC, the Chinese poet Chu Yuan wrote of his flight in a jade chariot at a high altitude over the Gobi Desert toward the snow-capped Kunlun Mountains in the west. Says researcher Andrew Tomas, "He accurately described how the aircraft was unaffected by the winds and dust of the Gobi, and how he conducted an aerial survey."[24]

Chinese folklore is replete with tales about flying chariots and other descriptions of flight. Tomas mentions that a stone carving on a grave in the province of Shantung, dated AD 147, depicts a dragon chariot flying high above the clouds.[24] In the fourth century AD Chinese historian Ko Hung might have been describing a type of helicopter when he wrote about "flying cars with wood from

120

the inner part of the jujube tree, using ox leather straps fastened to rotating blades to set the machine in motion."

Leonardo da Vinci had also designed a functional helicopter, possibly from Chinese designs. Helicopters, unlike gliders, do not need long landing areas, but they are much more difficult to control. However, a combination of a balloon with propellers to help move the craft would be a technical feat well within the capability of the dynastic Chinese. Even our own early aircraft, such as the plane made by the famous Wright Brothers at Kitty Hawk in North Carolina, were fairly crude constructs of wood, canvas and rope.

American adventurer Jim Woodman and his pals experimented with similar technology when they built a reed basket in Peru and then floated it above the Nazca Plain with a crude hot air balloon made of native fibers and woven cloth. The craft was named the *Condor I*, and Woodman wrote about it in the 1977 book *Nazca: Journey to the Sun*.[74] He and his friends rose to over 1,200 feet in the craft and landed successfully, with no one hurt. Woodman believed that the Nazca lines, which can only be fully viewed from the air, were seen by ancient Nazca priests who flew over the desert plain in primitive, but effective, hot air balloons.

This event—and the recreation of it—has been very popular in Japan, and a number of television documentaries have been produced in that country that have focused on early balloon exploits such as those theorized by Woodman. Indeed, stories of man-lifting kites are popular in Japan and a very well known tale is that of a 12th century samurai hero named Tametamo who helps his son escape from an island where they have been exiled by lashing him to a giant kite with which he is able to fly through the air to the Japanese mainland. Glider, balloon and man-lifting kite devices are fascinating in themselves, but when we consider many stories of ancient flight, we are looking at powered flight much as we have today. In this way we expect flying machine technology to be something similar to what we have today, including electricity and mechanical devices and controls.

In his book *Wonders of Ancient Chinese Science*[28] Robert Silverburg says that Chinese myths tell of a legendary people, the

Chi-Kung, who traveled in "aerial carriages." In the ancient Chinese chronicle *Records of the Scholars* it is recorded that the great Han Dynasty astronomer and engineer Chang Heng made a flying device. It was, says Silverburg, "[a] wooden bird with a mechanism in its belly that allowed it to fly nearly a mile."

The development of modern spaceflight, including experimentation with manned rockets, can be traced to the early use of gunpowder in China. Charcoal and sulfur had long been known as ingredients for incendiary mixtures. As early as 1044 the Chinese learned that saltpeter, added to such a mixture, made it fizz even more alarmingly. We do not know who first learned that if you grind charcoal, sulfur and saltpeter up very fine, mix them very thoroughly in the proportion of 1:1:3.5 or 1:1:4, and pack the mixture into a dosed container, it will, when ignited, explode with a delightful bang. It has been suggested that experimenters, believing that salt made a fire hotter because it made it brighter, tried various salts until they stumbled on potassium nitrate or saltpeter.

The rocket probably evolved in a simple way from an incendiary arrow. If one wanted to make a fire arrow burn fiercely for several seconds using the new powder, one would have to pack the powder in a long thin tube to keep it from going off all at once. It would also be necessary to let the flame and smoke escape from one end of the tube.

The Chinese created all manner of rocket-powered arrows, grenades and even iron bombs, very similar to those in use today. The first two-stage rocket is credited to the Chinese in the 11th century AD with their development of the "Fire Dragon" rocket. While on the way to its target, the "Fire Dragon" ignited fire arrows that flew from the dragon's mouth. An early two-stage cluster bomb rocket!

The Controversial Book *War in Ancient India*

Just at the end of WWII a controversial and scholarly book named *War in Ancient India*[50] was published by Oxford University Press in England. It was by a historian from southern India named Ramachandra Dikshitar. His 1944 book contained a fascinating chapter entitled "Aerial Warfare in Ancient India" that had the scholars of his day asking him why he would include such a chapter in his book? How could there have been aerial warfare in ancient India when quite obviously—as every scientist knows—the ancient Indians could not possibly have had airships?

Yet, the scholarly professor defended himself and said that he only wrote about these things because the ancient texts described such events as people flying in machines, well known as vimanas, and that these aircraft were also used in military actions. Aerial warfare, then and now, is an attractive option in that it is likely to inflict the most damage on the enemy with the least loss of life on the attacker's side. Aerial warfare, including the use of rockets and missiles, is a superior way to wage war, as long as one has that technology, advanced as it is.

Dr. Dikshitar begins the chapter called "Aerial Warfare in Ancient India" with several paragraphs on how interesting it is that India was an early contributor to the then (1944)newly-emerging science of aeronautics, including airplanes, zeppelins, blimps and other aircraft:

> No question can be more interesting in the present circumstance of the world than India's contribution to the science of aeronautics. There are numerous illustrations in our vast Puranic and epic literature to show how well and wonderfully the ancient Indians conquered the air. To glibly characterize everything found in this literature as imaginary and summarily dismiss it as unreal has been the practice of both Western and Eastern scholars until very recently. The very idea indeed was ridiculed and people went so far as to assert that it was physically impossible for man to use flying machines. But today what with balloons, aeroplanes and other flying machines a great change has come over our ideas on the subject.
>
> Turning to Vedic literature, in one of the *Brahmanas* occurs the concept of a ship that sails heavenwards. The ship is the Agnihotra of which the Ahavaniya and Garhapatya

fires represent the two sides bound heavenward, and the steersman is the Agnihotrin who offers milk to the three Agnis. Again in the still earlier *Rig Veda Samhita* we read that the Asvins conveyed the rescued Bhujya safely by means of winged ships. The latter may refer to the aerial navigation in the earliest times.

In the recently published *Samarangana Sutradhara* of Bhoja, a whole chapter of about 230 stanzas is devoted to the principles of construction underlying the various flying machines and other engines used for military and other purposes. The various advantages of using machines, especially flying ones, are given elaborately. Special mention is made of their attacking visible as well a invisible objects, of their use at one's will and pleasure, of their uninterrupted movements, of their strength and durability, in short of their capability to do in the air all that is done on earth. After enumerating and explaining a number of other advantages, the author concludes that even impossible things could be affected through them. Three movements are usually ascribed to these machines—ascending, cruising thousands of miles in different directions in the atmosphere and lastly descending. It is said that in an aerial car one can mount up to the Suryamandala 'solar region' and the Naksatra mandala (stellar region) and also travel throughout the regions of air above the sea and the earth. These cars are said to move so fast as to make a noise that could be heard faintly from the ground. Still some writers have expressed a doubt and asked 'Was that true?' But the evidence in its favour is overwhelming.

The make of machines for offence and defense to be used on the ground and in the air is described. ...Considering briefly some of the flying machines alone that find distinct mention in this work, we find that they were of different shapes like those of elephants, horses, monkeys, different kinds of birds, and chariots. Such vehicles were made usually of wood. We quote in this connection the following stanzas so as to give an idea of the materials and size, especially as we are in the days of rigid airships navigating the air for a very long time and at a long distance as well.[50]

The professor goes on to give some direct quotes, with Sanskrit text and then his English translation beneath them. He then provides us with the famous text from the *Samarangana Sutradhara* of Bhoja:

An aerial car is made of light wood looking like a great bird with a durable and well-formed body having mercury inside and fire at the bottom. It has two resplendent wings, and is propelled by air. It flies in the atmospheric regions for a great distance and carries several persons along with it. The inside construction resembles heaven created by Brahma himself. Iron, copper, lead and other metals are also used for these machines.[50]

Dr. Dikshitar goes on to defend himself in the face of the considerable criticism that was leveled at him when he first wrote about the sophistication and glory of ancient India, including aerial warfare:

All these show how far art was developed in ancient India in this direction. Such elaborate descriptions ought to [refute] the criticism that the vimanas and similar aerial vehicles mentioned in ancient Indian literature should be relegated to the region of myth.

The ancient writers could certainly make a distinction between the mythical which they designated *daiva* and the actual aerial wars designated *manusa*. Some wars mentioned in ancient literature belong to the *daiva* form, as distinguished from the *manusa*.[50]

Dr. Dikshitar tells the tale of King Satrujit who is presented with a magic horse that can convey him anywhere on earth he wishes and then discusses other "magical" conveyances including references in the *Ramayana*:

King Satrujit was presented by a Brahman Galava with a horse named Kuvalaya which had the power of conveying him to any place on the earth. If this had any basis in fact it must have been a flying horse. There are numerous references both in the *Visnupurana* and the *Mahabharata* where Krsna is said to have navigated the air on the Garuda. Either the accounts are imaginary or they are a reference to an eagle-shaped machine flying in the air. Subrahmanya used a peacock as his vehicle and Brahma a swan. Further, the Asura, Maya by name, is said to have owned an animated golden car with four strong wheels and having a circumference of 12,000 cubits, which possessed the wonderful power of flying at will to any place. It was equipped with various weapons and bore huge standards. And in the battle between the Devas and the Asuras in which Maya took a leading part, several warriors are represented as riding birds.

...Golikere draws attention to a number of instances where fierce duels have been fought between man and bird of prey resulting in the damage of the aeroplane and its inmates, in some cases leading to a forced landing. Again, the Raksasa Dronamukha offers his services to Ravana in his encounter with the vanara hosts to fight them either on the sea or in the sky or in subterranean regions. After the great victory of Rama over Lanka, Vibhisana presented him with the Pushpaka vimana which was furnished with windows, apartments, and excellent seats. It was capable of accommodating all the vanaras besides Rama, Sita and Laksmana. Rama flew to his capital Ayodhya pointing [out] to Sita from above the places of encampment, the town of Kiskindha and others on the way. Again Valmiki beautifully compares the city of Ayodhya to an aerial car.[50]

Finally, he goes on to say that it was a real science, with winged planes and tubular airships being used by royalty and military commanders in ancient times. Says Dr. Dikshitar:

> This is an allusion to the use of flying machines as transport apart from their use in actual warfare. Again in the *Vikramaurvasiya*, we are told that king Pururavas rode in an aerial car to rescue Urvasi in pursuit of the Danava who was carrying her away. Similarly in the *Uttararamacarita* in the fight between Lava and Candraketu (Act VI) a number of aerial cars are mentioned as bearing celestial spectators. There is a statement in the *Harsacarita* of Yavanas being acquainted with aerial machines. The Tamil work *Jivakacintamani* refers to Jivaka flying through the air.
>
> But it has to be inferred that being very costly, their use was more or less the exclusive privilege of kings and aristocrats.[50]

So, we have here a University scholar who tells us that there was flight in the ancient world. His comment at the very end is telling, that these craft are "the exclusive privilege of kings and aristocrats." It makes sense that somewhere there was a manufacturing facility for several types of aircraft—however crude or advanced they may have been. Perhaps as crude as a hot air balloon with steam-powered propellers or as advanced as an electro-gyroscopic vehicle like a flying saucer or the mysterious foo fighters of WWII.

And not just a few of these craft were made, but there were seemingly hundreds, probably made over many centuries and—just like an aircraft manufactured today—they were marketed to the kings and dictators of any country who could pay the price. The biggest problem with any flying device or even a steam locomotive is that is that without the machine being properly maintained it will eventually cease to function. It may be that the airships featured in the later tales were the last of their kind, relics of technology that could no longer be reproduced and therefore disappeared for some centuries.

We don't generally think of the world of 1000 BC as being

a time of airships, electric lamps and explosive weapons, but the ancient texts tell us otherwise. Airships may have been around for literally thousands of years by 1000 BC, and during this period the Egyptians, Hittites and many other civilizations built huge temples and granite statues that are of the finest stonework. Today we could not build huge edifices such as Karnak Temple or the Great Pyramid without power tools and heavy equipment.

With the technology of today, we have the ability to do all of these incredible things mentioned in the Bible and other texts. But we feel that the ancients could not do these things—even though they say they did them—because they lacked our technology. But did they?

Electrical devices, machines and aircraft were deluxe things to witness in ancient times but they are described enough to make us think that there must be some truth to the many stories in which they are featured. Let us now explore this fascinating topic of ancient electrical devices.

An old print of Ezekiel's vision of the Lord on a craft of four wheels.

CHAPTER SIX

ANCIENT ELECTRICITY AND THE ARK OF THE COVENANT

And thou shall put in the breastplate of judgment the Urim and the
Thummim; and they shall be upon Aaron's heart, when he goeth in
before the Lord; and Aaron shall bear the judgment of the children
of Israel upon his heart before the Lord continually.
—*Exodus 28:2-30*

While in the initial study of the Ark of the Covenant it may seem
a bit shocking, there is ample evidence that electricity was well
known in ancient times. We can picture someone like Benjamin
Franklin discovering electricity with a kite attached to a wire
during a lightning storm, but it is logical to think that the ancients
had been just as interested in this observable phenomenon. In fact,
archeologists have known for decades that direct current batteries
were used in the Middle East more than 2,000 years ago.

Lightning, ball lightning, static electricity, St. Elmo's Fire and
many other forms of electrical phenomena were observed over
thousands of years by the ancients and they made up their own
terms for them and even developed various devices. We know that
experiments concerning steam engines occurred many thousands of
years ago, and similarly, experiments concerning electricity must
have been conducted many thousands of years ago.

How long ago we simply do not know. But observations of
flashes of lightning—the weapons of Zeus—have been going on
since the beginning of man. Electricity in its many forms, and lights
of many kinds, may have been "invented" by ancient man many tens

of thousands of years ago. King Solomon was famous for saying that there is "nothing new under the sun." Indeed, electricity, power tools, flying machines and heavy equipment have probably been in use in one way or another for over 12,000 years—and possibly longer.

The ancient Greek and Egyptian stories of Atlantis remind us that the ancients believed that previous high-tech civilizations had existed before them and were destroyed in cataclysmic earth changes. Ancient astronaut theorists would surmise that extraterrestrials arrived on Earth many thousands of years ago and brought electricity, flying machines and ray guns with them. Either way, we have an ancient world in which many people lived very primitively, as they do today in isolated villages in the Amazon Basin or New Guinea, while others had marvelous temples with electric lamps and other cleverly made machines. One thing that is for sure is, a society with a high technology must have knowledge of electricity.

Electrical Batteries in the Ancient World

True technology of the advanced kind requires some kind of power, usually electricity. Think of the amazing array of devices that we use today, from automobiles to airplanes, from toaster ovens and refrigerators to power tools and computers—all of them use electricity in one form or another. That the ancients could harness electricity is absolutely essential to the belief that flight and other high technology once existed in the remote past.

Electric batteries were in use more than 2,000 years ago according to Dr. Wilhelm Koenig, a German archaeologist employed by the Iraq Museum in Baghdad, who discovered one in 1938 while conducting a dig at Khujut Rabu'a, not far to the south of Baghdad. The Museum had begun scientific excavations, and in the digging turned up a peculiar object that—to Koenig—looked very much like a present-day wet-cell. Other similar finds followed.

An article in the July, 1964 issue of *Popular Electronics* said that the ancient electrochemical batteries had central cell elements that included "...a copper cylinder containing an iron rod that had been corroded as if by chemical action. The cylinder was soldered with a 60/40 lead-tin alloy, the same solder alloy we use today." Two thousand years ago they not only had electricity, they also used exactly the same tin-alloy solder that we use today!

An earlier article on this amazing ancient technology appeared in the April 1957 issue of *Science Digest* entitled "Electric Batteries of 2,000 Years Ago." (Harry M. Schwalb, *Science Digest*, 41:17-19). Says the article:

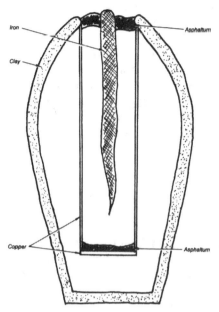

A diagram of the Baghdad battery.

...in Cleopatra's day, up-and-coming Baghdad silversmiths were gold-plating jewelry—using electric batteries. It's no myth; young scientist Willard F. M. Gray, of General Electric's High Voltage Laboratory in Pittsfield, Mass., has proved it. He made an exact replica of one of the 2,000-year-old wet cells and connected it to a galvanometer. When he flipped the switch—current flowed!

These BC-vintage batteries (made by the Parthians, who dominated the Baghdad region between 250 BC and 224 AD) are quite simple. Thin sheet-copper was soldered into a cylinder less than 4 inches long and about an inch in diameter—roughly the size of two flashlight batteries end to end. The solder was a 60/40 tin-lead alloy—'one of the best in use today,' Gray points out.

The bottom of the cylinder was a crimped-in copper disc insulated with a layer of asphaltum (the 'bitumen' that the Bible tells us Noah used to caulk the Ark). The top was closed with an asphalt stopper, through which projected the end of an iron rod. To stand upright, it was cemented into a small vase.

What electrolyte the Parthian jewelers used is a mystery, but Gray's model works well with copper sulfate. Acetic or citric acid, which the ancient chemists had in plenty, should be even better.

This is conclusive proof that the Babylonians did indeed use electricity. As similar jars were found in a magician's hut, it can be surmised that both priests and craftsmen kept the knowledge as a trade secret. It should be noted here that electroplating and galvanization were again introduced only in the first part of the nineteenth century.[24]

Andrew Tomas, in his 1971 book *We Are Not the First,* mentions that during his stay in India he was told about an old document, preserved in the Indian Princes' Library at Ujjain and listed as Agastya Samhita, which contains instructions for making electrical batteries:

> Place a well-cleaned copper plate in an earthenware vessel. Cover it first by copper sulphate and then by moist sawdust. After that put a mercury-amalgamated-zinc sheet on top of the sawdust to avoid polarization. The contact will produce an energy known by the twin name of Mitra-Varuna. Water will be split by this current into Pranavayu and Udanavayu. A chain of one hundred jars is said to give a very active and effective force.

Says Tomas, "The Mitra-Varuna now called cathode-anode, and Pranavayu and Udanavayu are to us oxygen and hydrogen. This document again demonstrates the presence of electricity in the East, long, long ago."[24]

Typical djed column of Osiris.

132

The bas relief at Dendera that seems to show djed columns and electric devices.

The Hathor Temple Electrical Device

At the Hathor Temple at Dendera, near Abydos in Egypt, can be found several unusual depictions of what appears to be an ancient Egyptian electrical device, probably used to light the temple. This large temple may have needed 20 or 30 of these devices to provide enough light inside the temple. Dendera is a beautiful and massive edifice with huge columns that tower over one's head like redwoods. The temple is of quite recent origin, built in the first century BC, but it encloses earlier temples. An inscription in one of the subterranean vaults says that the temple was built "according to a plan written in ancient writing upon a goatskin scroll from the time of the Companions of Horus." This is a curious inscription, essentially stating that the Ptolemaic (Greek) architects of the 1st century BC were claiming that the actual plan of the temple dated to the legendary prehistoric era when the "companions of Horus" ruled Egypt.

The temple is richly decorated with inscriptions and hieroglyphics. Probably most interesting to me were the bas reliefs in the room designated No. XVII that depict strikingly unusual scenes with what appear to be electrical objects. In these depictions, a large glass bulb with a snake-like filament is rested on a djed pillar, and it has a cable coming out the back of it.

133

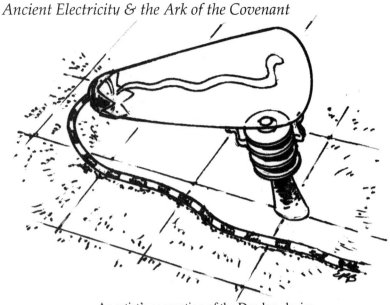

An artist's conception of the Dendera device.

The famous British scientist Ivan T. Sanderson discusses these wall decorations and ancient Egyptian electricity in his book *Investigating the Unexplained.*[51] Djed columns are interesting, as they are usually associated with Osiris. They are said to represent the column in which he was found at Byblos in Lebanon by Isis. The djed columns are explained as insulators, though they look like electrical generating devices themselves due to the odd "condenser" design at the top of the columns. An electrical engineer named Alfred Bielek explained the wall decoration to Sanderson as depicting some sort of projector with the cable being a bundle of many multi-purpose conductors, rather than a single high-voltage cable.

The mundane Egyptology explanation for this curious relief is that it is a lotus flower which is blooming, and the glass globe is the aroma of the blossom. No explanation is given for the serpent in the globe, or for the strange baboon figure or the miniature priests down by what appear to be cables.

Who are the giant figures standing behind these lighting devices? What is their job? Who are the miniature worshippers? Are they worshipping these electric devices? Why are they being held up by djed columns? The cables seem to be connected to a box, on which kneels a figure with a globe on his head. Is this box the source of

134

power for the lighting devices?

The more one looks at the scene, the more interesting it becomes. Egyptologists rarely make any mention of this scene, though it is shown to nearly all the tourists that visit the Temple of Dendera and it is the most famous image from that magnificent structure, apart from the well known zodiac. To my knowledge, the hieroglyphs on the image have not been translated and published.

Part of the evidence for ancient Egyptian electrics involves the mystery of how tombs and underground passages were highly painted and decorated. One ingenious theory was that the passageways and chambers were lit by a series of mirrors, bringing sunlight from the entrance. However, many tombs are far too elaborate, with deep and twisting turns, for this to work. The walls and ceilings show no signs of soot from fire torches, so how were the passageways illuminated

Baboons worshipping an orb held by an ankh and djed pillar. An electrical device?

to facilitate the work of the artisans?

Electric Lights in Ancient Egypt?

When looking at some of the odd things depicted on temple and tomb walls, and on papyrus scrolls or even pottery, we often see baffling depictions that seem like they are electrical devices of some sort. Many are manifestations of djed pillars, associated with the god Osriris, that have some sort of globe or disk on their heads.

Often these items look like some sort of machine and many appear to be a light or projector bulb of some sort, like the Dendera wall paintings and reliefs. Others seem to be glowing globes held up by a djed column. Might this be a lamp of some kind? Could an object like this have been the energy generator kept inside the Ark of the Covenant?

Osiris.

The exact explanation for why a djed pillar looks the way it does, typically a broad based column with four parallel bars, is actually lacking. Egyptologists cannot adequately explain this design, except to say that it is not an electrical device. Explanations range widely and include the following:

1. It is four pillars or columns seen as one behind the other.
2. It is a man's backbone, specifically Oriris'.
3. It is a cedar tree from Lebanon where Orisis once washed ashore.
4. It is a pole around which are tied sheaves of grain.

Djed columns were a popular design and fetish, with people carrying miniature ceramic djed columns. Were they clay replicas of important flashlight devices? The djed column was associated with the chief god of Memphis, Ptah, who was called the "Noble Djed." Ptah is often depicted as standing upright and holding a staff with a djed pillar at the top.

There was also a Djed Pillar Festival that occurred at harvest time on the first day of the month of Shemu. This involved raising a large wooden pillar to which cut sheaves of wheat were tied.

The djed pillar is associated with fertility, phallic symbols, harvest, death and rebirth. It is when it is seen accompanied by globes and serpents and ankhs that we wonder if these are not components of some larger device. The djed pillar might be the battery while the globe is a sealed glass ball with a gas or filament to be electrified by the battery—large or small. The ankh might represent the light and energy created, or simply be a form of decoration.

Another curious object was the Was Staff, sometimes carried by gods or men. It is theorized to be part survey staff and part divining rod. It may have been an electrical device as well, as Ptah was depicted with a staff that was similar to a Was Staff but had a djed pillar device at the top of it. A staff with certain jewels in it, such as rubies, with the proper electronics could be a small laser. The small handheld lasers of today use synthetic rubies and small batteries to power them.

Also, it is interesting to note the serpent design inside the bulbs of the Dendera wall reliefs. This serpent-plasma energy of gas inside an electrified light like a plasma ball or a neon sign may have been an important temple device in ancient Egypt. The serpent is used in other designs, as coiling around an egg or a staff. This would seem to indicate that the serpent represents an energy form, possibly a glowing plasma-gas like neon or maybe just a simple filament-resistor as in a light bulb.

When we look at the finely-crafted

Djed pillar with an ankh and orb.

137

granite and basalt statues from dynastic Egypt, they are so well cut and polished that it would seem that power tools were involved. These tools would need to be similar to the stonecutting tools that we use today. Engineer Christopher Dunn has written on exactly this topic in his books *Lost Technologies of Ancient Egypt*[91] and *The Giza Power Plant.*[92]

There are seemingly high-tech devices depicted in Egyptian hieroglyphic panels on a lintel at the Abydos Temple in southern Egypt. This is not far from the Dendera Temple. At Abydos hieroglyphics and symbols are carved into the granite rock which show what appear to be a helicopter, a rocket, a flying saucer and a jet plane. These unusual pictures may be interpreted by the reader as seems fit, but they are genuine. Mainstream Egyptologists have not commented on these hieroglyphs except to say that some are composites of two superimposed hieroglyphs.[30]

Electricity and Religion

A depiction from an 18th dynasty papyrus scroll shows "sacred baboons" and priests worshipping a djed column with an ankh with hands holding up an orb. Ivan Sanderson likens the object to static generators such as a Van de Graaff generator or Wimshurst generator. Sanderson had Michael R. Freedman, an electrical engineer, draw up plans for his version of a djed column static electricity generator. They indeed looked very similar to the

Osiris as the god Tat.

modern Van de Graaff generator found in many high school science laboratories.

In such a device, static electricity builds up in the orb, and, says Freedman:

> ...what better 'toy' for an Egyptian priest of ancient times? ...such an instrument could be used to control both the Pharaoh and fellahin (peasant), simply by illustrating, most graphically, the powers of the gods; of which, of course, only the priests knew the real secrets. Merely by placing a metal rod or metal-coated stave in the general vicinity of the sphere, said priest could produce a most wondrous display, with electric arcs and loud crashes. Even with nothing more elaborate than a ring on his finger, a priest could point to the 'life-symbol,' be struck by a great bolt of lightning, but remain alive and no worse for wear, thus illustrating the omnipotent powers of the gods—not to mention himself—in preserving life for the faithful.[51]

Though the device may have been some exotic, but simple, static generator, it might also have been a self-generating electric light tower and bulb. A glowing electric ball in the center of an ornate temple would have been an impressive sight. Did the Egyptians use electric lighting? It would seem so!

Authors such as Jerry Ziegler in his books *YHWH*[82] and *Indra Girt by Maruts*[89] claim that electrical devices of various sorts were used in temples and were often utilized as oracles or

Osiris as the god Asar.

139

awesome manifestations of deities. Ziegler cites a wealth of ancient sources on ancient lights, sacred fires and oracles in his books. He argues that the Ark of the Covenant as well as the sacred flames of Mithraic and Zoroastrian oracles were ancient electrical devices used for impressing the congregation.[82] Ancient Hebrew legends tell of a glowing jewel that Noah hung up in the ark to provide a constant source of illumination,[80] and in chapter five we noted the mention of similar objects in the palace of King Solomon about 950 BC.

Ancient electrics were apparently only used by special priesthoods and not by the masses. A similar book to Ziegler's is the book *Ka: A Handbook of Mythology, Sacred Practices, Electrical Phenomena, and their Linguistic Connections in the Ancient*

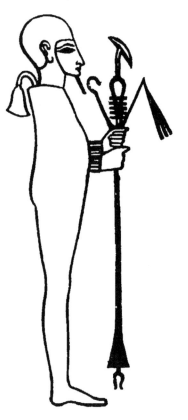

The god Ptah holding a special staff.

World, by Hugh Crosthwaite.[90] Crosthwaite's fascinating 1992 book maintains that the ancients built simple—and more complicated—electrical devices that were used in religious ceremonies. These sacred "fires" ranged from amber disks that created sparks of static electricity when rubbed together (easily seen in a darkened room) to static electrical condensers such as the famous Ark of the Covenant.

What is important about Crosthwaite's book is that he shows how much of early religion was built around electrical phenomena. The many famous temples of yore may have had as their center of attraction an electrical light of some sort that amazed the pilgrim and gave him something to genuinely wonder about. Small, rural towns would not have had electric lights and the majority of the people would be unfamiliar with electrical effects.

140

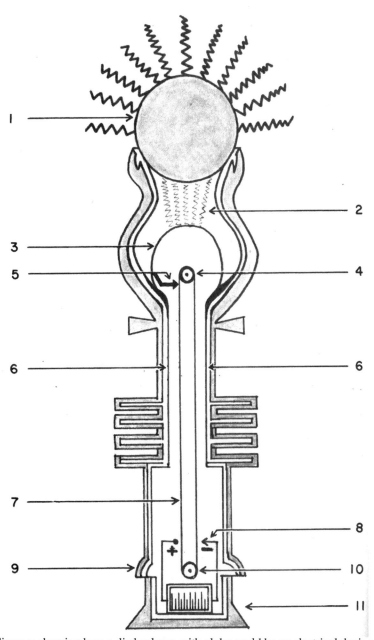

A diagram showing how a djed column with globe could be an electrical device.

Crosthwaite says the Ka of the ancient Egyptians is related to electrical phenomena and that much of the teachings of the so-called Mystery Religions, such as at Delphi in Greece, were related to various electrical devices as well. Over time, civilization slipped into the Dark Ages and the old religions were swept away by Christianity and Islam.

Electric Eternal Flames

Australian-Russian author and scholar Andrew Tomas, who was well versed on classical texts of both East and West, has a chapter entitled "Electricity in the Remote Past" in his 1971 book *We Are Not the First*.[24] This chapter has a long list of classical authors who have made many statements in their works testifying to the reality of ever-burning lamps in antiquity. Some of these ever-burning lamps may have used ancient electrical devices of various design.

Tomas mentions that Lucian (AD 120-180), the Greek satirist, gave a detailed account of his travels. In Hierapolis, Syria, he saw a shining jewel in the forehead of the goddess Hera that brilliantly illuminated the whole temple at night. Nearby, the Roman temple of Jupiter at Ba'albek was said to be lit by "glowing stones."[24]

A beautiful golden lamp in the temple of Minerva, said to burn for a year at a time, was described by the second-century historian Pausanias. Saint Augustine (AD 354-430) wrote of an ever-burning lamp which neither wind nor rain could extinguish.

Tomas relates that when the sepulcher of Pallas, son of Evander, immortalized by Virgil in his Aeneid, was opened near Rome in 1401, the tomb was found to be illuminated by a perpetual lantern that had apparently been alight for hundreds of years.[24]

Tomas also says that Numa Pompilius, the second king of Rome, had a perpetual light shining in the dome of his temple. Plutarch wrote of a lamp that burned at the entrance of a temple to Jupiter-Ammon,

The cosmic egg.

and its priests claimed that it had remained alight for centuries.

He claims that an ever-burning lamp was found at Antioch during the reign of Justinian of Byzantium (sixth century AD). An inscription indicated that it must have been burning for more than five hundred years. During the early Middle Ages a perpetual lamp made in the third century was found in England, and it had burned for several centuries.

Tomas also mentions a sarcophagus containing the body of a young woman of patrician stock that was found in a mausoleum on the Via Appia near Rome in April 1485. When the sealed mausoleum which had housed the sarcophagus was opened, a lighted lamp amazed the men who broke in. It must have been burning for 1,500 years! When the dark ointment preserving the body from decomposition had been removed, the girl looked lifelike with her red lips, dark hair, and shapely figure. It was exhibited in Rome and seen by 20,000 people.

Quoting Tomas on other examples of ancient lighting:

> In the temple of Trevandrum, Travancore, the Reverend S. Mateer of the London Protestant Mission saw 'a great golden lamp which was lit over one hundred and twenty years ago,' in a deep well inside the temple.
>
> Discoveries of ever-burning lamps in the temples of India and the age-old tradition of the magic lamps of the Nagas— the serpent gods and goddesses who live in underground abodes in the Himalayas—raises the possibility of the use of electric light in a forgotten era. On the background of the Agastya Samhita text's giving precise directions for constructing electrical batteries, this speculation is not extravagant.
>
> In Australia, the author learned of a village in the jungle near Mount Wilhelmina, in the western half of New Guinea, or Irian. Cut off from civilization, this village has "a system of artificial illumination equal, if not superior, to the 20th century," as C. S. Downey stated at a conference on street lighting and traffic in Pretoria, South Africa, in 1963.

Traders who penetrated this small hamlet lost amid high mountains said that they "were terrified to see many moons suspended in the air and shining with great brightness all night long." These artificial moons were huge stone balls mounted on pillars. After sunset they began to glow with a strange neon-like light, illuminating all the streets.

Ion Idriess is a well-known Australian writer who has lived amongst the Torres Strait islanders. In his *Drums of Mer* he tells of a story about the *booyas* which he received from the old aborigines. A *booya* is a round stone set in a large bamboo socket. There were only three of these stone scepters known in the islands. When a chief pointed the round stone toward the sky, a thunderbolt of greenish-blue light flashed. This "cold light" was so brilliant that the spectators seemed to be enveloped in it. Since Torres Strait washes the shores of New Guinea, one can perceive some connection between these *booyas* and the "moons" of Mount Wilhelmina.[24]

Other mysterious lights and "glowing stones" have been reported in lost cities around the world. Tibet is said to have such glowing stones and lanterns mounted on pillars in towers. Tomas relates that Father Evariste-Regis Huc (1813-1860), who travelled extensively in Asia in the 19th century, left a description of ever-burning lamps he had seen, while the Russian Central Asian explorer Nicholas Roerich reported that the legendary Buddhist secret city of Shambala was lit by a glowing jewel in a tower.

As Tomas avers:

> History shows that the priests of India, Sumer, Babylon, and Egypt, as well as their confreres on the other side of the Atlantic—in Mexico and Peru—were custodians of science. It appears likely that in a remote epoch these learned men were forced to withdraw into inaccessible parts of the world to save their accumulated knowledge from the ravages of war or geological upheavals. We still are not certain as to

what happened to Crete, Angkor, or Yucatan and why these sophisticated civilizations suddenly came to an end. If their priests had foresight, they must have anticipated these calamities.

In that case they would have taken their heritage to secret centers as the Russian poet Valery Briusov depicted in verse:

> The poets and sages,
> Guardians of the Secret Faith,
> Hid their Lighted Torches
> In deserts, catacombs and caves.[24]

Crystal Lenses, Solar Mirrors and Luminous Disks

Though there may be some doubt amongst the more conservative archaeologists that ancient societies like the Egyptians' had electricity, they all agree that ancient societies had relatively sophisticated glass technology as well as glass and crystal lenses. The ancient arts of glass smelting and metallurgy go back to the very dim mists of human civilization.

The British researcher Harold T. Wilkins mentions luminous disks in his 1952 book *Secret Cities of Old South America*.[55] Says Wilkins, "The Moslem Qu-ran, or Koran, says that old Noah planted an ebony tree and cut planks from it to make his great deluge ship, which is a not unlikely thing. We have a glimpse of some knowledge of physics and electro- or chemi-luminescence possessed by this old Atlantean Noah. The Qu-ran says he placed on the walls of the Ark *two luminous discs to make (or mark) day and night*." This is a slightly different version of the legend that mentioned Noah's glowing jewel.

The cosmic egg on a coin from Tyre.

145

A fascinating book on the use of ancient magnifying lenses is the 1953 book *The Ancient Secret: Fire from the Sun* by Flavia Anderson.[52] This is one of my favorite books on ancient technology, and Ms. Anderson is to be commended for having written this wonderful piece. Anderson says that the Grail legends are based on the existence of ancient lenses made of ground rock crystal that were once used in ancient ceremonies in the great temples of Egypt and the Eastern Mediterranean.

The lenses were set in elaborate supportive stands made of precious metals, and usually they had other precious gems set around the central lens. This central lens was an important sacred relic, yet it was no more than any common magnifying glass used today. These lenses were suspended in a device known as a monstrance. A monstrance (Anderson depicts a Spanish monstrance from the 16th century in her book) used screws to hold a rock crystal or glass lens into place on the silver/copper/gold stand. Anderson suggests that candles were lit with these lenses and they were used in religious ceremonies. Later they were used to develop telescopes, something that the Egyptians and others had known about earlier.

Anderson shows that crystal lenses were mounted in this manner by the Babylonians in what are termed "Grail Trees." The Grail Tree appears to be a lens held in the center of metal stand looking like a combination of a tree and the sun. Beside the Grail Tree, in her depiction, is a "Solar-hero in conflict with an Eagle-headed monster."

Anderson says that these crystal lenses were extremely valuable and often the symbol of nobility or authority. She gives several examples of crystal lenses being set in wonderful jewelry. Charlemagne, for instance, had a special crystal talisman. Says Anderson:

> At Denderah in Egypt there is a carving of Pharaoh presenting a wonderful necklace to the goddess Hathor on the face of the temple 'chapel,' known as the 'Birth Chamber' (where it was probable that the rebirth of the sun was celebrated yearly). The mysterious Arthurian queen in

the Prose Percival whose hand points to her necklace and its pendant 'star,' which it is claimed concerns the mystery of the Grail, could therefore be pointing to a crystal talisman such as that of Charlemagne. ...That the culture of Egypt and the Near East spread in some unknown fashion to Mexico and Peru has long been a supposition... The Spaniards recorded on their arrival in Peru that the heathen priests were accustomed to light their sacred fires from the sun's rays by means of a concave cup set in a metal bracelet.[52]

Anderson says that the legend of the phoenix bird, rising from the ashes of the fire that consumes it, may be based on certain rituals that used a magnifying crystal. The lens was used to focus the sun on some dry straw or other tinder and a trained bird then played in the fire. Anderson demonstrates in her book that a trained bird, a rook in this case, can play with fire in this manner and not be burnt or harmed in any way.

While crystal and glass lenses were apparently used by the ancients to focus the sun and light fires (often in religious ceremonies), this was probably a secondary technology to actual electric lights or other electrical devices such as Van de Graaff generators.

There are several famous stories from ancient literature that speak of giant lenses or mirrors that were used in battle. The most interesting of these stories is that of the Greeks using a fearsome 'solar mirror,' which Archimedes had cooked up in Syracuse in 212 to 215 BC, to incinerate the invading Roman fleet. He allegedly focused this giant solar mirror on the ships of the Roman fleet and set them on fire! Archimedes was credited with the naval victory, though the Romans eventually got the better of the Greeks in the long run.

To reenact and prove the Syracuse event, Tonnis Sakkas, an Athenian engineer, solar-focused seventy copper-backed mirrors, each measuring 90 cm. x 150 cm., and successfully set fire to a canoe in Skaramagas port at a distance of sixty meters.[54]

Robin Collins, in his book *Laser Beams from Star Cities*, says that old legends from China refer to the terrible 'yin-yang' mirror

147

used by warring supermen to burn the enemy. Another instrument of war possibly utilized by the ancients may have been immense electromagnets. Collins mentions that the Arabian Nights stories refer to giant magnets that withdrew the nails of ships as a means of conquering the enemy.[54]

Perseus possessed a magical helmet which, when placed upon his head, instantly rendered him invisible. Robin Collins asks, "Was the 'helmet' an electronic device to diffract or deflect light rays, thereby acting as a protective agent? The 'magic mist' produced by the Druids to render themselves invisible, may have been linked with light diffraction devices."[54]

Says Collins:

> It is not technically impossible for the solar mirrors to have reflected light and heat (and electromagnetic?) radiation from a central radiant core, e.g., a plasma radiation energy source positioned in the center of a crystalline/metallic alloyed mirror, and held by a magnetic field. Plastic jelly plasma photo-energy street lights are now experimental in the USSR, while in 1964 Columbia University scientists developed a 'free floating' plasma (ionized gas) only a few centimeters long which emitted heat radiation of +20,0000C, and a brightness three times more intense than the previous brightest artificial light source known to Man. The plasma was as bright, or brighter than the Sun! So, perhaps there is more than a grain of truth in the antiquated legends of the solar mirror engines of destruction?[54]

Many of the ancient tales of magic mirrors and "fire from heaven" may be stories of exceptionally advanced technology. For instance, crystals could be grown with phosphorescent or luminescent chemicals that would allow them to absorb solar energy during the day and be a glowing light of hard stone at night.

The idea that certain temples had fancy lights as well as steam motors or even electric ones that could open large doors automatically and thereby impress visitors even more upon their

148

visit is not so far-fetched. Such Wizard of Oz sort of temple antics may have been more common than we would like to think, with sacred oracles sitting upon their stools above a pit of vapor while green or blue glowing spheres light the huge stone walls of their sacred chambers. Even today many churches around the world use lighting and special effects like spotlights and Christmas lights to decorate their structures. Why not in ancient times?

Ark of the Covenant—Unplugged

It is my belief that the famous biblical Ark of the Covenant was in part an ancient electrical device that was Egyptian in origin. There were dangers in handling the Ark, which was generally done by the Levites who were said to have worn protective clothing.

By the time the Ark was in Israel and put in the special house near Shiloh it was over 40 years old. Yet it was still working just shortly before it was put in King Solomon's temple. The Bible reports this tragedy that happened to the priest Uzzah when the Ark was touched incorrectly. In 2 Samuel, Chapter 6, the Ark is being transported to Jerusalem by oxcart and this was giving the ark an unsteady ride. As the Bible says:

> And when they came to Nachon's threshing floor, Uzzah put forth his hand to the ark of God, and took hold of it, for the oxen shook it.
> And the anger of the Lord was kindled against Uzzah; and God smote him there for his error; and there he died by the ark of God.

Uzzah was immediately stunned to death by the force that was part of the Ark! However, it seems that others in the vicinity were not harmed, and only Uzzah was killed by the power of the Ark. Rather than thinking that God really wanted to kill Uzzah for trying to steady the Ark, it seems to be a tragic accident of a sudden discharge by a powerful electrical device. People did not understand how the Ark worked and therefore blamed the wrath of god for people being killed by it, the only possible explanation in their minds.

As we have seen before, if the Ark had not been grounded for some long period of time, the electrical charge built up in the box and statue could give a very nasty (even fatal) shock to someone who touched it. After the Ark had been discharged, however, it would be quite safe to touch. Since the chest was a sandwiching of wood and metal, a conductor and a non-conductor, it was what is known as an electrical condenser. A condenser such as the Ark would accumulate static electricity over a period of days (or years) until it was suddenly discharged onto a person, or grounded by means of a conductor, like a wire or metal rod touching the ground. But, perhaps it contained something very powerful, more powerful than a static build up.

Ark Radiations and Temple Electronics

In her book, *The Yahweh Encounters: Bible Astronauts, Ark Radiations and Temple Electronics*,[53] Ann Madden Jones says that the Bible reveals that the Scriptures are filled with technological data, and speak of a visitation to earth by celestial beings who created man. Interesting evidence is presented that the Exodus tabernacle and the Temple of Solomon, with the Ark as centerpiece, were microwave transceivers communicating with orbiting spaceships.

Jones, who holds degrees from George Washington University and the University of North Carolina, also examines biblical predictions of 21st century technology in her book, including orbiting thought-control devices and laser exterminators. She gives a comparison of ancient and modern UFOs and biblical descriptions of the horrors of a one-world dictatorship. She also details end-time cosmic disasters, to occur just before the return of Jesus and the spaceships.

According to Jones, the Ark of the Covenant is the centerpiece of a complicated communication system, and it she says it contained so much radioactive material that some 64,000 people died through its misuse! Three chapters in her book involve the details and circuitry of this system, and include diagrams of how the entire temple with the Ark was a huge microwave system.

The rest of the book is a discussion of Genesis through Revelation involving alien abductions and space flights, robot angels, SDI-type defense systems, nuclear war, genetic engineering, and control and resurrection through transplantation of the electrical pattern of the genetic code. Jones essentially takes modern technology and applies it to all the strange stories of the Bible.

In the three chapters on the temple's technology, she discusses biblical circuit descriptions involving plasma physics, crystal lasers, ionic loudspeakers, sonic holography, microwave resonators, and twelve six-foot diameter metal dish antennas on wheels. The details of the construction and operating procedures (rituals) she discusses are taken directly from the Bible passages of God's plans given to Moses and Solomon. As we shall see in the next chapter, these were very specific.

Early on in her book Jones questions whether Moses was shown the Promised Land via an airship at the very end of his life. She quotes Deuteronomy 34:1-3:

> Then Moses climbed Mount Nebo from the plains of Moab to the top of Pisgah, across from Jericho. There the Lord showed him the whole land—from Gilead to Dan, all of Naphtali, the territory of Ephraim and Manasseh, all the land of Judah as far as the Mediterranean Sea, the Negev and the whole region from the Valley of Jericho, the City of Palms, as far as Zoar.

Jones wonders how Moses, a frail old man, supposedly 120 years old, could have climbed Mount Nebo, a tall craggy mountain. And she says, even if he did climb the mountain, he could not have seen such far off places described, such as the land of Dan, the Mediterranean Sea, or the city of Zoar at the southern end of the Dead Sea. Says Jones:

> Is it possible Moses was flown across the Jordan river to a mountainous region on the west side [of the Dead Sea] to see some of the places (such as the promised land and the Mediterranean) he could not see from the eastern side?

The distances of the places mentioned which Moses was shown, the time which would have been required, and the difficulties for an aged man, in ascending the mountains by foot, or even riding an animal, are convincing that Moses was actually transported to these places effortlessly, in some kind of conveyance, most likely the spaceship called the "pillar of fire and cloud."[53]

Jones includes a discussion of the protective clothing worn by Moses' brother Aaron. She says that this protective clothing was to shield the priest in charge of the Ark from radioactivity, high voltage and microwaves.

She mentions that Exodus 39 speaks about the garment called the ephod which was a metallic woven waistcoat with straps over the shoulders. A large onyx stone was mounted on each of the shoulder straps. The ephod was then held in place with the "curious girdle" which had a pouch over the chest called the breastplate of judgment. It was in this pouch that the unidentified "crystal" objects called the Urim and Thummim were placed. Gold threads throughout the ephod make it a stiff and cumbersome waistcoat and girdle to wear. Says Jones:

The order in which the priestly vestments had to be worn reveals their protective function, and to some extent their part in the communication system. First, the linen or embroidered coat was donned, next to Aaron's skin. This was an insulating layer, since there was no mention of any gold cunning work.

...Over the coat was put the robe of the ephod, a long garment that reached from the neck to the ankles, of wool. ...attached to the robe's hem were gold bells that brushed the ground. It was stated that the bells made a noise to indicate to God that someone was in the tabernacle, so that person would not be killed. When the robe's golden bells brushed the ground, they would have provided an electrical ground for the entire outfit. Josephus wrote of sparks and crackling that was associated with the bells. The sounds could have been static electric discharges.

Over the robe of the ephod was the ephod itself, a long frock with much "cunning work" using gold interwoven into the fabric of wool linen, purple and scarlet. This piece would have been equivalent to a wire mesh or grid, or what we call today a Faraday cage. The function of a Faraday cage is to protect against exposure to electromagnetic radiations such as microwaves.

…A turban was worn on the high priest's head, with a gold plate attached to it by lace of blue at the front of the turban. This "blue" lay against the priest's forehead. [53]

Jones thinks that this gold plate in front of the priest's forehead, combined with the "crystals" and other stones on the ephod, created some sort of communication device for the priest wearing these clothes. Because it is in the vicinity of the Ark of the Covenant, itself a powerful transmitter, and the temple layout itself contributed to the effect, a mind-control communication system is activated and the priest gets instructions from a spaceship in orbit around planet Earth. This spaceship is occupied by our ancient astronaut controllers who orbit the Earth and occasionally interact with humans like Moses in order to move humanity in the direction that they desire. They are the angels of the Bible.

Not only is the priest receiving communication and mind-control signals through his protective clothing, but the entire temple, built with tons of gold and the Ark of the Covenant as a microwave resonator, is transmitting a mind-control message to the population of Jerusalem. Essentially, she is saying that the Ark, combined with the temple layout, could power an earth station that was "communicating" with an off-world spaceship.

Jones' book is a fascinating explanation of the Ark of the Covenant and many of the things associated with it, but it seems to go over the edge at times. She certainly seems to be on the right track about airships being involved in many of the strange incidents of the Old Testament, and that the Ark is some sort of energy device—a

153

microwave resonator in her case—and that the ephod was some sort of protective clothing that acted like a Faraday cage to protect the wearer from dangerous electromagnetic waves.

However, she is clearly an ancient astronaut theorist and believes that only extraterrestrials would have the technology of airships and microwaves in 1000 BC. The tales of vimana airships in the Hindu epics are not familiar to her, so her "angels in airships" must be ancient astronauts who have decided to use Moses as one of their tools on Earth. She goes one step beyond this and asserts that they are broadcasting a mind-control message via microwaves that affects a large portion of people who are in the vicinity of the grand device, which incorporates the entire massive temple structure.

While there may be ancient astronauts orbiting the Earth, I prefer to think that the energy device was something brought from Egypt during the Exodus. The pillar of smoke and fire does seem to be an airship of some kind, and Moses does seem to be interacting with beings in airships who are giving him directions and even military help. These beings were probably the same ones, or their descendants, who were responsible for the destruction of Sodom and Gomorrah. But, were they extraterrestrials?

It is difficult to look back at the ancient world as one that was entirely primitive. Megalithic constructions such as Baalbek in Lebanon and the Great Pyramid in Egypt are examples of an ancient world that included the ability to quarry and move huge stone blocks and then stack them up into walls of buildings that continue to amaze us today. How could the engineers and scientists responsible for these structures—obelisks included—have not known about electricity?

Similarly, the many magical and fabulous items that King Solomon had in his palaces and temples are still legendary today. Was it all given to him by extraterrestrials? King Solomon, it would seem, was also shown how to operate the Ark. Let us now look at this astonishing and legendary figure of history and his relationship to Ethiopia and India.

Plan of the Tabernacle and the Court

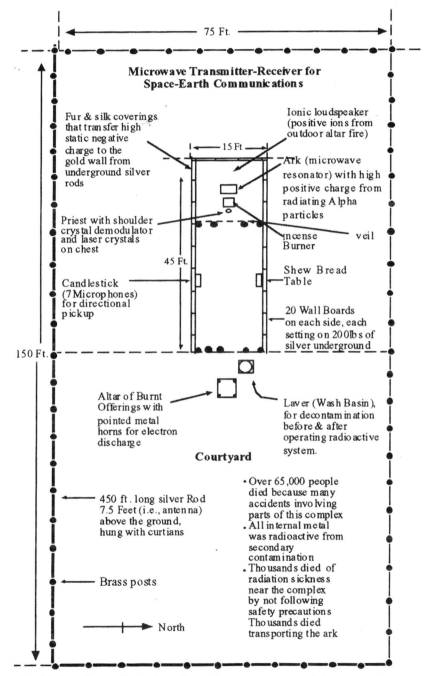

75 Ft.

**Microwave Transmitter-Receiver for
Space-Earth Communications**

Fur & silk coverings
that transfer high
static negative
charge to the
gold wall from
underground silver
rods

15 Ft

Ionic loudspeaker
(positive ions from
outdoor altar fire)

Ark (microwave
resonator) with high
positive charge from
radiating Alpha
particles

Priest with shoulder
crystal demodulator
and laser crystals
on chest

incense
Burner   veil

45 Ft.

Shew Bread
Table

Candlestick
(7 Microphones)
for directional
pickup

20 Wall Boards
on each side, each
setting on 200 lbs of
silver underground

150 Ft.

Altar of Burnt
Offerings with
pointed metal
horns for electron
discharge

Laver (Wash Basin),
for decontamination
before & after
operating radioactive
system.

Courtyard

• Over 65,000 people
died because many
accidents involving
parts of this complex
. All internal metal
was radioactive from
secondary
contamination
. Thousands died of
radiation sickness
near the complex
by not following
safety precautions
Thousands died
transporting the ark

450 ft. long silver Rod
7.5 Feet (i.e., antenna)
above the ground,
hung with curtians

Brass posts

North

Ann Madden Jones' illustration of her microwave resonator Ark of the Covenant.

CHAPTER SEVEN

KING SOLOMON'S SHIPS, AXUM & THE LAND OF OPHIR

King Solomon made a fleet of ships in Ezion-Geber, which is beside Eilat on the shore of the Red Sea in the land of Edom. And Hiram sent in the navy of his servants, shipmen that had knowledge of the sea, with the servants of Solomon. And they came to Ophir, and fetched from thence gold, four hundred and twenty talents, and brought it to King Solomon... Once in three years the fleet came in bringing gold, silver, ivory, apes, peacocks... a very great amount of red sandalwood and precious stones.
—I Kings 9:26-28

One of the curious things in the *Kebra Nagast* aside from the flying wagons, is that a war with India is mentioned. The connections Israel, Arabia, Egypt and Ethiopia had with the advanced civilization of ancient India has been well noted by numerous scholars. It seems the ancient Hindu epics were familiar to the early Christian bishops at the Council of Nicea as witnessed in the *Kebra Nagast*.

We have the same flying machines—vimanas, or wagons of Zion—mentioned in the epic books of India and Ethiopia. As we have seen, in the popular Hindu epic *Ramayana,* the prince Rama goes off to rescue his kidnapped wife. He is said to fly in his vimana across an ocean to the west of India to a land called Lanka. Lanka is ruled by a dark-skinned king named Ravana who is an expert

157

magician, technician and Shiva devotee.[37]

After several aerial battles and other adventures, Rama succeeds in rescuing his wife and they return to the Ayodha forests of northern India. The villain, Ravana, isn't such a bad guy in the story, as he is a king and a priest, but he does have dark skin. Is it possible that Ethiopia is the Lanka of the *Ramayana*? At the very least it would seem that the authors of the *Kebra Nagast* were trying to fit Ethiopian history into a similar framework as the Hindu epics, which everyone knew included aerial craft, battles and awesome weapons.

The Building of the Temple

The *Kebra Nagast* tells us that Solomon gave Sheba an airship, and later his son Menelik has one as well. While the Bible does not tell us about Solomon's airship, it does tell us that he and his kingdom became fabulously rich by sending a fleet of ships to a mysterious land of Ophir to bring back over 20 tons of gold, spices

An old print of the building of Solomon's temple.

and other goods.

We learn about King Solomon in the Old Testament books 1 Kings and 2 Chronicles. 1 Kings gives the general story of Solomon and of how Israel becomes powerful during his reign. It also tells of Solomon's death and the division of Israel into two states, Israel and Judah. 2 Chronicles continues to recount the life of Solomon and the building of the temple.

In the first chapters of 1 Kings, Solomon becomes the king of Israel. In 1 Kings 3 he makes an alliance with the Egyptian Pharaoh, marrying his daughter, and asks for wisdom from god in a dream.

In 1 Kings 5 we are told that the Phoenician King Hiram of Tyre (in what is today Lebanon) sends envoys to Solomon when he hears he has become king. Solomon wrote a letter to be taken to Hiram by the ambassadors stating his intention to build "a temple for the name of the Lord" now that there was relative peace in the region and he could turn his attention to this task. He asks that the cedars of Lebanon be cut for him, and sets up a rotation system for Israelite conscripted laborers to spend time in Tyre working alongside Hiram's expert wood- and stoneworkers. Says 1 Kings 5:17-18:

> At the king's command they removed from the quarry large blocks of high-grade stone to provide a foundation of dressed stone for the temple. The craftsmen of Solomon and Hiram and workers from Byblos cut and prepared the timber and stone for the building of the temple.

In 1 Kings 6 we are told more about Solomon building the great temple which was to house the Ark and impress anyone who entered it with the greatness of Yahweh. The temple is furnished with much gold and adornments and took seven years to build. In 1 Kings 6:7 we are told that no hammers or iron tools were used at the temple site:

> In building the temple, only blocks dressed at the quarry were used, and no hammer, chisel or any other iron tool was heard at the temple site while it was being built.

Because of this curious statement, a legend rose up that King Solomon possessed a magic substance—or "worm"—the size of a barleycorn, that could cut stone. This magical item was called the shamir and it could be used to cut any kind of metal or stone and was essentially harder than any other substance.

It is difficult to find a lot of information on the shamir but let us look at the Wikipedia entry under "Solomon's Shamir":

> In the Gemara [part of the Talmud], the shamir is a worm or a substance that had the power to cut through or disintegrate stone, iron and diamond. King Solomon is said to have used it in the building of the First Temple in Jerusalem in the place of cutting tools. For the building of the Temple, which promoted peace, it was inappropriate to use tools that could also cause war and bloodshed.
>
> Referenced throughout the Talmud and the Midrashim, the Shamir was reputed to have existed in the time of Moses. Moses reputedly used the Shamir to engrave the Hoshen (Priestly breastplate) stones that were inserted into the breastplate. King Solomon, aware of the existence of the Shamir, but unaware of its location, commissioned a search that turned up a "grain of Shamir the size of a barley-corn."
>
> Solomon's artisans reputedly used the Shamir in the construction of Solomon's Temple. The material to be worked, whether stone, wood or metal, was affected by being "shown to the Shamir." Following this line of logic (anything that can be 'shown' something must have eyes to see), early Rabbinical scholars described the Shamir almost as a living being. Other early sources, however, describe it as a green stone. For storage, the Shamir was meant to have been always wrapped in wool and stored in a container made of lead; any other vessel would burst and disintegrate under the Shamir's gaze. The Shamir was said to have been either lost or had lost its potency (along with the "dripping of the honeycomb") by the time of the destruction of the

First Temple at the hands of Nebuchadnezzar in 586 B.C.

According to the deutero-canonical Asmodeus legend, the shamir was given to Solomon as a gift from Asmodeus, the king of demons. Another version of the story holds that a captured Asmodeus told Solomon the Shamir was entrusted to the care of a woodcock. Solomon then sends his trusted aide Benaiah on a quest to retrieve it.

The shamir worm was also used by King Solomon to engrave gemstones. Apparently he also used the blood of the shamir worm to make carved jewels with a mystical seal or design. According to an interview with Dr. George Frederick Kunz, an expert in gemstone and jewelry lore, this led to the belief that gemstones so engraved would have magical virtues, and they often also ended up with their own powers or guardian angel associated with either the gem, or the specifically engraved gemstones.

So what was the shamir? It is tempting to think it was some sort of laser technology, with the "eye" of the shamir being the focused beam of light emitted from the laser, which could easily burn through stone, metal or wood. The first modern laser, developed in 1960, used a synthetic ruby crystal to beam red light, and the

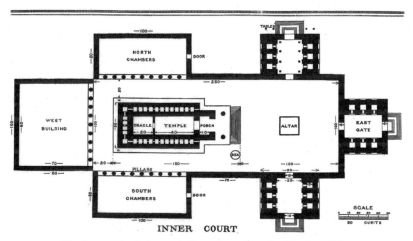
The layout for Solomon's Temple as described in the Bible.

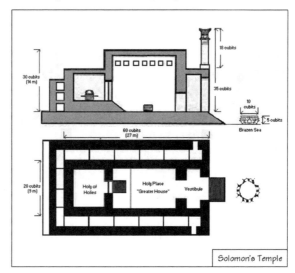

A plan of Solomon's Temple

shamir is associated with gems. Why did the shamir have to be kept in a lead box? Lead is usually used as a protective layer against excess radiation. "Laser" stands for Light Amplification by the Stimulated Emission of Radiation, and radiation injury is possible even from moderately powered beams. But having a laser device the size of a barleycorn seems far-fetched even by today's standards of miniaturization.

The general thought is that it is a diamond, the hardest substance in the mineral world. In fact, the shamir may have been some sort of diamond drill or saw that would cut other gems and saw and drill through such hard stones as granite or even basalt. To be "shown to the samir" may have been akin to having an object placed on a diamond lathe or saw. Today it is necessary to use diamond saws and drills to cut modern granite blocks at quarries and we might imagine that ancient stonecutters—some of them at least—had similar such tools.

Again, was some highly developed civilization, or several of them, producing diamond saws, diamond drills, iron tools, electrical devices and even airships? Countries like ancient Egypt, Babylonia, Hittite Hattusas, India and China were all capable, in my mind, of producing such things in ancient times. Other countries, such as ancient Israel, Greece or Ethiopia had to import these items and they were therefore "magical" objects and only owned by kings and important princes.

A fascinating website called BibleSearchers.com has some interesting information on the shamir, which was most likely composed of small pieces of diamond, sapphire and/or ruby, probably from India:

> In the Mishnah Avon 5:6, the Shamir was created on the sixth day of creation and was given to the hoopoe-bird (woodcock) who kept it in her custody throughout the ages in the Garden of Eden. This marvelous bird would on occasion take this worm and carry it across the earth, carrying it tightly in her beak, letting it down only to create a fissure on a desolate mountain peak so that the seeds of plants and trees could sprout and provide her food.
>
> When the Israelites were camped near Mount Horeb/ Sinai, the Lord brought the Shamir and gave it to Bezaleel to engrave the names of the twelve tribes on the twelve stones of the breastplate of the high priest, Aaron. Then the Lord gave it back to the custody of the hoopie-bird. Here she kept it in a leaden box, with fresh barley, wrapped in a woolen cloth. That is until Solomon needed it to build the Temple of the Lord in Jerusalem. Since that day, the Shamir has been lost.[56]
>
> As with all good rabbinic Talmudic debates, there was always a dissent. Judah R. Nehemiah claimed that the stones were quarried and then brought to the temple in a finished condition for the building of the temple. It appears that Rabbi Nehemiah's argument carried the debate as most scholars today believe this also to be true.
>
> Of course, most Talmudic arguments were debated during the Roman imperial rule. In Latin, the Shamir was known as *smirks corundum*, the substance of sapphires and rubies and the hardest known gem next to the diamond. The substance of legends has a kernel of truth and now we know the 'rest of the story.'

These Bible scholars think that there was more than one shamir and they were none other than power tools, specifically diamond drills and such. Says BibleSearchers:

> The whole passage in the Book of Kings suggests that there was a certain dignity and quietness, a decorum that was to be maintained as the contractors and the artisans could feel the presence of the Lord in the House that they were constructing. There was to be a spirituality of the Presence. They were not to hear the pounding or banging of instruments of iron. Was the literalness of the message also to have a spiritual connection? Yet within the House of the Lord, there [were] no injunctions of the Lord against the humming of diamond drill bits as they cut, polished and finished off the massive limestone walls, or trimmed the edges of the cedars of Lebanon, or engraved the wood on the porticoes, or drill holes into the limestone to set beams and stabilize pillars, to embellish the trimming on the ceilings of the Holy Place, place engraved images on the Molten Sea or on the large doors that entered into the temple proper. Is it not time to consider that Solomon with all his wisdom and wealth also had access to technologies that we think are modern, only to someday know that the ancients were using them too?
>
> ...Maybe within the hoard of the treasures of Solomon's temple, we will find evidence of the technological sophistication, such as diamond drills, diamond and corundum bit saws that scholars have long felt did not exist in the 11th century BCE.

BibleSearchers are giving a date for King Solomon between 1001 and 1100 BC, though others give the date at around 970 to 931 BC. No matter what the exact date for the building of Solomon's Temple, it was apparently a massive construction job, with some of the building consisting of huge ashlar stones, but these were likely already in place from a much earlier date.

Nearly all of this construction was done by Phoenicians from Tyre, Byblos and other Phoenician cities in the eastern Mediterranean. Indeed, it was Solomon's good fortune to have a Phoenician king who loved him and his countrymen and would go to great lengths to help Solomon build his nation into one of great prosperity.

Solomon Installs the Ark of Covenant in the Temple

In 1 Kings 7 we are told that Solomon took 13 years to build his palace in Jerusalem, which he named the House of the Forest of Lebanon, apparently an acknowledgement of the huge amount of cedar wood that went into the construction. The chapter continues with his work on the temple at Jerusalem. It is here that we are introduced to an exceptional individual from Tyre named Hiram, but he was an artisan, not the king. Says 1 Kings 7:13-14:

> King Solomon sent to Tyre and brought Hiram, whose mother was a widow from the tribe of Naphtali and whose father was from Tyre and a skilled craftsman in bronze. Hiram was filled with wisdom, with understanding and with knowledge to do all kinds of bronze work. He came to King Solomon and did all the work assigned to him.

In 2 Chronicles 2:14, King Hiram writes to Solomon about the craftsman he is sending to aid in the temple construction, and he credits Hiram with even more extensive skills:

> He is trained to work in gold and silver, bronze and iron, stone and wood, and with purple and blue and crimson yarn and fine linen. He is experienced in all kinds of engraving and can execute any design given to him. He will work with your skilled workers and with those of my lord, David your father.

Hiram apparently served as the supervisor of all the different kinds of work being done to complete the temple. The specifications of many aspects of the temple are quite detailed and overwhelming, but really fine constructs and furnishings were turned out. It is interesting to note that this Hiram is the archetypal figure of Freemasonry. The group utilizes a lot of imagery surrounding the "widow's son" in its third level rites, and the two pillars recreated at most lodges are a direct reference to the work of Hiram. According to 2 Chronicles 3:15-17:

> For the front of the temple he made two pillars, which together were thirty-five cubits long, each with a capital five cubits high. He made interwoven chains and put them on top of the pillars. He also made a hundred pomegranates and attached them to the chains. He erected the pillars in the front of the temple, one to the south and one to the north. The one to the south he named Jakin and the one to the north Boaz.

Two gigantic statues of winged cheubim covered with gold stood were constructed to adorn the Most Holy Place within which the Ark was to be kept. In 2 Chronicles 3:10-13 we are told:

> For the Most Holy Place he made a pair of sculptured cherubim and overlaid them with gold. The total wingspan of the cherubim was twenty cubits. One wing of the first cherub was five cubits long and touched the temple wall, while its other wing, also five cubits long, touched the wing of the other cherub. Similarly one wing of the second cherub was five cubits long and touched the other temple wall, and its other wing, also five cubits long, touched the wing of the first cherub. The wings of these cherubim extended twenty cubits. They stood on their feet, facing the main hall.

Details like this stand out as being somewhat odd, especially given Ann Madden Jones' theory of circuitry at the temple. Why do the wings of the cherubim exactly touch each wall, and each other in the center?

In 1 Kings 8, Solomon has the Ark placed inside the temple. Says 1 Kings 8: 1-11:

> Then Solomon assembled the elders of Israel and all the heads of the tribes, the leaders of the fathers' houses of the people of Israel, before King Solomon in Jerusalem, to bring up the ark of the covenant of the Lord out of the city of David, which is Zion.
>
> ...And they brought up the ark of the Lord, the tent of meeting, and all the holy vessels that were in the tent; the priests and the Levites brought them up.
>
> ...Then the priests brought the ark of the covenant of the Lord to its place in the inner sanctuary of the house, in the Most Holy Place, underneath the wings of the cherubim.
>
> For the cherubim spread out their wings over the place of the ark, so that the cherubim overshadowed the ark and its poles.
>
> And the poles were so long that the ends of the poles were seen from the Holy Place before the inner sanctuary; but they could not be seen from outside. And they are there to this day.
>
> There was nothing in the ark except the two tablets of stone that Moses put there at Horeb, where the Lord made a covenant with the people of Israel, when they came out of the land of Egypt.
>
> And when the priests came out of the Holy Place, a cloud filled the house of the Lord, so that the priests could not stand to minister because of the cloud, for the glory of the Lord filled the house of the Lord.

The cloud emanating from the Ark and filling not just the Holy of Holies but the entire temple was apparently a dark cloud that terrified the people—not surprising given the history of deadly encounters associated with the Ark and cloud. In the next verse, Solomon tries to calm the crowd, saying "The Lord said he would dwell in a dark cloud."

167

Apparently, no one was hurt in this incident, and the people of Jerusalem and Israel were happy with the temple. Then we are told that Solomon gifts King Hiram twenty towns for all the supplies and help he has contributed to Solomon's building program. Says 1 Kings 9: 10-12:

> At the end of twenty years, during which Solomon built these two buildings—the temple of the Lord and the royal palace—King Solomon gave twenty towns in Galilee to Hiram king of Tyre, because Hiram had supplied him with all the cedar and juniper and gold he wanted. But when Hiram went from Tyre to see the towns that Solomon had given him, he was not pleased with them.

So Hiram apparently suggests that they gain access to the Red

Sea, through the neighboring land of Edom, and make a fleet of Phoenician ships that could sail out to the Indian Ocean and bring back gold and other valuable cargo. In 1 Kings 9:26-28 we are a told:

> And King Solomon made a navy of ships in Ezion-Geber, which is beside Eilat on the shore of the Red Sea, in the land of Edom.
> And Hiram sent in the navy his servants, shipmen who had knowledge of the sea, with the servants of Solomon.
> And they came to Ophir and fetched from thence gold, four hundred and twenty talents, and brought it to King Solomon.

This is the first time we learn of a fabled land called Ophir, which we learn later is a three year voyage, a place of plentiful gold, spices and other valuable items.

King Solomon's Fleet Goes to the Land of Ophir

Sometime around 950 BC Solomon and Hiram built a port and a fleet of ships at Ezion-Geber, at the very northern end of the Red Sea. These ships made a series of three-year voyages to the mysterious land of Ophir. This amazing port and fleet were not even in Israel or Phoenicia, but in the Kingdom of Edom. Edom had its own port, Eilat, but through marriage and diplomacy Solomon was able to have the Phoenicians build a quasi-military harbor on the Red Sea.

This gave Israel the advantage of having ports on the Mediterranean and on the Red Sea with access to the Indian Ocean. Since Solomon's ships would be largely manned by highly-skilled Phoenicians, Solomon's fleet was a de facto Phoenician navy in the Indian Ocean. And a Phoenician navy in the Indian Ocean could reach such far-flung places as Southeast Asia and Indonesia. They could even have voyaged into the Pacific. Wherever they were going, their home port was Ezion-Geber.

Traces of the port are lost to time and historians are not sure where the ancient port of Ezion-Geber actually was. Some historians

169

doubt that it even existed. In the late 1930s, the famous Israeli archaeologist Nelson Glueck discovered ruins at Tell-el Kheleifeh of what he identified as copper smelting furnaces and metal forges that dated back to the tenth century BC. These findings led to the belief that this was part of King Solomon's port city of Ezion-Geber. Further work at the site proved that it went back no further than the 8th century BC, and Glueck reversed his opinion in 1965.[7,48]

The British archeologist Alexander Flinder located Ezion-Geber on an island just offshore of Eilat and relates this discovery in his 1985 book *Secrets of the Bible Seas*.[48] In this book he claims that a small island off the Eilat coast—called Coral Island or Jezirat Fara'un—was the location of Ezion-Geber. Flinder did an archeological underwater recovery on an ancient ship near this island and says that it is a natural harbor. This island and a port on the coast were probably used together. Some think that Ezion-Geber lies beneath the modern Jordanian port of Aqaba.

The ships built at Ezion-Geber were built out of cedar trees from Lebanon brought across the desert of Edom to the Red Sea, a mammoth feat in itself.

Expert Phoenician shipmakers then helped Solomon's crew construct a fleet of ships, perhaps six or more. Seamen from the two countries then made the three-year journey to Ophir and back. A long strange trip indeed! Where did they go?

The Land of Ophir

The mysterious land of Ophir is a place that is reached via the Red Sea and Indian Ocean, and could be in various places such as Africa, India, Indonesia, Australia or even Peru. Scholars remain confused over where Ophir is—or was—and many places have been proposed.

Another mysterious place mentioned in the Bible is Uphaz. This may be another name for Ophir, but scholars are not sure. Uphaz is mentioned only twice in the Bible, in Jeremiah and Daniel:

> Hammered silver is brought from Tarshish and gold from Uphaz. What the craftsman and goldsmith have made

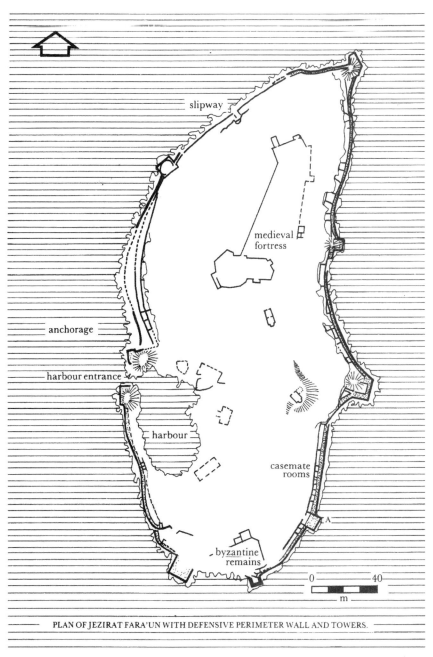

slipway

medieval
fortress

anchorage

harbour entrance

harbour

casemate
rooms

A

byzantine
remains

0 ———— 40
m

PLAN OF JEZIRAT FARA'UN WITH DEFENSIVE PERIMETER WALL AND TOWERS.

Alexander Flinder's map of the island of Jezirat Fara'un which he says is Ezion-Geber

is then dressed in blue and purple—all made by skilled workers. (Jeremiah 10:9)

I looked up and there before me was a man dressed in linen, with a belt of fine gold from Uphaz around his waist. (Daniel 10:5)

Some scholars think that Uphaz (Ophir?) is a place near the river Hyphasis of northwest India, in the southeast of the Punjab, which today is partially in India and partially in Pakistan. In fact, this is the core area of the Indus Valley civilization. Others suggest that Uphaz was an Indian colony in Yemen. India had colonies in Oman and southern Yemen and the dress and customs of these areas was very similar to that in India. Naturally, a great deal of naval traffic occurred from the west coast of India and Sri Lanka to Yemen, Oman and various Gulf Kingdoms.

From ports in Oman and Yemen there was also a great deal of naval traffic to East Africa with islands such as Lamu, Pemba and Zanzibar becoming city-states that were governed from Oman. This sort of trade must have been going on since at least 2000 BC and the settlement of Madagascar from Southeast Asia would have happened in this time period as well, culminating in a huge migration from Borneo around 350 BC. It is from the early exploration of these many islands that we get the stories of Sinbad in the Tales of the Arabian Nights. Sinbad was an Omani sea captain who traditionally

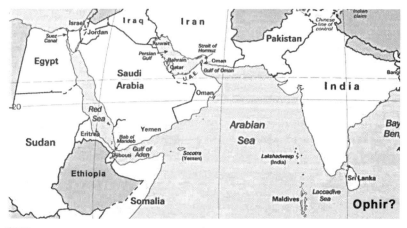

A satellite photo of the Red Sea from the Sinai to the Gulf of Aden.

had a home on the Kenyan island of Lamu.

Biblical scholars, archaeologists and others have tried to determine the exact location of Ophir. Vasco da Gama's companion Tomé Lopes reasoned that Ophir would have been the ancient name for Great Zimbabwe in Zimbabwe, the main center of sub-African trade in gold in the Renaissance period, though the ruins at Great Zimbabwe are now dated to the medieval era, long after Solomon lived. Milton, in his epic poem Paradise Lost, identified Sofala in Mozambique as Ophir, and this was common among many other works of literature and science.

Ophir is generally thought to be somewhere in India, though various 19th century writers like H. Rider Haggard in *King Solomon's Mines* (1885) placed Ophir in South Africa or Zimbabwe. But, ruins in Zimbabwe and other ruins in Mozambique were deemed as not old enough to be King Solomon's mines, and places like Somalia were too close to the Red Sea. Still, historians remain constantly unaware of the many connections between far-flung ancient civilizations, and would place the land of Ophir along the coast of Arabia that was only a few days' sail from Ezion-Geber.

The myopic attitude of biblical scholars and historians may be summed up by this statement from Manfred Barthel, the German scholar who wrote *What the Bible Really Says*: "Zimbabwe was too recent, India too far away, the Urals too cold... It does seem likely that Ophir was somewhere on the shores of the Red Sea."[43]

Similarly, the German scholars Hermann and Georg Schreiber

say in their book *Vanished Cities:*

> At one time the idea arose that the Ophir of the Bible may have been in what is now called Peru. But that is out of the question; no merchant fleet sailed so far in the tenth century B.C. The Solomon Islands, north of Australia, have also been suggested. But that is pure nonsense; all these have in common with King Solomon is the name, by which they were first called in 1568. Moreover, there is no gold in the Solomon Islands. It is also impossible to equate Ophir with the Spanish port of Tartessus, as a modern church lexicon does; no one who wanted to sail from Palestine to Spain would build his ships on the Red Sea!
>
> Flavius Josephus, the great Jewish historian of the first century A.D., guessed that Ophir was located in Farther India. But India was more interested in importing than in exporting gold.
>
> The search for the famous land of gold has therefore been restricted fundamentally to southern Arabia and the African coast. Arabia, however, is also out of the question. If Ophir had been situated there, as some scholars still maintain, Solomon would not have needed the assistance of the King of Tyre; he would simply have used the ancient caravan routes of the Arabian peninsula.[7]

The Schreibers have many good points but at the same time they fall into the strange logic of the isolationists, those who believe that ancient man never ventured far from land or the known. Manfred Barthel is typical of the isolationist at his worst, because for him, even India is too far away for Solomon's fleet.

Today, scholars have little doubt about the extensive maritime trade between the Red Sea and India. The real question is how long would it take to make a trip to India and back from the Red Sea? Three years?

A voyage in a Phoenician trireme (three sets of oars plus sails) from Ezion-Geber to the Axumite port of Adulis would take maybe a week. A further few weeks would get the ship to ports along the southern Arabian coast. From Oman to ports along the coast of western India would be another several weeks. Even a trip from Ezion-Geber to the southern Indian port of Poovar would only take about six months. This is almost certainly the voyage that King Solomon's ships were taking. It would seem that the first major stop they made was to a port at the southern tip of India.

Poovar is the southernmost port on the west coast of India, and it has a natural harbor. Poovar was a trading center of sandalwood, timber, ivory and spices. Gold was probably traded here as well, but it came from another source, apparently a place called Parvaim.

Poovar is mention by the Roman writer Pliny the Elder, and the great traveler Marco Polo wrote of Poovar's connections with Greece and Rome. This ancient port would have been easy to reach by ships from Ezion-Geber, Adulis, Yemen or Oman as well as from Sumatra, Borneo, Java and other places in Southeast Asia.

Wikipedia gives us this information on Ophir being in India or a name for India in general:

> A dictionary of the Bible by Sir William Smith published in 1863, notes the Hebrew word for peacock Thukki, derived from the Classical Tamil for peacock Thogkai and Cingalese "tokei," joins other Classical Tamil words for ivory, cotton-cloth and apes preserved in the Hebrew Bible. This theory of Ophir's location in Tamilakkam is further supported by other historians. Ophir, referring to the country of the port Tarshish may well refer to the nation of the Tamil Velir-Naga tribe Oviyar in ancient Jaffna, who lived around the famous port towns of Mantai and Kudiramalai, home to the historic Thiruketheeswaram temple.
>
> …Earlier in the 19th century Max Müller and other scholars identified Ophir with Abhira, near the Indus River in modern-day state of Gujarat, India. According to Benjamin Walker Ophir is said to have been a town of the Abhira tribe.
>
> Easton's Bible Dictionary (1897) adds a connection to "Sofir," the Coptic name for India. Josephus connected it

with "Cophen, an Indian river, and in part of Asia adjoining to it," (*Antiquities of the Jews* 1:6), sometimes associated with a part of Afghanistan.

In my book *Lost Cities of Ancient Lemuria and the Pacific*[60] I proposed that Australia was the land of Ophir. I suggested that mining was being done by Phoenicians and other settlers in Western Australia. This small colony set in a mining zone would ultimately see Solomon's ships depart with a cargo of gold, silver, copper and precious stones, headed for a port such as Poovar.

Curiously, there are petroglyphs on the Finke River in Australia which show no less than ten traditional Jewish candlesticks or menorah.[93] Did these petroglyphs show the way to King Solomon's Ophir?

There is evidence that Egyptian explorers have been in eastern Australia. At the town of Gympie in Queensland, an alleged pyramid was found, now destroyed, along with a three-foot-high statue of the Egyptian god Thoth in the form of a baboon, and numerous Egyptian and Phoenician relics all currently in the local museum. What is more, the same place became known as "The Town that Saved Queensland" because of a gold rush in the late 1800s.

On a trip to Australia in July, 2015, I was part of a group that was shown a series of Egyptian hieroglyphs on a rock cleft in northern New South Wales near the town of Gosford that are said to chronicle an expedition to Australia. Some Australian historians say that it is an elaborate fake while others think that they are genuine hieroglyphics that are thousands of years old. It is a popular notion in Australia that Egyptians and others explored the country, with various Egyptian inscriptions and artifacts being reported.[60]

If Australia was Ophir, then on leaving the continent the fleet would have probably stopped in Sumatra and then docked at Poovar on the southern tip of India. Here they would have obtained the ivory, sandalwood, spices and peacocks, and then made the voyage back to Yemen and up the Red Sea. In this theory, the voyage to Ophir was a trip to India and then to Australia, where the ore had to be crushed and smelted. This would have taken some time, probably an entire year.

176

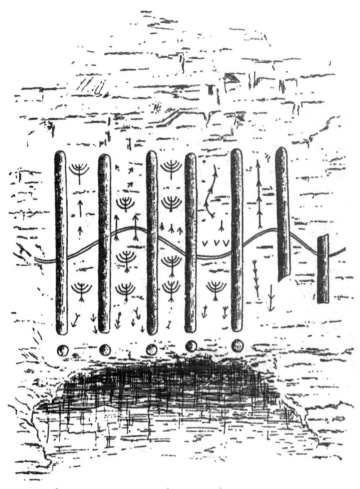

An old print of the Finke River petroglyphs, discovered in 1873.

Was South America the Land of Ophir?

It would seem obvious that Ophir is well beyond Arabia and probably beyond Poovar on the tip of India. It seems that the three-year voyage actually took the seafarers to India, Indonesia and beyond. If you knew where you were going, could you cross the Pacific to Mexico or Peru and return in three years? The answer is probably yes.

Some early New World explorers wondered if Peru or Mexico could have been the source of Solomon's fortune as told in the

177

Bible. One such explorer was the Spanish admiral Alvaro Mendana who discovered the Solomon Islands in 1568 while searching for the lost land of Ophir.

Alvaro Mendana (October 1, 1542–October 18, 1595) was a Spanish navigator and is best known for the two voyages he led from Peru into the Pacific in 1567 and 1595 in search of Terra Australis. A Spanish chronicler named Sarmiento had said the Inca wealth had come from a land further to the west, and when Mendana and his crew set out to find this land, they ran across the Solomon Islands. They attempted to establish a colony but eventually returned to Peru.

Mendana and his group believed that the island group was the land of Ophir from Bible and therefore gave it the name "Solomon's Islands." Though there are some gold mines in the Solomons no historians actually think that the Solomon Islands are the land of Ophir. But it may be that the ships of the ancients passed the Solomon Islands on their way to Mexico and Peru. Mendana thought that the land of fabulous gold was a group of islands west of Peru, when actually the Andes Mountains themselves may have been the source of Solomon's gold. Ancient places like Tiwanaku and Puma Punku had gold sheets fixed to all the walls. Gold was so plentiful in Peru at the beginning of the Spanish conquest that nearly every conquistador became very rich.

The theologian Benito Arias Montano proposed in 1571 that Peru was Ophir. In fact, the origin of the name Peru is not really known and Montano suggested that the name was really O-Per. Montano reasoned that the native Peruvians were thus descendants of the person named Ophir (mentioned in one of the biblical genealogies of Genesis) and Shem. Montano also believed that the Yucatan was named after Ioktan, father of Ophir, whom he surmised had been an Inca queen. A major problem with this theory is that the Bible genealogy names Ophir as the son of Ioktan.

Whether Peru was named somehow after Ophir is unlikely, but a voyage from the Indian Ocean into the Pacific to Peru is not out of the question. Such a journey would take about a year, the length specified by the Bible. There would be plenty of time in Peru to help smelt the gold and prepare the cargo. Also to grow food for the trip

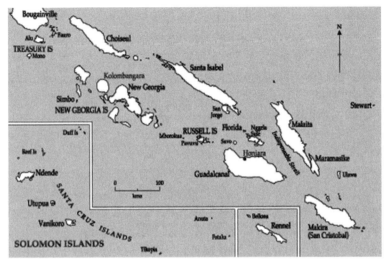

A map of the Solomon Islands, once thought to be Ophir.

home.

The return voyage might take them first to Easter Island as Thor Heyerdahl theorized, and then westward to Polynesia and Melanesia and eventually to the Hindu ports that were in Indonesia at that time. Then they would stop in southern India to pick up sandalwood and exotic goods and head home. The ballast for these ships was literally a cargo of pure gold.

Barry Fell, in his book *Saga America*,[21] maintains that the Egyptians were mining gold on Sumatra. Phoenicians would have taken these mines over, and mined them for King Solomon. Indeed, in 1875 an article in the Anthropological Institute Journal examined the subject of Phoenician alphabet characters in Sumatra.[33] Were these Phoenician characters left by the sailors of Solomon's fleet?

Likewise, Thor Heyerdahl shows clearly in his book *The Maldive Mystery*[49] how ancient seafarers like the Phoenicians would have had to pass through the equatorial channel in the Maldives, stop at the Sun Temple there, and then sail on to Sumatra, and of course, further on to Australia, New Zealand and the Pacific. That the Egyptians and Phoenicians, as well as the ancient Indians and Chinese, were exploring the vast Pacific many thousands of years ago is discussed in my book *Lost Cities of Ancient Lemuria & the Pacific*.[60]

Suddenly, we see that the idea of Solomon's ships reaching as far as Peru is not so far-fetched at all, and is in fact, quite plainly within the achievement of the ships. Phoenicians were brave and excellent sailors, and their ships were large and well equipped, much better than the ships of Columbus. The land of Ophir had to be a land of gold, and Peru certainly was such a place.

Orville Hope, in his book *6000 Years of Seafaring*,[45] asserts that King Solomon's Ophir was actually in New Mexico, where Hebrew inscriptions, refineries, and fortifications have been found near Albuquerque. While these ancient Hebrew inscriptions may be authentic, it is unlikely that Solomon's ships would have sailed out of the Red Sea around Africa, and west to the Gulf of Mexico on their way to such mines.

It may well be that the Hebrews, sailing with their buddies, the Phoenicians, did go to the east coast of the Americas as well, but these voyages probably went from Mediterranean ports out into the Atlantic, along a route the Phoenicians and their successors the Carthaginians had been using for many hundreds of years.

The Mysterious Gold of Parvaim

Another mysterious place mentioned in the Bible is Parvaim. What was Parvaim gold? Only one time in the Old Testament is the use of Parvaim gold recorded. When Solomon began the construction of the House of the Lord, he used this special type of gold in the Holy Place.

We learn in 2 Chronicles 3:3-7:

> The foundation Solomon laid for building the temple of God was sixty cubits long and twenty cubits wide (using the cubit of the old standard). The portico at the front of the temple was twenty cubits long across the width of the building and twenty cubits high.
>
> He overlaid the inside with pure gold. He paneled the main hall with juniper and covered it with fine gold and decorated it with palm tree and chain designs. He adorned the temple with precious stones. And the gold he used was

gold of Parvaim. He overlaid the ceiling beams, doorframes, walls and doors of the temple with gold, and he carved cherubim on the walls.

Apparently, the word Parvaim is a unique word in Hebrew and is used only once in the scripture as noted above. The Bible often talks about pure gold, but Parvaim gold is a special gold, possibly reddish in color, from the mysterious region of Parvaim. Where was Parvaim? It turns out that Parvaim is a Sanskrit word, coming from the word "purva." From Smith's Bible Dictionary at Biblesudtytools. com we have this definition:

> Parvaim: (Oriental regions), the name of an unknown place or country whence the gold was procured for the decoration of Solomons temple. (2 Chronicles 3:6) We may notice the conjecture that it is derived from the Sanscrit *purva*, "eastern," and is a general term for the east.

So once again we are brought back to India as an area from which Solomon was importing gold and other valuable goods. There seems little doubt that ancient Israel and ancient India were connected in many ways. If King Solomon had possession of an airship, possibly a vimana made in India, would he have made trips from Jerusalem to India to visit the kings there and make his trade deals?

By actually visiting some of these far-flung destinations in his vimana, including for instance the metalworks at Tiwanaku, King Solomon and his admirals could determine the best way to sail and which remote ports could be ports of call. Some voyages need to be made by air and some voyages need to be made by sea. Even though we have aircraft in our own era, most of our cargo is moved over long distances by ships.

As for a fleet of ships making the long journey to Peru—make no mistake about the possibility of sailing across the Pacific Ocean in a few months without even stopping at islands for water or food; it has been done many times in the past. Captain Bligh made the journey in a small open boat from Tahiti to Indonesia without seeing any islands along the way. Similarly Magellan crossed the entire Pacific and reached the Philippines without ever sighting another island.

Certainly India was involved in the importation of valuable goods from Ophir and was an important stop for the fleet, but it seems too close to Ezion-Geber to be a three-year journey. Gold from India may have been Parvaim gold, and worth more than "pure gold." The other gold, worth less than Parvaim gold was the bulk of the gold, from Australia, Sumatra, Peru or elsewhere.

It would seem that a return trip to a port like Poovar in southern India should really be a one-year trip. Did the fleet spend two years to do work for a sultan in India before heading home? Was it really a three-year trip to Ophir and back? And what exactly were the ships of Tarshish?

Ships of Tarshish

The Phoenician seagoing vessels were often called "ships of Tarshish," after the Phoenician port or island called Tartessos. This important naval center was perhaps on the island of Sardinia or a port in southern Spain called Tartessos.

Tarshish was a well-known land of silver, and it was different from Solomon's mines and the gold coming through Ezion-Geber. It is in the Mediterranean somewhere, and Sardinia may well have been the island center for the huge navy of cargo ships equipped with bronze battering rams roaming the Mediterranean. They not only roamed the Mediterranean, they controlled it, and with the founding of Carthage on the North African coast as well as Lixus and Morodor on the Atlantic coast of Morocco, they were the dominant traders of the western world at that time.

The vessels of the Phoenician fleet constructed by ship makers from Israel, Tyre and Byblos at Ezion-Geber were also called ships of Tarshish, although they did not ply the Mediterranean. In Isaiah 60:9 we get the picture that these ships and others roamed far and abroad, carrying out elaborate trade:

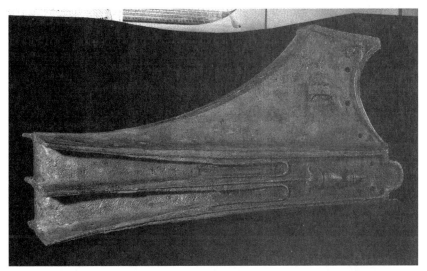

A huge bronze battering ram that was secured to the front of a Phoenician ship.

They are ships from the ends of the earth, from lands that trust in me, led by the great ships of Tarshish. They are bringing the people of Israel home from far away, carrying their silver and gold. They will honor the Lord your God, the Holy One of Israel, for he has filled you with splendor.

After Solomon, his heir Jehoshaphat also had a fleet of Phoenician ships built at Ezion-Geber to go to Ophir but apparently a storm wrecked the fleet and the voyages to Ophir come to a halt. In 1 Kings 22:48 we are told:

Jehoshaphat made ships of Tarshish to go to Ophir for gold, but they did not go, for the ships were wrecked at Ezion-Geber.

The ships of Tarshish are now referred to in modern translations of the Bible as simply "trading ships." Curiously, it seems Tarshish is the main center for the Phoenician navy rather than Tyre, Byblos or other cities of the eastern Mediterranean. But where was Tarshish? I found the following interesting discussion on the website hope-of-Israel.org:

It is significant that the main home base for the "ships of Tarshish" was not Tyre, but a place just outside the pillars of Hercules, called by the Romans "Gades." This was on the Atlantic side of Gibraltar, near the mouth of the Guadalquivir River in south-western Spain. This port came later to be called Cadiz—in about the 12th century. In more modern times it became the chief base for the navy of Spain under Philip II. In Davis' *The Dictionary of the Bible* we find it definitely identified with Tarshish: "It is believed that Tarshish was Tartessus in the south of Spain, near Gibraltar... ships of Tarshish were originally ships trading to and from Tarshish; but ultimately ships of first-rate size to whatever place their voyages may have been made."

Thus, it is seen that large sea-going ships carried goods in trade from Tarshish to the four points of the compass. We know from Ezekiel's words that "ships out of Tarshish" traded in iron, tin and lead. Although there were mines in Spain producing tin, these became exhausted and the ships sailed elsewhere in quest of their much-prized tin and lead. They found it in Cornwall and Somerset, in England. They also traded in the much-prized North Sea amber.

Some agree that Tarshish was probably Tartessus, but others think the place was off the mainland. Bits of scripture posted on Wikipedia relating to Tarshish seem to make a distinction between Tarshish and the coastlands. One quote tells inhabitants of the coast to "cross over to Tarshish." After some prophesied calamity obliterates Tyre and the surrounding coastland, survivors will be sent to Tarshish and other places, including coastlands that are far away. Says a discussion of this on Wikipedia:

> Psalm 72 (Psa 72:10), a Psalm often interpreted as Messianic in Jewish and Christian tradition, has "May the kings of Tarshish and of the coastlands render him tribute; may the kings of Sheba and Seba bring gifts!" This verse is

the source text of the liturgical antiphon *Reges Tharsis* in Christian Cathedral music. In 2013, Thompson and Skaggs recognized that this passage is composed formulaically with a chain of scaled correlates that indicate Tarshish was a large island.

Isaiah contains three prophecies mentioning Tarshish. First 2:16 "against all the ships of Tarshish, and against all the beautiful craft," then Tarshish is mentioned at length in Chapter 23 against Tyre. 23:1 and 14 repeat "Wail, O ships of Tarshish, for Tyre is laid waste, without house or harbor!" and 23:6 "Cross over to Tarshish; wail, O inhabitants of the coast!." 23:10 identifies Tyre as a "daughter of Tarshish." These prophecies are reversed in Isaiah 60:9 where "For the coastlands shall hope for me, the ships of Tarshish first, to bring your children from afar," and 66:19 "and I will set a sign among them. And from them I will send survivors to the nations, to Tarshish, Pul, and Lud, who draw the bow, to Tubal and Javan, to the coastlands far away, that have not heard my fame or seen my glory. And they shall declare my glory among the nations."

As mentioned earlier, Jeremiah says that Tarshish is a source of silver and mentions the mysterious Uphaz, saying, "Beaten silver is brought from Tarshish, and gold from Uphaz."

Therefore, it seems silver is largely coming from Tarshish and Mediterranean ports and gold is coming from the Red Sea port of Ezion-Geber, bringing gold from India and beyond.

The Queen of Sheba and Axum

The ships to Ophir are mentioned amid a description of the visit of the Queen of Sheba to Solomon's court. Although the comments about the navy seem to be an aside interrupting the narrative, we get the idea that the ships may have been stopping at a port on the Red Sea that was in her kingdom, and she heard the tales of King Solomon from the sailors. In 1 Kings 10:1-15 we are told:

And when the queen of Sheba heard of the fame of Solomon concerning the name of the Lord, she came to test him with hard questions. And she came to Jerusalem with a very great train, with camels that bore spices and very much gold and precious stones; and when she had come to Solomon, she communed with him about all that was in her heart. And Solomon told her all her questions; there was not any thing hidden from the king which he told her not.

And when the queen of Sheba had seen all Solomon's wisdom, and the house that he had built, and the meat of his table, and the sitting of his servants, and the attendance of his ministers, and their apparel, and his cupbearers, and his ascent by which he went up unto the house of the Lord, there was no more spirit in her.

And she said to the king, "It was a true report that I heard in mine own land of thy acts and of thy wisdom. However I believed not the words until I came and mine eyes had seen it; and behold, the half was not told me. Thy wisdom and prosperity exceedeth the fame which I heard. Happy are thy men, happy are these thy servants, who stand continually before thee and who hear thy wisdom. Blessed be the Lord thy God, who delighted in thee, to set thee on the throne of Israel! Because the Lord loved Israel for ever, therefore made He thee king to do judgment and justice."

And she gave the king a hundred and twenty talents of gold, and of spices a very great store, and precious stones; there came no more such abundance of spices as these which the queen of Sheba gave to King Solomon.

And the navy also of Hiram, that brought gold from Ophir, brought in from Ophir a great plenty of almug trees and precious stones. And the king made of the almug trees pillars for the house of the Lord and for the king's house, harps also and psalteries for singers. There came no more such almug trees, nor were seen unto this day.

And King Solomon gave unto the queen of Sheba all her desire, whatsoever she asked, besides that which Solomon gave her of his royal bounty. So she turned and went to her own country, she and her servants.

Now the weight of gold that came to Solomon in one year was six hundred threescore and six talents of gold, besides what he had from the merchants, and from the traffic of the spice merchants, and from all the kings of Arabia, and from the governors of the country.

Was the Queen of Sheba traveling from Axum? Where was Ophir? Where was all this gold coming from, not only Solomon's, but Shebas?

The Land of Saba

It is quite apparent that the Queen of Sheba ruled over a rich country heavily involved in trade. In fact, the *Kebra Nagast* says that it was from a wealthy merchant that Sheba learned of Solomon.

For various reasons, many modern historians are doubtful that the Queen of Sheba existed, and if she did, they doubt that she was from Axum. I think they are wrong on both counts, and certainly millions of Ethiopians believe that she was a queen from Axum just as millions of Hindus in India believe that Krishna and Rama were real people.

The Queen of Sheba's visit to King Solomon was something of a trade trip, as the Queen brought with her some hundred and twenty talents of gold plus a multitude of spices and precious stones. As the Bible records, "there came no more such abundance of spices as these which the Queen of Sheba gave to King Solomon." The Queen also wished to test the wisdom of Solomon, and see for herself his magnificent court. As she leaves, Solomon gives her anything she wants, in addition to his royal bounty. "So she turned and went to her own country, she and her servants." (I Kings)

So, the 120 talents of gold were largely for trade, with the Queen taking the "royal bounty" in return. Yet, scholars to this day are divided as to who the Queen of Sheba was and where she came from. She is not given a name in the Bible, just the title, Queen of Sheba, or Saba.

The actress Betty Blythe as the Queen of Sheba in 1921.

The Sabeans are mentioned in the Quran twice. The Quran mentions the Queen of Saba and names her Bilqis in the 27th chapter. In this chapter Suleiman (Solomon) gets reports from the hoopoe bird about the kingdom of Saba. It is ruled by a queen whose people worship the sun and planets instead of God. Suleiman (Solomon) sends a letter inviting her to submit fully to the One God, Allah, Lord of the Worlds.

The Queen of Saba is unsure how to respond and asks counsel of her advisors. They reply that the country is "of great toughness" in a reference to their willingness to go to war if necessary. She replies that she fears if they were to lose, Suleiman might behave as most other kings would: "entering a country, despoiling it and making the most honorable of its people its lowest."

She decides to meet with Suleiman and sends him a letter. Suleiman receives her response to meet him and asks if anyone is able to bring the queen's throne to him before she arrives. A djinn under the control of Suleiman then tells the king that he will bring him the throne of Bilqis before Suleiman can rise from his seat.

This is done and when the queen arrives at his court she is shown the throne and asked: does your throne look like this? She replies to them that the throne was as her own. When she enters Solomon's crystal palace she accepts Abrahamic monotheism and the worship of one God alone, Allah.

But this curious story from the Quran does not say exactly where Bilqis is from, except that she was the queen of Saba. Where exactly was Saba? Most scholars agree that southwestern Arabia (much of today's Yemen) was part of the kingdom of Saba. But was Saba on both sides of the Red Sea, in Eritrea and Ethiopia as well? It would seem so. If this was the case, there would have been many cities in Saba; was Axum the capital at one point as the *Kebra Nagast* claims?

The famous Arabian explorer H. St. John Philby, in his book *The Queen of Sheba,*[88] maintains that the popular Arabian legend that Bilqis was the Queen of Sheba is wrong. He points out, as does the famous archeologist Wendell Phillips, that the name of Bilqis does not appear in any Sabean records, which Phillips says go back as far as 800 BC.[87,88]

Philby believes the real Queen of Sheba actually came from Northern Arabia and is somehow confused with the legends of Zenobia, the last queen of Palmyra in Syria. This is an unlikely identification, as Zenobia lived in the third century AD and doesn't fit the profile in any way. Yet, Philby wrote an entire book on the subject; it is clear that, like many scholars, he does not want to admit that some great court like Sheba's existed in southern Arabia or Ethiopia.

It seems that the land of Sheba was far more extensive than most scholars will dare to admit, not because there is not evidence to support it, but just because historians have preconceived notions of the ancient world, and this part of the world has sort of been forced out of history—Ethiopia especially. Indeed, the brief story of the visit of the Queen of Sheba gives us, three thousand years later, clues to life in the South of Arabia and the Horn of Africa in the first and second millennia BC.

The kingdom of Saba is quite likely older than 800 BC, and some of the structures at Axum may help prove that. As I have mentioned before, one problem with the *Kebra Nagast*'s claim that the Queen of Sheba, named Makeda, was from Axum is that many historians do not think that the city existed at the time. I think those historians are wrong on this, and we will discuss the antiquity of Axum shortly. The stories of the *Kebra Nagast* predate the Quran, but it would seem that Mohammed was unaware of the book. As we have seen, however, there is some question as to when the stories were gathered together in one volume.

Though not much is known about ancient Saba, I contend that it was a huge country, with wealthy port cities on both sides of the Red Sea; some of the world's most impressive megaliths exist at Axum. There is good evidence that these megaliths are over three thousand years old, as we shall see.

That the Queen's caravan was loaded with spices is only natural. Not only would the queen's realm have included the Dhofar region of the Hadramut, a major source of frankincense in the world, but it controlled the thriving trade with India and the spice islands of Indonesia. Saba controlled nearly all the production of frankincense, which is grown in southern Arabia, Ethiopia and northern Somalia. Today northern Somalia is the largest producer of frankincense, and the Vatican is the main buyer of the crop.

The lost city of Ubar was rediscovered in the early 1990s in Oman using satellite photography, and it is believed to have been an eastern center of the frankincense trade along the "Incense Road." Ubar and Oman are on the eastern edge of the frankincense production zone.

As the German scholar Joachim Leithauser once pointed out, if it were not for the incredible demand for spices and aromatics, almost all of which came from Southeast Asia or India, the world would never have been explored. Nutmegs, cloves, cinnamon, cardamom and other spices were literally worth their weight in gold. Frankincense, however, came from southern Arabia and the Horn of Africa.

Trade in spices had been going on for thousands of years before King Solomon's time and it seems only natural that the empire of Sheba was in control of a portion of that trade during the Queen's time. The Babylonians and Persians had their own trading vessels that made the easy voyage, but it was Saba that controlled the trade in the Red Sea. Ports such as Adulis and Aden controlled traffic to the trading cities in Egypt, Israel and the eastern Mediterranean. Some of the major cities in Saba were Axum, Wiqro and Adulis in Ethiopia and Najran, Zafar, Marib, Aden, Timna and Qana in southwest Arabia.

The ancient kingdom of Saba—the land of Sheba—must have existed circa 1200 BC and even earlier. There seems little doubt that during the early dynasties of Egypt there was trade and contact going on with Ehiopia and Arabia, including maritime traffic. Saba would have included most of Southern Arabia and northern Ethiopia during the time of King Solomon. The question is whether Axum could have been the capital. Most historians say that the capital of Saba was at Marib, a desert oasis to the east of Sana'a in present-day Yemen. However, Marib was more likely a later capital of Saba when the country began to fall apart around the third century BC, some six hundred years after Solomon, Sheba—and Menelik—were exchanging gifts and flying over oceans.

The great dam at Marib is thought to have been built about 800 BC, before it became the capital of Saba; The area was conquered by the Himyarites around 100 AD. Marib seems like an unusual site for the capital of a united Saba, especially since some of its most important cities were ports on the Red Sea. It would seem that Saba was centered on Axum in its early days, and Marib became the dominant city later. The *Kebra Nagast* basically tells us this but historians have continually doubted the antiquity of Axum.

191

Thoth and the Baboons of Saba

Living in both Ethiopia and Yemen is the hamadryas baboon (dog-faced baboon), the northernmost of all the African baboons. This baboon is native to the Horn of Africa and the southwestern tip of the Arabian Peninsula, essentially the area of ancient Saba. The hamadryas baboon is smaller than other baboons. They live in semi-desert areas and require cliffs for sleeping so they can avoid predators, which are leopards or hyenas. The hamadryas baboon is omnivorous and is adapted to its relatively dry habitat. How did this baboon get on both sides of the Red Sea? Presumably via a land bridge, but they were sacred in Egypt and even kept as pets. Many tomb scenes show the animal led on a leash, or playing with the children of the household. It is believed that some baboons were trained by their owners to pick figs from the trees for them.

The hamadryas baboon appears in various roles in ancient Egyptian religion, and so is sometimes called the "sacred baboon." Baboons are not native to Egypt, however, and were imported from Ethiopia or Yemen. Hamadryas baboons were even trained as temple guardians or something similar. This was essentially the plot of Michael Crichton's book *Congo* (1980) which was made into a film in 1995, in which generations of trained gorillas have been guarding an Egyptian diamond mine that also contains temples.

The Egyptian god Thoth was often depicted in the form of a hamadryas baboon, sometimes carrying a crescent moon on his head. Thoth was also represented as an ibis-headed figure. Hapi, one of the Four Sons of Horus that guarded the organs of the deceased in ancient Egyptian religion, is also represented as having the head of a dog-faced baboon. Hapi protected the lungs and therefore a baboon's head is the lid of the canopic jar that held the lungs.

Thoth played many prominent roles in Egyptian mythology, including maintaining the universe, arbitrating godly disputes, and being one of the two deities (the other being Ma'at) who stood on either side of Ra's boat. Thoth was also associated with the arts of magic, the development of science, and the system of writing.

As Thoth's sacred animal, the baboon was often shown directing scribes in their task. Baboons were said to carry out Thoth's duties

Thoth, Egyptian god of science and knowledge, depicted as a baboon.

as the god of measurement. They are sometimes seen with the scales that weighed the heart of the deceased in the judgment of the dead and are depicted at the spout of water clocks.

So we see that Egypt had close relations with not just Nubia to its south, but also to Ehiopia. Important rivers feeding the Nile begin in Ethiopia including the Blue Nile which originates at Lake Tana. When we look at Axum its similarities to Egyptian cities like Aswan or Luxor are astonishing. Like these cities, Axum has megalithic buildings and obelisks which are thousands of years old. Luxor Temple with its obelisks is dated to approximately 1400 BC. Could Axum be from this same time period?

The Antiquity of Axum

Among the many things in the *Kebra Nagast* that modern historians tend to discount is the antiquity of Axum and its monuments. The book describes events that supposedly took place

An old print of the obelisks of Axum by the British artist Henry Salt, 1809.

circa 950 BC or earlier. Yet, the book starts at the Council of Nicea and is clearly a collection of works compiled around 400 AD or later. The accounts of flying wagons and the removal of the Ark of the Covenant from Jerusalem are all considered to be fictitious fantasy by modern scholars. Also, Axum could not have been the city of the Queen of Sheba as historians say that it was probably not in existence in 950 BC.

But, is it possible that the *Kebra Nagast* is telling a story that is largely true? Certainly millions of Ethiopians believe the account to be a true version of what happened thousands of years ago. Is Ethiopia as important as the *Kebra Nagast* claims it is? Did they have some sort of flying vehicles at this time? Was the Ark of the Covenant—or a replica—removed from Jerusalem and taken to Ethiopia?

Graham Hancock, in his 1992 book *The Sign and the Seal*,[4] makes no mention of the flying wagons, but does discuss the Ark of the Covenant flying, as we have seen.

Hancock thinks that the Ark of the Covenant may have been taken from Jerusalem and then through Egypt, as described in the *Kebra Nagast,* and then brought to Lake Tana, the source of the Blue Nile. However, this did not happen during the time of Menelik but in the time just after the reign of King Uzziah (c.781-740 BC).

Hancock thinks that Uzziah might have been standing in front of the Ark of the Covenant circa 730 BC when he was struck with leprosy as mentioned in 2 Chronicles 26: 16-21:

> But after Uzziah became powerful, his pride led to his downfall. He was unfaithful to the Lord his God, and entered the temple of the Lord to burn incense on the altar of incense. Azariah the priest with eighty other courageous priests of the Lord followed him in. They confronted King Uzziah and said, "It is not right for you, Uzziah, to burn incense to the Lord. That is for the priests, the descendants of Aaron, who have been consecrated to burn incense. Leave the sanctuary, for you have been unfaithful; and you will not be honored by the Lord God."
>
> Uzziah, who had a censer in his hand ready to burn incense, became angry. While he was raging at the priests in their presence before the incense altar in the Lord's temple, leprosy broke out on his forehead. When Azariah the chief priest and all the other priests looked at him, they saw that he had leprosy on his forehead, so they hurried him out. Indeed, he himself was eager to leave, because the Lord had afflicted him.
>
> King Uzziah had leprosy until the day he died. He lived in a separate house —leprous, and banned from the temple of the Lord. Jotham his son had charge of the palace and governed the people of the land.

Hancock thinks that sometime shortly after the reign of Uzziah the Ark of the Covenant was taken to a Jewish community on Elephantine Island in southern Egypt and then to Lake Tana. It was kept for some time in a temple on one of the many islands in this large lake in the mountains of western Ethiopia; there are many ancient churches and temples on these islands to this day. Hancock thinks that the Ark would have arrived here sometime around 640 BC and eventually it was moved to Axum, where the Ethiopian Coptic Church says it resides today.

It is reasonable to think that the sacred ark of the Ethiopians did reside at Lake Tana (Hancock says specifically the island of Tana Kirkos), and now resides at the Church of Our Lady Mary of Zion in Axum. Perhaps the Ark was first brought from Jerusalem to Axum by Menelik and then later, during an invasion, it was taken to the island of Tana Kirkos. Later it was returned to Axum. But, is it the genuine Ark of the Covenant from Jerusalem or a copy? If it is genuine, why should we not believe the ancient book the *Kebra Nagast*? Just as we should believe certain accounts of the books of Exodus, Numbers and Kings, I think that we must believe that at least some of the things in the *Kebra Nagast* are true. Ethiopians would certainly want to think that!

The problem is that mainstream historians don't think that Axum was a capital in 950 BC, and prefer to date the Axumite kingdom to beginning around 400 BC. Mainstream historians think that the earliest monumental buildings in Ethiopia are those at Yeha, to the east of Axum, which are dated to circa 700 BC. So the question is whether Axum is older than Yeha as the *Kebra Nagast* claims.

First, let us look at Axum, its amazing monumental works and the Axumite dynasty. Axum is said to be the oldest continually

A photo from the 1906 German archeological expedition of the excavation of Stela 6.

196

A photo from the 1906 German archeological expedition of a gigantic statue base.

inhabited place in Africa. Though it is many days' walk inland it was the capital of a maritime empire that extended to Arabia and across the Indian Ocean. However, not much is written or known of the extensive naval voyages by the Axumite kings from their port of Adulis on the Red Sea out into the Indian Ocean. One would imagine as well that ships from the Persian Gulf, India, Sri Lanka and Indonesia would have arrived at the port of Adulis. Other voyages would have gone along the eastern African coast.

Says Wikipedia about Axum and the Axumite dynasty:

> Axum was a naval and trading power that ruled the region from about 400 BC into the 10th century. In 1980 UNESCO added Axum's archaeological sites to its list of World Heritage Sites due to their historic value. Located in the Mehakelegnaw Zone of the Tigray Region near the base of the Adwa mountains, Axum has an elevation of 2,131 meters (6,991 ft).
>
> Axum was the center of the marine trading power known as the Axumite Kingdom, which predated the earliest mentions in Roman era writings. Around 356, its ruler was converted to Christianity by Frumentius. Later, under the reign of Kaleb, Axum was a quasi-ally of Byzantium against the Persian Empire. The historical record is unclear, with

ancient church records the primary contemporary sources.

It is believed it began a long slow decline after the 7th century due partly to the Persians (Zoroastrian) and finally the Arabs contesting old Red Sea trade routes. Eventually Axum was cut off from its principal markets in Alexandria, Byzantium and Southern Europe and its trade share was captured by Arab traders of the era. The Kingdom of Axum was finally destroyed by Gudit, and eventually some of the people of Axum were forced south and their civilization declined. As the kingdom's power declined so did the influence of the city, which is believed to have lost population in the decline, similar to Rome and other cities thrust away from the flow of world events. The last known (nominal) king to reign was crowned in about the 10th century, but the kingdom's influence and power ended long before that.

...The Kingdom of Axum had its own written language, Ge'ez, and developed a distinctive architecture exemplified by giant obelisks, the oldest of which (though much smaller) date from 5000–2000 BC. The kingdom was at its height under King Ezana, baptized as Abreha, in the 4th century (which was also when it officially embraced Christianity).

The Ethiopian Orthodox Church claims that the Church of Our Lady Mary of Zion in Axum houses the Biblical Ark of the Covenant, in which lie the Tablets of Law upon which the Ten Commandments are inscribed. The historical records and Ethiopian traditions suggest that it was from Axum that Makeda, the Queen of Sheba, journeyed to visit King Solomon in Jerusalem. She had a son, Menelik, fathered by Solomon. He grew up in Ethiopia but traveled to Jerusalem as a young man to visit his father's homeland. He lived several years in Jerusalem before returning to his country with the Ark of the Covenant. According to the Ethiopian Church and Ethiopian tradition, the Ark still exists in Axum. This same church was the site where Ethiopian emperors were crowned for centuries until the reign of Fasilides, then again beginning with Yohannes IV until the end of the empire. Axum is considered to be the holiest city in Ethiopia and is an important destination of pilgrimages.

So, we already have a problem with the Wikipedia entry on Axum in that Axum wasn't a thriving kingdom with a seaport until around 400 BC but the oldest of the city's many obelisks are said to be from 5000-2000 BC! While Wikipedia says that these older obelisks were much smaller than the later ones, I would disagree and say that the largest obelisks are probably the oldest. The most massive Axum obelisk, the Great Stele, is broken into a number of pieces and once weighed an astonishing 520 tons (estimated)!

It would seem that these huge obelisks are from the same time frame that the large obelisks in Egypt were being erected, and that would be around 2000 BC or earlier. That is a difference of 1600 years in the founding of the Axumite Empire and the construction of its earliest monuments—and they are gigantic in size. It would seem that the Axumite Empire, or at least the city of Axum, was founded long before 400 BC and must easily go back to 3000 or 5000 BC, perhaps earlier. The monuments at Axum are clearly the most stupendous in the whole country of Ethiopia—which has a wealth of amazing buildings and megaliths—and clearly the oldest. They are so old that there is no history as to the erecting of these

A 1949 photo of the obelisks of Axum.

obelisks—at least the oldest ones—and how they were cut, dressed, moved and erected is a complete mystery to archeologists. Many of them envision elephants helping to haul these massive stone towers down the road to their erection site. The quarry is about four miles west of the obelisk park in the center of the city.

Graham Hancock has this interesting interchange with the high priest of the church that supposedly holds the Ark in his book *The Sign and the Seal*:

> "How powerful?" I asked. "What do you mean?"
>
> The guardian's posture stiffened and he seemed suddenly to grow more alert. There was a pause. Then he chuckled and put a question to me: "Have you seen the stelae?"
>
> "Yes," I replied, "I have seen them."
>
> "How do you think they were raised up?"
>
> I confessed I did not know.
>
> "The Ark was used," whispered the monk darkly, "the Ark and the celestial fire. Men alone could never have done such a thing."[4]

A 1949 photo of the fallen obelisk of Axum that weighs over 520 tons.

Indeed, the gigantic obelisks (stelae) at Axum are as impressive as any in Egypt and it would seem that Axum was some sort of Egyptian satellite city, and the same engineers, stonemasons and architects who were building the megalithic structures in Egypt were doing the same in Axum. Lake Tana is the source of the Blue Nile and has papyrus growing in it that is made into reed boats, same as in Egypt. Axum is further north than Lake Tana but sits near the Takazze River which feeds into the Atbara River, which meets the Nile north of Khartoum. Certainly there was a strong trade connection with Egypt and the Nile, and it is easy to see how Axum and Lake Tana could once have been early colonies of Egypt.

Let us look at the obelisks that are found at Axum.

The Great Stele is 33 meters long, 3.84 meters wide, 2.35 meters deep, weighing 520 tons.

The Obelisk of Axum, also called the Rome Stele (24.6 meters high, 2.32 meters wide, 1.36 meters deep, weighing 170 tons) had fallen and broken into three pieces (supposedly in the 4th century AD). It was removed by the Italian army in 1937, and returned to Ethiopia in 2005 and reinstalled July 31, 2008.

The next tallest is King Ezana's Stele. It is 20.6 meters high above the front baseplate, 2.65 meters wide, 1.18 meters deep, and weighs 160 tons.

Three more stelae measure as follows: 18.2 meters high, 1.56 meters wide, 0.76 meters deep, weighing 56 tons; 15.8 meters high, 2.35 meters wide, 1 meter deep, weighing 75 tons; 15.3 meters high, 1.47 meters wide, 0.78 meters deep, weighing 43 tons.

Standing in the Northern Stelae Field in 2014, I gazed in amazement at the Great Stele, thought to be the largest single block of stone ever erected. For some reason archeologists seem to believe it fell and broke during construction. I could not really see why this would be, and it seems just as likely that it stood erect for hundreds or even thousands of years and then fell, maybe in an earthquake around 400 BC.

When this gigantic 520-ton obelisk fell, it collided with the massive 360-ton slab of stone that is the ceiling of the central chamber of what is called Nefas Mawcha's tomb. This shattered

A 1949 photo of the tallest standing obelisk at Axum.

the upper portion of the obelisk and collapsed the tomb's central chamber, scattering the huge roof supports about like broken twigs.

Says the Lonely Planet guide to Ethiopia:

> The megalithic Tomb of Nefas Mawcha consists of a large rectangular central chamber surrounded on three sides by a passage. The tomb is unusual for its large size, the sophistication of the structure and size of the stones used for its construction (the stone that roofs the central chamber measures 17.3 m by 6.4 m and weighs some 360 tons!). The force of the Great Stele crashing into its roof caused the tomb's spectacular collapse.
>
> Locals believe that under this tomb is a 'magic machine,' the original implement the Axumites used to melt stone in order to shape the stelae and tombs. The same type of machine was apparently also used to create some of the rock-hewn churches of Tigray.[19]

This magic machine is pretty interesting, and there seems to be a parallel to what Graham Hancock was told in 1983 by the high priest of the church that holds the Ark.

Clearly this priest believed that the Ark had the power to use celestial fire to cut and lift megaliths, and would also believe that the Ark was brought here circa 950 BC by Menelik. Therefore it would seem that this priest, and others, believed that the obelisks were erected at this time.

Parts of the Great Stele are so huge that the tourist path at one point goes under the main section of the obelisk that lies at an angle on the partially excavated slope. In fact, very little archeological work and excavation have been done here and it is thought that some obelisks lie buried in the park.

Curiously, the mainstream dating for this huge obelisk and the gigantic collapsed structure called Nefas Mawcha's tomb is the late 4th century AD, near the time of the conversion to Christianity of much of Ethiopia.

This massive block had to be quarried and dressed on the

mountain to the west of town and then somehow dragged here to central Axum. It then had to be stood up and aligned vertically to the ground. How this was done is not known and there are no records of the raising of any of the obelisks, though some are ascribed to certain ancient kings. The Great Stele is sometimes referred as King Ramhai's Stele. An amazing structure at the northernmost corner of the Northern Stelae Field is known locally as the Tomb of King Ramhai, but is usually called the Tomb of the False Door. There, a large stone slab is carved with a false door very reminiscent of the many such carvings in Egyptian temples and tombs.

It would seem that the obelisks are from the time when the

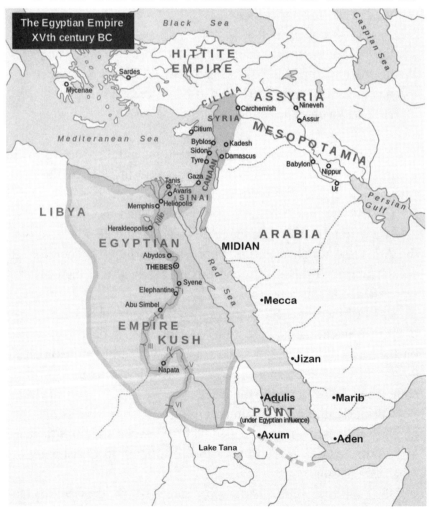

obelisks of Egypt were being erected, circa 2000 BC. Over time, burials were made around the obelisks and therefore today they are mistakenly associated with burials. It is thought that somehow each stele is there to mark a tomb. This is far from obvious, and in Egypt obelisks and stelae are not associated with burials at all but are boundary markers and monuments—supposedly representing a ray of the sun.

None of the Ethopian obelisks has any inscriptions, but most have some articulation and carving on them. It seems at the time that Christianity was being introduced into Ethiopia, circa 350 AD, several of the obelisks either fell down or were purposely pushed over. It is said that King Ezana (c.321-360 AD) introduced Christianity to Ethiopia. He was influenced to become a Christian by his childhood tutor Frumentius, a Christian monk from Syria. Frumentius became the first bishop and founder of the Ethiopian Orthodox Church. At that time the Axumite kings ruled over Ethiopia, Eritrea, Yemen, Southern Saudi Arabia, northern Somalia, northern Sudan and southern Egypt. It was a mighty empire that spanned both sides of the Red Sea. They worshiped the sun and moon and a god they named Astar. It is also acknowledged that there was a large Jewish community within the empire.

King Ezana is said to have banished the pagan practice of erecting burial stelae and they became neglected. Over time, many of these stelae fell to the ground, but one of the large obelisks remained standing. It was called the King Ezana Stele, however it would seem he did not erect it. This stele is the centerpiece of the famous painting "Sight of Axum" by Henry Salt (1780–1827).

So it would seem that modern archeologists have fallen into a familiar trap: mistaking the time of some megalithic monuments' destruction with the time that they were built. What modern archeologists are suggesting is that these massive and intricately-carved monoliths were erected in a short time during the beginning of King Ezana's reign with two of the three largest obelisks immediately falling down. And, even more incredibly, shortly after erecting his own giant monolith—God knows how—he banned the whole practice and said it was against his religion.

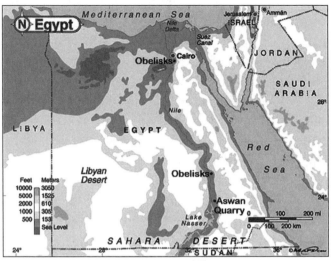

A map of the obelisks in Egypt, all smaller than the largest at Axum.

It is painfully obvious to me that most of the stelae in the park are the oldest megaliths in Ethiopia and that King Ezana had nothing to do with the erection of any them. Rather, he may have been responsible for having some of them toppled over. King Ezana issued a number of coins but none of them depict an obelisk—which seems strange if he had erected one of these gigantic 200-ton monsters, a feat of engineering as amazing as any in the ancient world.

There is no written record of King Ezana erecting any stelae and the *Kebra Nagast* makes no mention of the erection of any objects, as great a feat as it would have been. The *Kebra Nagast* speaks of all sorts of amazing and unbelievable things like the flying wagon of Zion, but it does not mention King Ezana and his obelisks.

Modern archeologists admit that they don't know how obelisks were transported and lifted into place. They also admit that it must have taken a pretty amazing effort to do this. They theorize thousands of workers and thousands of meters of rope and rolling logs or sleds and such. The whole thing, it would seem, was a massive undertaking that required hammering these huge objects from the rock, using saws and chisels to square and engrave them, and then some apparatus to move them for several miles to the site. They would then have to have been stood up, either by building a huge

206

crane and hauling them up with pulleys (which is what the Romans did with the Egyptian obelisks they took back to Rome circa 200 BC) or the people might have created mounds to drag the obelisks onto and then tip them down to the ground and use rope to stand them completely upright. Either way some large scaffolding would have to have been erected, even after they were already standing up.

The whole thing is a difficult and, frankly, baffling task. We don't know why anyone would go through the difficult process of quarrying and erecting an obelisk, and this is the same with Egyptian obelisks. Egyptologists have no good explanation for the penchant of Egyptians in the early dynasties to erect obelisks. They are said to be monuments to Ra the sun god, and the typically 300-ton obelisks represent a ray of the sun, giver of life.

The so-called Unfinished Obelisk at Aswan was left in its quarry because during the process of removing it from the mother-granite it was discovered that a natural crack was in the stone, and therefore

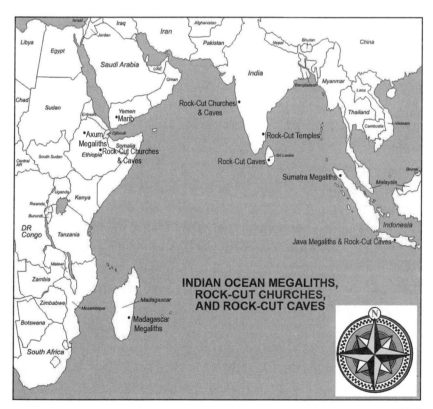

INDIAN OCEAN MEGALITHS, ROCK-CUT CHURCHES, AND ROCK-CUT CAVES

the obelisk would have a small crack in it. It was abandoned as unusable.

Obelisks were also erected at Carnac in Brittany, and the Devil's Arrows of Yorkshire are a series of three obelisks. Obelisks like this have been found in Morocco and Algeria, and it is believed by some archeologists, such as Pierre Honore, that Tiwanaku and Puma Punku in Boliva had obelisks, now fallen and broken.

Erecting obelisks is very tricky and making the very tall ones stand up securely on their bases must have been an engineering difficulty only for the most skillful. Modern archeologists rarely experiment with erecting an obelisk. A PBS television crew for a show called "Nova" tried to erect a small obelisk in Egypt with levers and counterbalances and a cage, but were unable to stand it up. Later a different technique was used in the USA and a small obelisk was successfully raised by hauling it onto a mound of sand, about half as high as the obelisk, and then digging out the sand beneath the base and tipping the obelisk in to a small hole in the ground and then standing it up.

We do not know how the Egyptians raised their obelisks. Despite a wealth of paintings and inscriptions from that culture, the erecting of obelisks is never described. The Ethiopians believe that their obelisks were raised with some sort of anti-gravity power of the Ark of the Covenant. As I looked at the huge stones around me at the Axum obelisk park, I could honestly believe that something like that may indeed have happened.

Obelisks are one of the great mysteries in archeology, and the two countries most known for their obelisks are Egypt and Ethiopia. One would think that the Egyptian obelisks are the largest, but the Great Stele of Axum is the largest known obelisk ever erected. Even if it fell while being erected, it must have stood tall for a few moments, long enough to fall from its great height and break the megalithic slab structure near it as it shattered into five gigantic pieces.

The fall of this obelisk must have been an awesome sight! It certainly highlights the difficulty of raising an obelisk and keeping it erect. Obelisks in Egypt, France and Britain have been standing

208

for over 4,000 years and will probably stand for another 4,000 years. Hopefully Axum's obelisks will last the next 4,000 years as well—God willing.

A photo of one of the obelisks being moved to Italy.

Two photos from 1949 of the massive stone building known as Yeha.

CHAPTER EIGHT

PRESTER JOHN AND THE THREE INDIAS

From that place to the city of the people called Auxumites
there is a five days' journey more; to that place all the ivory
is brought from the country beyond the Nile through the
district called Cyeneum, and thence to Adulis.
—*Periplus of the Erythraean Sea*, Chapter 4

For some reason, Ethiopia has largely been written out of world
history. Despite being the home of "Lucy," one of the oldest
"human" skeletons ever found, mainstream historians maintain that
civilization did not come to Ethiopia until around 700 BC at Yeha,
a short distance east of Axum. It would seem that civilization in
Ethiopia is much older than that. It seems that Axum was a trading
center for ivory, gems, incense, spices and gold for many thousands
of years.

It was probably in Ethiopia that the donkey was domesticated,
an animal used widely throughout the Egypt, the Middle East and
the Mediterranean. They were essentially the original beasts of
burden. Donkeys were an important part of life in ancient Egypt,
but they originated in the fertile highlands of Ethiopia where the
African wild ass still exists today in remote areas. By at least 3000
BC donkeys were exported to Egypt, Arabia and India, where the
Hindu goddess Kalaratri is typically depicted as riding a donkey.
Naturally, donkeys would have arrived in India by boat and there
has been historically a great deal of trade and cultural interaction
between the two countries, though modern historians do not seem

to recognize this.

Ethiopia and its port of Adulis, today located about 30 miles south of the modern port of Massawa in the Gulf of Zula, was an important maritime trade center and it would have received ships from all over coastal Arabia and East Africa as well as ships coming directly from India. Ethiopia was truly one of what geographers called "the three Indias." It was a green and prosperous country with a dense population, intense agriculture, religious temples, thriving markets and vast herds of sheep and cattle.

Ethiopia is today, as in ancient times, a mountainous land of many villages, farms and fields. Millions of sheep, goats, donkeys and cattle roam throughout the land (including the village streets) and a wide variety of crops are grown—it is the birthplace of coffee. It is a land of incense and spices and the Ethiopians make a similar spicy curry as that made in India. The people look and dress much as they do in India, with women often wearing what is similar to an Indian sari.

It seems that Axum in 950 BC was the controller of the important port cities of Adulis, Muza (Mocha), Qana and Aden, which was called Eudaemon. Ancient Sabean script can be found in Tigray near Axum. The gigantic obelisk in Axum, when standing, weighed over 520 tons. It is carved out of single piece of granite, and is as impressive as any Egyptian obelisk and must have had Egyptian engineers to oversee the difficult engineering project.

In Lalibela are monolithic rock-cut churches built in the thirteenth century AD. It seems that, like the Nabateans who are credited with carving Petra, the Ethiopians were fond of carving structures into solid rock. Similar rock-cut temples are found in western India such as those at Elora, Ajanta and Elephanta Island just off of Mumbai. Did Indian technicians—with diamond tools— come to Ethiopia to cut the monolithic churches of Lalibela? The Ethiopian legends of the site claim that angels came down during the night and did the work. This work was cutting extremely hard granite at a considerable rate. It would seem that power tools were being used here.

The closest port to Axum was Adulis; other important ports

were mainly on the Arabian side of the Red Sea, which then opened up to the Indian Ocean. Sailors could continue down the coast of what is today Somalia to various ports in East Africa of that time. Or the ships could sail along the Arabian coast, or directly across the Arabian Sea to ports on the west coast of India. For many centuries the first stop on the Arabian coast was Eudaemon (Aden), a popular port for ships from India.

The port of Eudaemon was a major transshipping port in the Red Sea and Indian Ocean trade network. This city and the surrounding country were dubbed in Latin "Arabia Felix" (Happy Arabia), an abundant area of spices, coffee, mutton and various imported goods, mostly from India. Eudaemon (which means "good spirit" in Greek), was described in the *Periplus of the Erythraean Sea* (circa 85 AD) as a city in decline. Says Wikipedia:

> Of the auspiciously named port we read in the periplus that "Eudaemon Arabia was once a full-fledged city, when vessels from India did not go to Egypt and those of Egypt did not dare sail to places further on, but came only this far. " The new development in trade during the 1st century CE avoided the middlemen at Eudaemon and made the courageous direct crossing of the Arabian Sea to the coast of India.

With Saba as a large region on both sides of the Red Sea it was a center for all sorts of trading goods coming from central Africa, the Horn of Africa, southern Arabia and India. It was a land of ships, ports, roads and donkey carts. As noted above, Ethiopia is a very good place to raise sheep and cattle and the country has an abundance of these animals, as well as hundreds of thousands of donkeys. Areas of Saba on the Arabian side of the Red Sea would have had a smaller number of animals, being more of a desert.

Saba was not able to hold together and began to break up into separate empires, with the Axumite empire on the African side. The Arabian side broke up into countries called Saba, Qataban, Himyar and Hadramut. After the time of the First Council of Ephesus (431

AD) and then the conquest of Arabia by Mohammed's armies in 630 BC, Ethiopia basically disappears from Western history. It became the "hidden empire."

The Hidden Empire

Known as the Hidden Empire, Ethiopia's official name, until recently, was Abyssinia. Its history fades back into the mists of time. As we have seen, Ethiopia was apparently an Egyptian satellite country that later became the Saba kingdom of the Horn of Africa, controlling much of present-day Yemen, Ethiopia and Somalia. In later years while Europe, North Africa and the Middle East continued to trade and exchange ideas, their commerce centered on the Mediterranean and the Black Sea and Ethiopia was largely excluded. A great deal of trade was going on in the Indian Ocean, centered around India, and Ethiopia was part of this commerce. Around this time coffee, the traditional drink of Ethiopia, began gaining popularity in Arabia and Egypt. The former Sabean port of Muza became the coffee-hub known as Mocha, giving its name to a type of roasted coffee bean and later to a hot drink combining coffee and chocolate.

Ethiopia's major port of Adulis was an important trading hub, yet it was virtually unknown to European historians, who only vaguely knew that India and China were in eastern Asia. In fact, beyond Persia it was said that there were three Indias; they could be reached by boat from the Red Sea, but Europeans did not seem to be cognizant of this fact—this knowledge was largely lost by the time of Marco Polo. Rather, journeys to India were almost exclusively by camel caravan. If one is with knowledgeable sailors and in a good boat, then voyage by sea is probably preferable. When Marco Polo's group returned from China they came by boat, but not through the Red Sea, which would have been the better route.

Marco Polo, with his father and uncle, reached the court of Kublai Khan circa 1275 AD and presented sacred oil from Jerusalem and papal letters to the Khan. The Polos had accumulated a great deal of knowledge and experience in their journeys that were useful to the Khan, plus they spoke a number of languages and had now mastered

An old print of Ethiopia as Abyssinia, showing the lack of knowledge of the area.

Chinese. They became ambassadors of a sort for the Khan and they embarked on many imperial visits to China's southern provinces, the far south and Burma. These journeys were in huge Chinese ships and there is evidence from one of the maps that Marco Polo brought back to Italy that they may have made a trip to Alaska.

The Polos continually asked the Khan if they could leave China but he would not accede. Marco says that they began to worry that they might not be returning home, and that if the Khan died they may not be in favor with the next ruler.

But then, in 1292, representatives arrived from Persia where the Kublai Khan's great-nephew was the ruler. The ruler was in search of a wife, and once a suitable bride had been found it was decided that the Polos would accompany the group for the return to Persia.

This was a wedding party of 600 people including the Polos, and it was to return to Persia by boat, rather than by caravan. The group left that same year from the port of Zaitun in southern China with a fleet of 14 junks, the crews of the ships adding to the total number of people aboard. With about 80 people in each boat these ships must have been fairly large and luxurious for the important passengers that they carried.

The fleet sailed down the coast of Vietnam to the area of Singapore and then travelled northwest to Sumatra. They crossed the Bay of Bengal to the Tamil port of Jaffna in northern Sri Lanka. From there they voyaged up the west coast of India. Eventually the Polos were in the Arabian Sea and docked at the Persian port of Ormuz.

It had been a perilous two-year journey from Beijing and of the 600 passengers that began the voyage only 18 survived to reach Persia. The three Polos were among them, as well as the bride. Ironically, her intended husband had died before the ill-fated fleet set sail.

The Polos then travelled overland to Terbil in Persia and to the port of Trebizond on the Black Sea. From there they took a ship to Constantinople and finally back to Italy. They had clearly travelled in waters that were well known to the seafarers of India, Southeast Asia and Indonesia. They did not go through the Red Sea because the fleets' destination was the Persian Gulf. But the Red Sea would have been a faster route back to Italy and the Mediterranean. One person who must have taken this route is Thomas, "the twin," one of the apostles of Jesus of Nazareth.

How Did St. Thomas Cross to India?

Supposedly, each of the 12 apostles of Jesus was to write a book and go forth into the world and spread the gospel. Thomas the Apostle was given the name Didymus in the Gospel of John, which means "the twin"; he is sometimes known as "doubting Thomas" because he expressed doubt when hearing of the resurrection of Jesus. According to most historians, Thomas arrived in India about the year 52 and quickly established a Christian ministry there. How did he get to India?

Texts such as The Acts of Thomas say that he arrived via the

216

Red Sea and Indian Ocean at the port of Muziris, a major port in the state of Kerala on the west coast of India known as the Malabar coast. Muziris had a Jewish community at the time and Kerala still has several small Jewish communities even today. Had they also come via the Red Sea?

Muziris was destroyed by massive flooding and earth changes that rearranged the southern Indian coasts in 1341 AD. Muziris was near the modern port of Kodungalloor in Kerala state. In 1983, a large hoard of Roman coins was discovered at a site about six miles from Kodungallur in a small town called Pattanam, and this town is now thought to be on the former site of Muziris. Excavations carried out at Pattanam from 2007 to 2011 have uncovered over 20,000 articles including ceramic objects, beads, amphora pieces, cannonballs and more.

An old print of the shrine of St. Thomas at Meliapore, India.

217

Once Thomas the Apostle reached Muziris he founded a group that today are known as Saint Thomas Christians or Nasranis. The Acts of Thomas identifies his second mission in India with a kingdom ruled by King Mahadeva, one of the rulers of a 1st-century dynasty in southern India. After carrying out the second mission, he died, circa 72 AD in Mylapore near Madras.

A stamp of St. Thomas.

Early scholars wondered how Thomas the Apostle would have arrived at the Kerala coast in 52 AD because they had no knowledge of the lively trade between Egypt, Ethiopia and India. Every year the monsoon winds blow east and west across the Indian Ocean and can carry ships from the Horn of Africa directly to and from the Malabar coast.

The trade between Rome and India during this period is a little-understand portion of history, but the discovery of large hoards of Roman coins show that there was a thriving trade, with Roman ships leaving Red Sea ports in Egypt. In addition, thriving Jewish colonies were to be found at the various trading centers, thereby furnishing obvious bases for the apostolic witness. Jewish and Christian colonies were reported on the island of Socotra in this period and the southern Arabian kingdom called Himyar was a Christian kingdom, like Ethiopia.

Thomas most likely crossed to India by joining a ship at an Egyptian-Roman port somewhere near the northern end of the Red Sea. His ship would have continued south down the Red Sea to ports such as Adulis in Ethiopia, where he may have spent some time preaching the Christian gospel. Upon leaving Adulis he would have gone on to Socotra or Aden and then, when the monsoon winds were right, he would have crossed directly across the Arabian Sea to Kerala. What is more, there was an entire manual for this voyage describing ports all over the Indian Ocean. It was a small manual written in Greek called the Periplus of the Erythraean Sea.

The Periplus of the Erythraean Sea

A periplus was a manuscript typically carried by ship captains and navigators that listed the ports and coastal landmarks of a certain voyage along a coast. The ports and landmarks would be discussed in the order they would be visited and with approximate intervening distances. Navigators added various notes to the periplus as time went by, and editions would sometimes be updated.

Periplus is the Latinization of the Greek word periplous, literally "a sailing around," and it became a standard term in the ancient navigation of Phoenicians, Greeks, and Romans. The Periplus of Hanno the Navigator is an example of a pretty interesting periplus as it records the voyage of Hanno, a Carthaginian colonist and adventurer who explored the coast of Africa in the sixth or fifth century BC from present-day Morocco as far south as Senegal.

Maps, charts, and logs such as a periplus were important to any captain's chest since seafaring began. It can't be stressed how important and valuable maps and charts were in ancient times. Each had to be hand-copied and, like a rare book, they sold at a high price. With the early printing of high quality maps in Germany, Holland and Belgium, a powerful industry of mapmaking began: Prints of various maps—accurate or not—were eagerly consumed by the public, starting with sea captains and governments. In many ways, the craze for maps and accompanying commentary, like a periplus, created the modern travel book, whether a guide or a personal account, such as Marco Polo's or Jack Kerouac's.

To the Greeks, and to the Phoenicians prior to them, the Erythraean Sea (or Eritrean Sea) was the Red Sea and beyond, including the Indian Ocean and the Persian Gulf. Even places like Sumatra, Java and Bali were probably considered part of the Erythraean Sea. One has to wonder if Greek sailors, coming mainly from Ptolemaic Egyptian ports on the Red Sea, would have voyaged as far as Indonesia and possibly Melanesia—what an adventure that would have been!

The Periplus of the Erythraean Sea was originally written in Greek with no author credited. It initially gives the ports, trading

219

opportunities and navigation tips for the trip from Roman Egyptian ports like Berenice along the west coast of the Red Sea, and then along the Horn of Africa to East Africa. At chapter 19 it switches to describing a trip along the eastern side of the Red Sea to Arabia and then to ports on the Indian subcontinent. The actual date of the text is not given, but it is thought to have been written circa 50 AD. This is the approximate period of Thomas the Apostle and his journey to

An old map from 1609 of the places mentioned in the Periplus of the Erythraean Sea.

India.

The Periplus says that a direct sailing route from the Red Sea to southern India across the open ocean was discovered by the Greek navigator Hippalus (first century BC). Pliny the Elder claimed that Hippalus discovered not the route but the monsoon wind, which was really the same thing. Arabian sailors were well aware of the monsoon winds, which Greeks also called Hippalus (or Hypalus).

Prior to this discovery of the Greeks, it was thought in the West that the Indian coast stretched from west to east. Remember that King Solomon's ships of Tarshish had made the same voyage and must have correctly known the geography. This shows how knowledge was lost from the time of 900 BC to the period of about 100 BC, a dark age of sorts in the first millennium BC.

Hippalus learned of the route from other sailors in the Red Sea, and of the north-south orientation of the western coast of India. Realizing that the Indian spice trading ports of the Malabar coast of Kerala lay to the south, across the open water, a much faster journey could be made than following coastal routes.

This quick route to southern India, which received ships from the spice-rich islands of Indonesia, greatly contributed to the prosperity of Roman ports in Egypt during the period 100 BC to 300 AD. The Romans, having defeated Carthage, could now finally do what the Phoenicians had been able to do through their alliance with King Solomon—sail the Indian Ocean from ports on the Red Sea, as well as cruise the Mediterranean and Atlantic. From Red Sea ports, large Roman ships crossed the Indian Ocean to the southern Indian kingdoms of the Cholas, Pandyas, and Cheras in present day Kerala and Tamil Nadu.

The Periplus consists of 66 chapters, most of them about the length of a long paragraph in English. No chapter is more than one paragraph long, as this was the writing style of the time. Some chapter-paragraphs are very short, including the first chapter, which reads in its entirety:

1. Of the designated ports on the Erythraean Sea, and the market-towns around it, the first is the Egyptian port of

221

Mussel Harbor. To those sailing down from that place, on the right hand, after eighteen hundred stadia, there is Berenice. The harbors of both are at the boundary of Egypt, and are bays opening from the Erythraean Sea.

In many cases, the description of places is sufficiently accurate to identify their present locations but some ports remain mysterious and unknown. For instance, a place called "Rhapta" is mentioned as the farthest port south on the East African coast, which is called "Azania." Rhapta could be one of over five locations matching the description. Going in the other direction, the Periplus mentions the Ganges River and then, in the final chapters about a land called "This," describes China as a "great inland city Thina" that is a source of raw silk.

The Periplus ends with this short chapter-paragraph:

66. The regions beyond these places are either difficult of access because of their excessive winters and great cold, or else cannot be sought out because of some divine influence of the gods.

Axum is mentioned in chapter-paragraph four of the periplus as being eight days inland from the port of Adulis and being an important marketplace for ivory and even rhinoceros horn, which were exported throughout the ancient world:

4. Below Ptolemais of the Hunts, at a distance of about three thousand stadia, there is Adulis, a port established by law, lying at the inner end of a bay that runs in toward the south. Before the harbor lies the so-called Mountain Island, about two hundred stadia sea-ward from the very head of the bay, with the shores of the mainland close to it on both sides. Ships bound for this port now anchor here because of attacks from the land. They used formerly to anchor at the very head of the bay, by an island called Diodorus, close to the shore, which could be reached on foot from the land;

by which means the barbarous natives attacked the island. Opposite Mountain Island, on the mainland twenty stadia from shore, lies Adulis, a fair-sized village, from which there is a three-days' journey to Coloe, an inland town and the first market for ivory. From that place to the city of the people called Auxumites there is a five days' journey more; to that place all the ivory is brought from the country beyond the Nile through the district called Cyeneum, and thence to Adulis. Practically the whole number of elephants and rhinoceros that are killed live in the places inland, although at rare intervals they are hunted on the seacoast even near Adulis. Before the harbor of that market-town, out at sea on the right hand, there lie a great many little sandy islands called Alalaei, yielding tortoise-shell, which is brought to market there by the Fish-Eaters.

According to the next chapter of the Periplus, the ruler of Axum (c. 50 AD) was a king named Zoscales, who, besides ruling in Axum also held under his sway two harbors on the Red Sea, Adulis (near Massawa in Eritrea) and Avalites (the port of Assab). This Axumite king is said to control sub-Saharan Africa from Axum to the Berber area of southern Algeria and to have been familiar with Greek literature as we are told in chapter-paragraph 5:

> 5. These places, from the Calf-Eaters to the other Berber country [Algeria-Morocco], are governed by Zoscales; who is miserly in his ways and always striving for more, but otherwise upright, and acquainted with Greek literature.

Another port on the Horn of Africa that may have been part of Saba-Sheba-Axum was the port city of Malao, situated at present-day Berbera on the northern coast of Somalia. Malao is mentioned in chapter-paragraph 8 of the Periplus:

> 8. After Avalites there is another market-town, better than this, called Malao, distant a sail of about eight hundred

stadia. The anchorage is an open roadstead, sheltered by a spit running out from the east. Here the natives are more peaceable. There are imported into this place the things already mentioned, and many tunics, cloaks from Arsinoe, dressed and dyed; drinking-cups, sheets of soft copper in small quantity, iron, and gold and silver coin, not much. There are exported from these places myrrh, a little frankincense, (that known as far-side), the harder cinnamon, duaca, Indian copal and macir, which are imported into Arabia; and slaves, but rarely.

The port city of Muziris in the Chera kingdom, and Nelcynda of the Early Pandyan Kingdom are mentioned in the Periplus as major ports for the purchase of pepper, other spices, metalwork, and semiprecious stones. Says the Periplus in chapter-paragraph 54 about the intense Greek trade with Muziris:

54. Tyndis is of the Kingdom of Cerobothra; it is a village in plain sight by the sea. Muziris, of the same Kingdom, abounds in ships sent there with cargoes from Arabia, and by the Greeks; it is located on a river, distant from Tyndis by river and sea five hundred stadia, and up the river from the shore twenty stadia. Nelcynda is distant from Muziris by river and sea about five hundred stadia, and is of another Kingdom, the Pandian. This place also is situated on a river, about one hundred and twenty stadia from the sea.

The Periplus of the Erythraean Sea even records that special consignments of grain were sent to places like Muziris, and historians suggest that these deliveries were intended for Roman-Greek residents of these ports, which included large Jewish populations. These Greco-Romans needed something to supplement the local diet of rice.

It is clear that Axum, Ethiopia and the Horn of Africa were important in trading areas of the time and that trade with India was crucial. But shortly after 300 AD knowledge of the importance of Axum, Ethiopia and its claim to possessing the Ark of the Covenant was forgotten by the world. Ethiopia disappeared from history. With the later advent of Islam the country was cut off from the rest of the world and the trade between Europe and India virtually came to a halt.

The Mysterious Kingdom of Prester John

The rise of Islam in the seventh century caused Ethiopia to withdraw into itself and move its capital from Axum to the mountain fortress of Gonder (perhaps where J.R.R. Tolkien got the name for the Kingdom of Gondor in his trilogy *Lord of the Rings*). At this time the Christian Ethiopians began to lose control of the coastal areas, but the inner highlands were too rugged for the invading Muslim armies to conquer.

Ethiopia entered a long period of isolation which was well summed up by the seventeenth-century historian Gibbon, who said, "Encompassed on all sides by the enemies of the religion… Ethiopia slept near a thousand years, forgetful of the world by whom they were forgotten."

Even though Ethiopia was completely surrounded by the enemies of its religion, it clung to the Coptic Christian faith, a religion that teaches reincarnation, karma and that Jesus and Christ were different personalities with Christ entering the body of Jesus at the time of his baptism by his cousin, John the Baptist. This story is also told in the popular book *The Aquarian Gospel of Jesus the Christ*. Like Nestorian Christians and Gnostic Christians, the Coptics did not sign the Nicene Creed in the 4th century AD, and were essentially banished from further participation in the church councils at the time.

These eastern churches neither recognized the Pope nor the editing and censorship of the New Testament that was taking place at the time under the orders of Emperor Constantine. Heretical books such as the Book of Enoch were part of the canon of the Ethiopian church. What eventually grew out of Ethiopia's Christian isolation was the legend of a Christian king who battled the Muslims and wanted to free Jerusalem from their grasp.

Crusaders began hearing legends of a Christian king named Prester (Priest or Pastor) John who was a direct descendant of one of the magi who had visited the Christ child. A letter from Bishop Hugh of Gebal (in Syria) sent to the Pope in 1145 AD mentioned that Prester John's armies had defeated the Muslim kings of Persia, and were intending to march on to Jerusalem but were impeded by the difficulties of crossing the Tigris River.

Many historians think that the battle the letter refers to is probably the battle between the Mongol Khan Yeh-Lu Ta-shih and the Muslim Persian army at Qatwa, Persia, in the year 1141 AD. Historians think that Yeh-Lu Ta-shih's title, Gur-kan was changed phonetically in Hebrew to Yohanan and then to Latin as Johannes, or John. The legend of Prester John had been established, but his kingdom was thought to be in Central Asia somewhere. Indeed, there were large communities of Nestorian Christians in Central Asia and China at the time.

Others thought that Prester John was in India; because of the text of The Acts of Thomas the clergy was familiar with the Apostle Thomas and his work in India. This was one of the few texts about India that were available, and the Christian sects that Thomas founded were imagined to have become a powerful nation. Furthermore it was a popular belief that there were three Indias, and I think that Ethiopia was one of them.

The Three Indias

Around 1165 AD a mysterious letter addressed to Manuel Comnenus, Emperor of Byzantium, began circulating around Europe. It was from a Prester John who claimed to "exceed in riches, virtue and power all creatures who dwell under heaven. Seventy-two kings pay tribute to me. I am a devout Christian and everywhere protect the Christians of our empire… Our magnificence dominates the Three Indias, and extends to Farther India, where the body of St. Thomas the Apostle rests. It reaches through the desert toward the place of the rising sun, and continues through the valley of deserted Babylon close by the Tower of Babel…"

The three Indias are, in my opinion, Ethiopia, India and Indonesia. Visiting these areas would be taking essentially the same route as King Solomon's ships. India proper was a land of many spices and exotic goods, but some of the most popular spices came from islands in Indonesia. Most of Indonesia was Hindu until the seventh century AD. Ports in southern India are a logical place to begin a journey to Sumatra, Java, and the kingdoms of Cham and Khmer in Southeast Asia.

What little knowledge of Ethiopia, India and Indonesia that existed in the West largely came from sailors who traded at Greek and later Roman ports at the northern end of the Red Sea. It was at these ports in Egypt, such as Suez or Eilat or Aqaba on the eastern end of the Red Sea, that Europeans learned of the countries to the south and east that were the three Indias, and of the exotic spices, incense, perfumes, nuts and dried fruits, plus silks and fine cottons that could be had there. Exotic live animals such as monkeys, peacocks, parrots and even larger animals would show up at these ports.

European/North African/Mediterranean sailors would also crew on these ships and make the many long voyages south down the Red Sea and then into the Indian Ocean. They would stop at Adulis, the island of Socotra and ports in Oman along the way and then cross the Arabian Sea to the west coast of India. From

A depiction of Prester John from an old map.

southern India the sailors may have crewed on other ships that went to Sumatra and Java. Many of these sailors would have traded down the east coast of Africa as well. That trade was going on between Ethiopia and the Indies is evident.

Europeans took great heart from this letter from Prester John. They took encouragement in their struggle with the Muslims from the knowledge that they were not alone in that struggle. In a historical context, it is important to note the far-reaching influence of Prester John. His description of his realm as being so extremely opulent made "the Indies" an almost legendary destination in the minds of medieval men. Searches for his kingdom largely spurred on the Age of Exploration by Europeans, and was particularly important in the development of Portugal into a naval powerhouse and master of the spice trade. The Catholic kings of that country devoted huge amounts of state revenues to expeditions around the tip of Africa to secure hegemony in the spice trade, but also in search of the Christian king who could help stop the spread of Islam.

The Search for Prester John

The search for the kingdom of Prester John was underway, yet the Europeans' knowledge of geography was so poor that they hardly knew where to begin. Many believed erroneously that Prester John's kingdom was in Central Asia, even though the letter says that he is the ruler of at least one of the Three Indias. Even Marco Polo hoped to find the Christian kingdom of Prester John in Central Asia.

Michael E. Brooks, in his doctoral dissertation on Prester John for the University of Toledo, notes that the great gold wealth of sub-Saharan kingdoms like Ghana and Mali had garnered some attention in Europe by the 14th century. When Europeans started taking a closer look around Africa, it was natural to zoom in on the Christian kingdom of Ethiopia. Says Brooks:

> What is clear is that, by the end of the fourteenth century, there was a growing European belief that the location of the kingdom of Prester John centered on the region of Nearer India, or Abyssinia. The historical roots of the Ethiopian

locus for the priest-king can be traced to 1306, when thirty Ethiopian envoys stopped in Genoa after visiting Avignon and Rome. The stated purpose of their voyage was the establishment of an alliance between the emperor of Ethiopia and the rulers of the kingdoms of Castile and Aragon. The Ethiopian monarch had apparently heard of the Iberian struggles against the forces of Islam, and believed that some type of linkage might offer mutually beneficial possibilities. It is not known if this mission ever reached the Spanish sovereigns, but documented evidence exists that Pope Clement V received the envoys. In any case, the visit by distant Christian delegates certainly made an impression on those aware of the mission and intent.

Europeans called the king of Ethiopia "Prester John" even after Ethiopian ambassadors sent by Emperor Zara Yaqob attended the Council of Florence in 1441 and told the members that they never called the emperor that name. However, the name stuck. John was much easier to say than the Ethiopian names. Ethiopian emperors did have several names; as we have seen, Menelik I changed his name to David once he returned from Jerusalem with the Ark of the Covenant, according to the *Kebra Nagast*.

The Portuguese finally reached Ethiopia around 1490. The explorers Alfonso de Paiva and Pero da Covilha were commissioned by King John II to find out where cinnamon and others spices could be found, and also to find Prester John. Covilha went to India while Paiva went to Ethiopia; he died before the two could make their planned rendezvous in Cairo. On hearing of Paiva's death, Covilha decided to go to Ethiopia. He was welcomed by Emperor Eskender in 1492 or 1493, but then not allowed to leave; he died there in 1526. He wrote letters to Portugal describing Ethiopia, but it was not until 1520 that the first Portuguese expedition finally arrived. Even though the Ethiopians had never heard of Prester John, The Portuguese were content that they had found his fabled kingdom, and they were probably right.

The Letter of Prester John

The letter said to be sent by Prester John to several European heads of state is quite the work of literature, full of grandiosity and fanfare. Note that it mentions the Apostle Thomas, thusly confirming that Ethiopia and India are in an association as the land of Prester John. Says the lengthy letter:

> John, priest by the almighty power of God and the might of our Lord Jesus Christ, King of Kings and Lord of Lords, to his friend Emanuel, prince of Constantinople, greeting, wishing him health, prosperity, and the continuance of divine favor.

> Our Majesty has been informed that you hold our Excellency in love and that the report of our greatness has reached you. Moreover, we have heard through our treasurer that you have been pleased to send to us some objects of art and interest that our Exaltedness might be gratified thereby. Being human, I have received it in good part, and we have ordered our treasurer to send you some of our articles in return...

> Should you desire to learn the greatness and excellency of our Exaltedness and of the land subject to our sceptre, then hear and believe: I, Presbyter Johannes, the Lord of Lords, surpass all under heaven in virtue, in riches, and in power; seventy-two kings pay us tribute...In the three Indies our Magnificence rules, and our land extends beyond India, where rests the body of the holy apostle Thomas; it reaches towards the sunrise over the wastes, and it trends toward deserted Babylon near the Tower of Babel. Seventy-two provinces, of which only a few are Christian, serve us. Each has its own king, but all are tributary to us.

> Our land is the home of elephants, dromedaries, camels, crocodiles, meta-collinarum, cametennus, tensevetes, wild asses, white and red lions, white bears, white merules, crickets, griffins, tigers, lamias, hyenas, wild horses, wild oxen, and wild men—men with horns, one-eyed men, men with

eyes before and behind, centaurs, fauns, satyrs, pygmies, forty-ell high giants, cyclopses, and similar women It is the home, too, of the phoenix and of nearly all living animals.

We have some people subject to us who feed on the flesh of men and of prematurely born animals, and who never fear death. When any of these people die, their friends and relations eat him ravenously, for they regard it as a main duty to munch human flesh. Their names are Gog, Magog, Anie, Agit, Azenach, Fommeperi, Befari, Conei-Samante, Agrimandri, Vintefolei, Casbei, and Alanei. Theses and similar nations were shut in behind lofty mountains by Alexander the Great, towards the north. We lead them at our pleasure against our foes, and neither man nor beast is left undevoured, if our Majesty gives the requisite permission. And when all our foes are eaten, then we return with our hosts home again.

These accursed fifteen nations will burst forth from the four quarters of the earth at the end of the world, in the times of the Antichrist, and overrun all the abodes of the saints as well as the great city Rome, which, by the way, we are prepared to give to our son who will be born, along with all Italy, Germany, the two Gauls, Britain, and Scotland. We shall also give him Spain and all of the land as far as the icy sea.

The nations to which I have alluded, according to the words of the prophet, shall not stand in the judgement on account of their offensive practices, but will be consumed to ashes by a fire which will fall on them from heaven.

Our land streams with honey and is overflowing with milk. In one region grows no poisonous herd, nor does a querulous frog ever quack in it; no scorpion exists, nor does the serpent glide amongst the grass, nor can any poisonous animals exist in it or injure anyone.

Among the heathen flows, through a certain province, the River Indus. Encircling Paradise, it spreads its arms in manifold windings through the entire province. Here are found the emeralds, sapphires, carbuncles, topazes, chrysolites, onyxes, beryls, sardius, and other costly stones. Here grows the plant Assidos which, when worn by anyone, protects him from the evil spirit, forcing it to state its business and name—consequently the foul spirits keep out of the way there. In a certain land subject to us all kinds of pepper is gathered and is exchanged for corn and bread, leather and cloth...

At the foot of Mount Olympus bubbles up a spring which changes its flavor hour by hour, night and day, and the spring is scarcely three days' journey from Paradise, out of which Adam was driven. If anyone has tasted thrice of the fountain, from that day he will feel no fatigue, but will, as long as he lives, be as a man of thirty years. Here are found the small stones called Nudiosi which, if borne about the body, prevent the sight from waxing feeble and restore it where it is lost. The more the stone is looked at, the keener becomes the sight.

In our territory is a certain waterless sea consisting of tumbling billows of sand never at rest. None have crossed this sea—it lacks water all together, yet fish of various kinds are cast up upon the beach, very tasty, and the like are nowhere else to be seen.

Three days' journey from this sea are mountains from which rolls down a stony, waterless river which opens into the sandy sea. As soon as the stream reaches the sea, its stones vanish in it and are never seen again. As long as the river is in motion, it cannot be crossed; only four days a week is it possible to traverse it.

Between the sandy sea and the said mountains, in a certain plain, is a fountain of singular virtue which purges Christians and would-be Christians from all transgressions. The water stands four inches high in a hollow stone shaped like a mussel-shell. Two saintly old men watch by it and ask the comers whether they are Christians or are about to become Christians, then whether they desire healing with all their hearts. If they have answered well, they are bidden to lay aside their clothes and to step into the mussel. If what they said be true, then the water begins to rise and gush over their heads. Thrice does the water thus lift itself, and everyone who has entered the mussel leaves it cured of every complaint.

Near the wilderness trickles between barren mountains a subterranean rill which can only by chance be reached, for only occasionally the earth gapes, and he who would descend must do it with precipitation, ere the earth closes again. All that is gathered under the ground there is gem and precious stone. The brook pours into another river and the inhabitants of the neighborhood obtain thence abundance of precious stones. Yet they never venture to sell them without having first offered them to us for our private use. Should we decline them, they are at liberty to dispose of them to strangers. Boys there are trained to remain three of four days under the water, diving after the stones.

Beyond the stone river are the ten tribes of Israel which, though subject to their own kings, are, for all that, tributary to our Majesty.

In one of our lands, Height Zone, are worms called salamanders. These worms can only live in fire, and they build cocoons like silk-worms which are unwound by the ladies of our palace and spun into cloth and dresses which are worn by our Exaltedness. These dresses, in order to be cleaned and washed, are cast into flames...

When we go to war, we have fourteen golden and bejewelled crosses borne before us instead of banners. Each of these crosses is followed by ten thousand horsemen and one hundred thousand foot soldiers, fully armed, without reckoning those in charge of the luggage and provision.

When we ride abroad plainly we have a wooden, unadorned cross without gold or gems about it, borne before us in order that we meditate on the sufferings of our Lord Jesus Christ; also a golden bowl filled with earth to remind us of that whence we sprung and that to which we must return;

but besides these there is borne a sliver bowl full of gold as a token to all that we are the Lord of Lords.

All riches, such as are upon the world, our Magnificence possesses in superabundance. With us, no one lies, for he who speaks a lie is thenceforth regarded as dead—he is no more thought of or honored by us. No vice is tolerated by us. Every year we undertake a pilgrimage, with retinue of war, to the body of the holy prophet Daniel which is near the desolated site of Babylon. In our realm fishes are caught, the blood of which dyes purple. The Amazons and the Brahmins are subject to us.

The palace in which our Superemincency resides is built after the pattern of the castle built by the apostle Thomas for the Indian king Gundoforus. Celings joists, and architrave are of Sethym wood, the roof ebony, which can never catch fire. Over the gable of the palace are, at the extremities, two golden apples, in each of which are two carbuncles, so that the gold may shine by day and the carbuncles by night. The greater gates of the palace are of sardius with the horn of the horned snake inwrought so that no one can bring poison within. The other portals are of ebony; the windows are of crystal; the tables are partly of gold, partly of amethyst; the columns supporting the tables are partly of ivory, partly of amethyst. The court in which we watch the jousting is floored with onyx in order to increase the courage of the combatants. In the palace at night, nothing is burned for light, but wicks supplied with balsam...

Before our palace stands a mirror, the ascent to which consists of five and twenty steps of porpyry and serpentine... This mirror is guarded day and night by three thousand men. We look therein and behold all that is taking place in every province and region subject to our sceptre.

Seven kings wait upon us monthly, in turn, with sixty-two dukes, two hundred and fifty-six counts and marquises. Twelve archbishops sit at table with us on our right and twenty bishops on the left, besides the patriarch of St.

Thomas, the Sarmatian Protopope, and the Archpope of Susa…

Our high lord stewart is a primate and king, our cup-bearer is an archbishop and king, our chamberlain a bishop and king, and our marshal a king and abbot.

[The letter reportedly ends with a description of Prester John's church, the stones of which it is built, and the virtues of those stones.]

While some scholars believe the Prester John affair to be a misunderstanding involving a hoaxed letter, others have little doubt that the letter referred to India and Ethiopia, and that it had been written by some monk who was a traveler that had knowledge of Ethiopia and of Thomas in India. There seems no question that parts of the letter were completely fabricated, but there are some ties to the real world, and Ethiopia is at the root. The letter mentions the Three Wise Men of the New Testament. One of the Three Wise Men was said to be an Ethiopian; when the three are portrayed, one of them is traditionally shown as having dark skin. It was part of the Prester John mythos that he was decended from the magi.

Ethiopia and the Christian-Jewish colonies in India may have made up some joint kingdom that was Prester John's in the mythology that grew up around this character, but it seems to me that the initial rumors that developed into Prester John were of the great Christian "hidden kingdom" of Ethiopia. Ethiopia was still a powerful and abundant country that still had strong connections to India but had been cut off from the Western world for a thousand years. Many wonderful things could be found in this reclusive mountain country. Could the Ark of the Covenant have been kept in secret here for thousands of years? It is a fantastic thought!

CHAPTER NINE

IS THE ARK OF THE COVENANT IN ETHIOPIA?

Lady of Heaven,
She puts on the garment of heaven;
She valiantly ascends towards Heaven.
Over all peopled lands, She flies in her MU…
—*Hymn to Ishtar*

So, to recap, the Queen of Sheba, circa the year 950 BC, as recorded in the *Kebra Negast*, left Axum, then the capital of Saba, and journeyed to the Axumite port of Adulis. From there she went by boat across the Red Sea to present day Yemen and then by camel caravan along the western coast of Saudi Arabia to Jerusalem where she met King Solomon.

On the way back to Axum the book says that she gave birth to Solomon's son, Menelik. Menelik later as a young man visited his father in Jerusalem. When leaving, he and some young Israelite nobles took the Ark of the Covenant from the Holy of Holies inside the temple and returned to Axum with the important relic.

Menelik was King Solomon's son and he was the first king in the Solomonic lineage that is still important in Ethiopia today. This line of Solomonic kings was supposedly unbroken for three thousand years until the death of Emperor Haile Selassie in 1975. Haile Selassie was the 225th Solomonic ruler of Ethiopia and died under house arrest in August of 1975 after a military coup. Before taking on his imperial moniker he was known as Ras Tafari, and it is from this name that the Jamaican "cult" of Rastafarianism took its appellation.

The big question is whether the Ethiopian ark is a copy of the Ark of the Covenant, or the real thing. Is the *Kebra Nagast* giving us genuine history or is it a document created to give legitimacy to the royal lineage of Ethiopian kings—a lineage that has been fabricated? Even if the *Kebra Nagast* is largely a true document, did the real Ark remain at the temple in Jerusalem, and was a duplicate ark actually taken to Axum?

Perhaps the Ethiopian ark was brought to Lake Tana and Axum at a later time, like 600 BC, via the Jewish community at Elephantine Island in Egypt as Graham Hancock suggests in his book *The Sign and the Seal*.[4] In that book he concludes that the Ethiopian ark may be the genuine Ark of the Covenant, but it was not brought to Ethiopia by Menelik.

To this day millions of Ethiopians believe that the Ark of the Covenant is held in the small chapel—a church that has a single priest as its caretaker—known as the Chapel of the Tablet, or otherwise called the Chapel of the Ark, next to the original Church of Our Lady Mary of Zion, near Axum's fabled obelisks. The Ark is carefully guarded behind a series of walls and fences and Ethiopians would probably say that it is the most valuable object in the entire country—and, yes, people would want to steal it.

We were told by our guide in Axum in October of 2014 that earlier in the year, two German men had suddenly rushed to the iron gate of the church and tried to climb it in order to enter the sacred inner sanctum. Presumably they wanted to steal the Ark. They were arrested and the story made all the newspapers in Ethiopia where the vast majority of the people are aware that the Ark of the Covenant is said to reside in the church.

By his own account, one of the few people to ever see the Ethiopian ark was Dr. J.O. Kinnaman, who organized the National Museum of Ethiopia at the request of Haile Selassie in the 1950s. As a mark of special respect and appreciation, Dr. Kinnaman claimed, he was permitted to spend many hours in the immediate presence of the Ark at the small sanctuary in Axum. His request to photograph the Ark was denied, but he says he was permitted to take exact measurements and make sketches of the details. One imagines that he was allowed to view and measure a wooden chest with gold ornamentation. It seems that he did not see what was kept inside the chest, which was probably "the Tablet."

Only males are permitted entry into the Old St. Mary's Cathedral. The New Cathedral of St. Mary of Zion stands next to the old one, and was built to fulfill a pledge by Emperor Haile Selassie to honor Our Lady of Zion for the liberation of Ethiopia from the Italian occupation under the fascist dictator Mussolini.

This church is neo-Byzantine in style. Work on the new cathedral began in 1955, and it took ten years to complete the construction. This church allows the admittance of women. Emperor Haile Selassie interrupted the 1965 state visit of Queen Elizabeth II to travel to Axum to attend the dedication of the new cathedral. A few days later Elizabeth II arrived in Axum and visited the cathedral with Selassie. Between the two cathedrals is the Chapel of the Tablet which was built at the same time as the new cathedral.

Emperor Haile Selassie's consort, Empress Menen, paid for the Chapel of the Tablet's construction from her private funds. Admittance to the chapel is closed to all but the single guardian monk who resides there. Entrance is even forbidden to the Patriarch of the Orthodox Church, and to the ruler of Ethiopia. The two cathedrals and the Chapel of the Ark are the focus of pilgrimage and considered the holiest sites in Ethiopia to members of the Orthodox Church.

The original cathedral is said to have been built by King Ezana (who allegedly erected all the obelisks, but failed to mention this incredible feat in any of his inscriptions or documents). This original church, built around 340 AD, was said to be a massive structure with 12 naves. This church was burned to the ground by the Jewish warrior queen Gudit, of the Beta Israel, around the year 960 AD (more about her below).

It was then rebuilt, and then destroyed again during the Muslim Gragn wars of the 1500s. It was again rebuilt by Emperor Gelawdewos (completed by his brother and successor Emperor Minas). Finally, the Emperor Fasilides replaced that structure with the present one in 1665.

One of the destroyers of the early Our Lady Mary of Zion Cathedral was the Ethiopian warrior queen named Gudit (Judith

239

spoken in the Ge'ez language). Gudit was a legendary, anti-Christian queen of the Ethiopian Jewish mega-tribe known as the Beta Israel (House of Israel). Her deeds are mainly recorded in oral traditions and she is said to have killed the Beta Israel emperor and then reigned for 40 years. Queen Gudit brought her Jewish army out of Gonder and the Lake Tana area around 960 AD with the goal of laying waste to Axum and its countryside. Gudit was determined to exterminate all the members of the Axumite dynasty and destroyed palaces, churches and monuments all over the ancient land of Tigray. Accounts of her violent misdeeds are still related among peasants in the north Ethiopian countryside, often while they are pointing to standing stones and other large ruins as signs of the destruction wrought by Gudit. But who populated this powerful Jewish mega-tribe called the Beta Israel? How did they get to Ethiopia?

The Beta Israel and the Ark

The Beta Israel comprised Jewish communities located for centuries in more than 500 villages in a large area around Lake Tana and in the Amhara and Tigray regions of northwestern Ethiopia. Over time many converted to Christianity or were killed in various wars. Most of the remaining Beta Israel people have now moved to Israel.

Israeli officials decided in March of 1977 that the Israeli Law of Return applied to the Beta Israel of Ethiopia. The Israelis, helped by the American government, mounted a series of airlift operations to transport the Beta Israel people out of Ethiopia to Israel. These airlifts to Israel included operations called Moses, Joshua, Solomon and others.

Operation Solomon took place in 1991 and consisted of non-stop flights of 35 Israeli aircraft to transport 14,325 Ethiopian Jews to Israel. Done in only 36 hours, the airplanes were all stripped of their seats and up to 1,122 passengers were boarded on a single plane. Many of the immigrants came with nothing except their clothes and cooking instruments, and several pregnant women gave birth on the planes.

The population of the Beta Israel in Ethiopia is currently around 25,000 although they once numbered about a million people, and at times they controlled much of the country. How is it that Ethiopia

The Church of the Tablet in Axum, believed by Ethiopians to house the Ark of the Covenant.

King Solomon receives the Queen of Sheba. (*Giovanni de Min, 1850*)

An Egyptian papyrus scene showing the Ethiopian donkey at work.

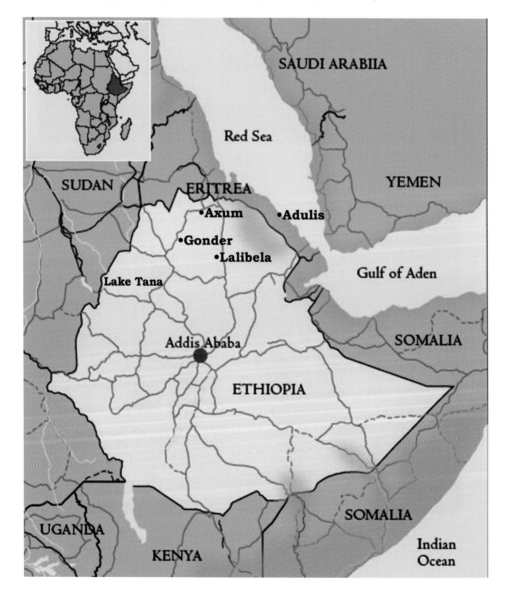

Periplous of the
Erythraean Sea

Περίπλους τῆς
Ἐρυθράς Θαλάσσης

1st century AD

Beyond these places, the fierce winters
and great ice formations make travelling
hard, and by the powers of the gods,
these places are unexplored

Beyond these places, the unexplored ocean
curves around towards the west and mingles
with the western sea

- - - - Periplous
· · · · Land route

Roman
Empire

Himyarite
Kingdom
King Charibael

Indo-Scythian
Kingdom
King Nambanus

Pandian

Parthian
Empire

Kingdom of Aksum
King Zoscales

Nabataean kingdom
King Eleazu

Cheras

Damirica

Others

Spices

Wine

Gold

Ivory

Metals

Cloth

Aromatic
flowers

Silk

Precious
stones

A map of the Periplus of the Erythraean Sea (*George Tsiagalakis*)

Some of the standing obelisks at the central area of Axum.

One of the tall obelisks still standing at Axum.

Keystone cuts for metal clamps can be seen on ancient structures at Axum, just like in Egypt;

Portions of the broken Great Obelisk at Axum landed on this gigantic structure called the Tomb of Nefas Mawcha.

Portions of the broken Great Obelisk at Axum, once weighing 520 tons.

A photo of 12 stones to be mounted on a priest's breastplate,
carved with the names of the 12 tribes of Israel.

A color photo taken by Tom Crotser of the "Ark" he claimed he saw on Mount Pisgah.

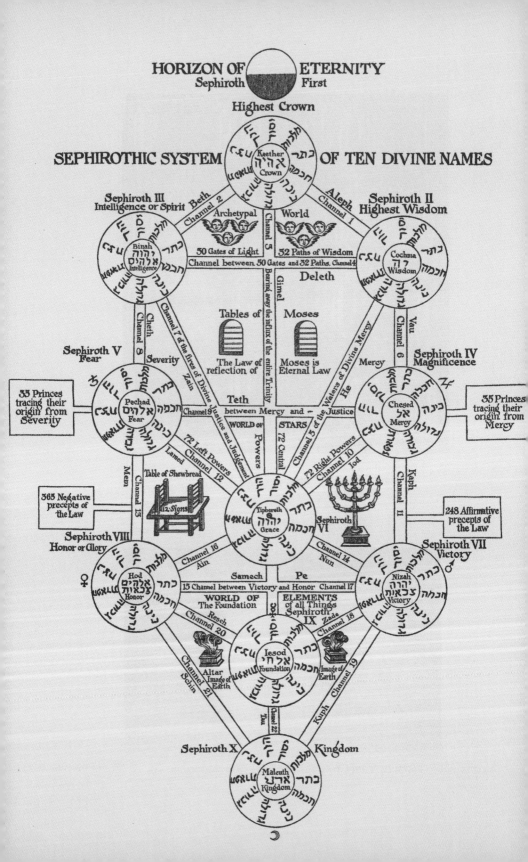

had such a large Jewish community? Did the Beta Israel come to Ethiopia with the Ark of the Covenant?

Curiously, there does not appear to be an ancient tradition on the origin of the Beta Israel, also known as the Falasha (which means wanderer or landless—considered a derogatory term by the Beta Israel). The standard belief in Ethiopia is that these Jewish Ethiopians were descendants of King Solomon, Sheba and Menelik, plus the young Jewish aristocrats of Israel commanded to go with Menelik as related in the *Kebra Nagast*.

We have no reason to doubt this part of the *Kebra Nagast*, as it is recorded in the Old Testament that the Queen of Sheba came to visit Solomon circa 950 BC. There are also Hebrew traditions that Moses was the king of Ethiopia at one point. According to jewishencyclopedia.com one of the legends of Moses is that he left Egypt for Ethiopia after killing the slave driver:

> The fugitive Moses went to the camp of King Nikanos, or Kikanos, of Ethiopia, who was at that time besieging his own capital, which had been traitorously seized by Balaam and his sons and made impregnable by them through magic. Moses joined the army of Nikanos, and the king and all his generals took a fancy to him, because he was courageous as a lion and his face gleamed like the sun. When Moses had spent nine years with the army King Nikanos died, and the Hebrew was made general. He took the city, driving out Balaam and his sons Jannes and Jambres, and was proclaimed king by the Ethiopians. He was obliged, in deference to the wishes of the people, to marry Nikanos' widow, Adoniya (comp. Num. xii.), with whom he did not, however, cohabit.

Moses definitely had an Ethiopian wife, and such legends demonstrate that Ethiopia was a powerful country in 1200 BC, and cities like Axum and Adulis were probably already major economic centers. That northern Ethiopia, possibly once ruled by Moses, would become an early Jewish state is not surprising, and that is one Beta Israel story.

There are, however, other traditions that have the

An old print of the Beta Israel farmers around Lake Tana.

forefathers of the Beta Israel coming from Egypt at a later time than that of Moses or Menelik. At the time of the destruction of the First Temple by the Babylonians in 586 BC a group of Israelites were led to safety by a Hebrew priest whose name was On. They remained in exile in Egypt for a few hundred years until the reign of Cleopatra.

These Jewish Egyptians had a community on Elephantine Island at the major Nile city of Aswan in southern Egypt. The Egyptian Jews had supported Cleopatra in her war against Augustus Caesar but when she was defeated it became dangerous for these Jews to remain in Egypt; they are said to have migrated to Ethiopia via Nubia (Sudan) starting around 39 BC. These Egyptian Jews settled in northern Ethiopia and some apparently went to Yemen. But were there already many Jews living in Ethiopia? It appears so.

The Beta Israel claim that there were several migrations to Ethiopia beginning with origins that go back to the time of Moses. They claim that a portion of the Tribe of Dan parted from other Jews right after the Exodus and moved south to Ethiopia. Another remnant of the Tribe of Dan was said to have arrived later.

In the 9th century AD an Ethiopian rabbi-drifter named Eldad ha-Dani (Eldad the Danite) began turning up in the Jewish communities of Cairo and Spain. Eldad was a man with dark skin who one day arrived in Cairo and created a great stir in the Egyptian Jewish community there with claims that he had come from a Jewish kingdom of pastoralists far to the south. The only language he spoke was a hitherto unknown dialect of Hebrew. He carried Hebrew books with him that supported his explanations of halakhah, or Jewish Law, and he was able to cite ancient authorities

242

in the sagely traditions of his own people.

He said that the Jews of his kingdom derived from the tribe of Dan that had resettled in Egypt after fleeing the civil war in Israel between Solomon's son Rehoboam and Jeroboam the son of Nebat. From there they moved southward up the Nile into Ethiopia. The Beta Israel say the stories of Eldad the Danite confirm that they are descended from the tribe of Danites. The Danites were known as great sailors and fighters—the Biblical hero Samson was a Danite, for example. Of the many tribes of Israel, they seem like the most likely to take off on the adventurous course of migrating from Israel to Ethiopia. The Danites were also a very large group of people, many of them warriors.

Dan the patriarch was born to Jacob and Rachel's maidservant Bilhah (Genesis 30:1-9), because Rachel wanted children but was incapable of having any. Genesis says that Dan was a rambunctious youth, and multiplied greatly during the sojourn of the Israelites in Egypt (Exodus 1:7-9, 12). When Moses led the children of Israel out of Egypt, the tribe of Dan was said to number some 62,700 men old enough to make war (Numbers 1:38-39).

In the book of Judges, we learn that the tribe of Dan is a seafaring tribe like the Phoenicians. In the song of Deborah and Barak, during the time of the Judges, the score asks, "Why did Dan remain in ships?" (Judges 5:17).

Essentially, the tribe of Dan was the seafaring tribe, allied with the Phoenicians, who made voyages through the Mediterranean and into the Atlantic. They were the ones who went to Ophir on the three-year voyages for King Solomon. They lend their name to Denmark and the Danes, as well as to the legendary Tuatha de Dannon of Ireland. In many cases, such as with the Tuatha de Dannon, the tribe of Dan carried an ark with them in their ships. Almost anywhere the name Dan appears in ancient geography it is related to this "lost tribe" of Israel. Apparently, like the Phoenicians, they were scattered all over the world.

Travel along the Nile or Red Sea was usually done in smaller Egyptian plank ships or reed ships, and these same craft were used on the core area of the Beta Israel—Lake Tana, Ethiopia—which is a virtual inland sea. These Danites built a fleet of ships for this lake and began to occupy the islands in the lake as well. Legends say that the Ethiopian Ark was kept at various islands here for centuries.

Eldad said that his country could be found on "the other side of the river of Kush" where dwelt the Bene Mosheh (tribe of Moses). He said that the Bene Mosheh dwell in beautiful houses, and no unclean animal is found in their land. Their cattle and sheep as well as their fields bear twice a year. No child dies during the lifetime of its parents, who live to see a third and fourth generation. He said they do not close their houses at night, for there is no theft or wickedness among them. They speak Hebrew, and never swear by the name of God. Indeed, he seems to be describing the land of Ethiopia very well.

Eldad said that he had started his journey from Ethiopia in a ship, apparently going to Yemen and the Arabian Gulf, with a man of the tribe of Asher. Their ship was wrecked in a great storm but Eldad and his companion were miraculously "saved by God," who provided them with a large plank of wood to cling to until they reached a shore. Here they were captured by cannibals who ate Eldad's companion, but thought Eldad too skinny to eat.

A sun-worshipping tribe then attacked these people and Eldad was taken prisoner by them. He remained a prisoner for four years and was taken by boat to various places around the Arabian Sea, apparently being forced to work as a sailor. He apparently made it to a Jewish community in India where his freedom was purchased by a Jewish merchant for 32 pieces of gold.

He was now a free man and apparently went to Nepal or some area of northwest India and travelled with the tribe of Issachar. They lived high in the mountains near Media and Persia, and "They are at peace with all, and their whole energy is devoted to the study of the Law; their only weapon is the knife for slaughtering animals." This knife sounds like the kukri knife of Nepal made famous by the Gurkha soldiers of that country.

The tribe of Issachar was one of the 12 tribes of Israel and became one of the ten "lost" tribes after the Assyrians conquered the area in 722 BC. They disappeared from history but, Eldad is essentially saying that the Jewish communities along the Malabar Coast of Kerala were the tribe of Issachar.

Eldad eventually made it from India to Byzantium to Cairo, from whence he went on to Spain. Scholars recorded his amazing tales of his travels and of the peaceful and bountiful life in his Jewish homeland. Several books were written about Eldad by European historians in the 19th century.

Eldad indicates that there were at least three waves of Jewish immigration into his region, creating other Jewish tribes and kingdoms, including the earliest wave that settled in the remote kingdom of the "tribe of Moses." His tribe of Danites came later, plus there were other Jewish groups, including some from Yemen, which at this time was the Jewish-Christian Himyar nation. Eldad painted Ethiopia as the strongest and most secure Jewish kingdom that ever existed, with farming villages, cities, lots of domesticated animals and great wealth.

It seems that the strong Jewish communities of Ethiopia existed around Lake Tana and northern Ethiopia—including Axum—since the time of Moses, who clearly must have spent some time in that green, pastoral country. When Makeda, the Queen of Sheba converted to Judaism from the sun- and moon-worshipping Sabean religion, most of Ethiopia and Yemen would have become Jewish. Hinduism, Zoroastrianism and Sabaeism would continue to be influential in the eastern part of Arabia in places such as Oman and the Gulf States.

Later, as Ethiopia became Christian over time, there was strife between the Beta Israel and the Christian kings, based either in Gonder or Axum.

The Beta Israel had something of a Golden Age between the years 858 and 1270 AD when the Jewish kingdom flourished for one last time. During that period the world Jewry heard for the first time the stories of Eldad the

The former lands of the Beta Israel around Lake Tana.

245

Danite and his impressive accounts of his Jewish kingdom of happy pastoralists. Marco Polo mentions an independent Ethiopian Jewish kingdom in his writings from that period, though he did not visit Africa on his voyages.

This period came to a close after the rise of a new Solomonic-Christian dynasty. In 1270 AD, the lineage described by the *Kebra Nagast* was "restored" after the crowning of a monarch who claimed descent from the single royal prince who managed to escape Queen Gudit's uprising. For the next three centuries, the Solomonic dynasty emperors conducted a series of long, armed confrontations with the Jewish kingdom.

The Muslim Invasion of Ethiopia

During the reign of the Solomonic Emperor Yeshaq (1414–1429) the Jewish kingdom of the Beta Israel was invaded by Christian forces and annexed. Yeshaq divided the occupied territories of the Jewish kingdom into three provinces which were controlled by commissioners appointed by him. He reduced the Jews' social status to one below that of Christians and attempted to force Jews to convert with the threat that they would lose their land if they refused. Yeshaq decreed, "He who is baptized in the Christian religion may inherit the land of his father, otherwise let him be a Falasi," or Falasha as they are called now.

However, by the year 1450 AD the Jewish kingdom managed to regain its independence and began to prepare an army to invade Axum. The Beta Israel forces attacked the Christians in the year 1462 AD, but lost the campaign and its army was decimated.

Meanwhile, starting around 1415 AD the Muslim Adal Sultanate began to grow in the Horn of Africa. Centered on the port city of Zeila near present-day Djibouti and the fortress towns of Harar and Dakar, the Adal Sultanate controlled much of northern Somalia, Djibouti and Ethiopia at one point.

Starting in the year 1529 and continuing until 1543 the Muslim Adal Sultanate armies, with some assistance from forces from the Ottoman Empire, invaded and fought the empires deep in the Ethiopian highlands, including the Beta Israel around Lake Tana.

These Muslim forces were led by Ahmad ibn Ibrahim al-Ghazi (c. 1506-February 21, 1543) popularly known in Ethiopia as Ahmed

Gragn (the left-handed) who was a Somali imam and general of the Adal Sultanate. Several times Ahmed Gragn left his fortress town of Harar and marched his Muslim army north where he defeated several Abyssinian emperors and even occupied islands on Lake Tana for a brief period.

The leaders of the kingdom of Beta Israel saw the Muslim armies as a potential ally in their fight with the Christians and began supporting Ahmed Gragn and the Adal Sultanate. However, the Adal Sultanate armies felt that they did not need this support and refused it. The Muslim armies conquered different regions of the

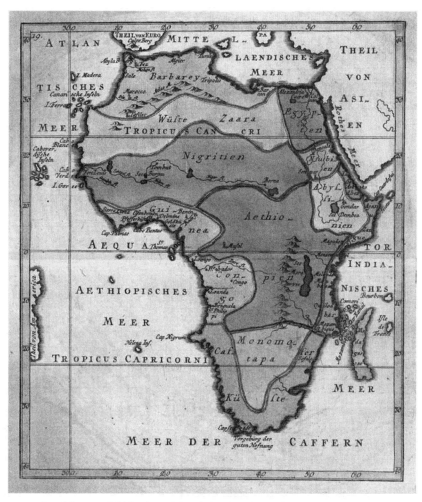

An old map of Ethiopia as Abyssinia, showing Lake Tana prominently.

Jewish kingdom and looted it for livestock and food.

The forces of the Ethiopian empire did succeed eventually in conquering the Muslims and freeing Ethiopia from Ahmed Gragn, but not until more battles were fought.

On October 28, 1531 Ahmed Gragn defeated the Christian Emperor Lebna Dengel at the Battle of Amba Sel. Then the army marched northward to loot the island monastery of Lake Hayq and the stone churches of Lalibela.

Shortly after this the Muslim army reached Axum, where Ahmed Gragn destroyed the Church of Our Lady Mary of Zion. Presumably the Ethiopian Ark was removed from the church before this time and hidden until the church could be rebuilt.

At this point the Christian Solomonic emperor Gelawdewos asked the Portuguese for military help. Portuguese military advisors with cannons and muskets landed at the port of Massawa on February 10, 1541. This Portuguese force was led by Cristoval da Gama and included 400 musketeers as well as a number of artisans and other noncombatants.

Da Gama's force met the army of Ahmed Gragn on April 1, 1542 at a place called Jarte. Knowing that victory lay in the number of firearms an army had, Ahmed Gragn sent to his fellow Muslims for help and had received 2,000 musketeers from Arabia, plus artillery and 900 Ottoman soldiers to assist him.

Da Gama's force had been reduced to 300 musketeers, but they were determined to fight Ahmed Gragn's larger force. At the end of the seasonal rains, Imam Ahmad attacked the Portuguese camp and through sheer numbers killed all but 140 of da Gama's troops. Da Gama was badly wounded and was captured with 10 of his men. Back at Gragn's camp they refused an offer to have their lives spared if they would convert to Islam. Ahmed Gragn had them executed.

The survivors of the Portuguese force were able to meet up with the forces of Emperor Gelawdewos and attacked Ahmed Gragn on February 21, 1543 in the Battle of Wayna Daga. In this important battle, Ahmed Gragn was shot and killed by a Portuguese musketeer. who was mortally wounded in avenging da Gama's death. The battlefield was thrown into disarray and the 9,000 Ethiopian and Portuguese troops managed to defeat the 15,000 Muslim soldiers.

After the victory against Ahmed Gragn in 1543, the Ethiopian

Christian empire decided to declare war against the Jewish kingdom, giving as their justification the Jewish leaders' change of positions during the Ethiopian–Adal War.

With the assistance of Portuguese forces from the Order of the Jesuits, the Ethiopian empire under the rule of Emperor Gelawdewos invaded the Jewish kingdom and executed the Jewish king, whose name was Joram. The Beta Israel were given a certain amount of autonomy, but the kingdom continued to shrink and Jews on the outer edges of the kingdom began converting to Christianity.

Finally, around the year 1620, the Beta Israel autonomy in Ethiopia came to an end. The Emperor Susenyos I confiscated most of their lands and forcibly baptized or enslaved people. Much of the traditional Ethiopian Jewish culture changed or was lost.

The Beta Israel community was not entirely exterminated and even appears to have continued to flourish. The capital of Ethiopia at the time, Gonder, was surrounded by Beta Israel lands and these Ethiopian Jews served as craftsmen, masons, and carpenters. They continued to farm as well. Starting around 1630 AD the emperors used these craftsmen extensively, and such trades were shunned by most Ethiopians as lowly and less honorable than farming.

According to contemporary accounts by Portuguese, French and British diplomats and merchants, the Beta Israel numbered about one million persons in the 17th century. Even after the airlifting of tens of thousands of Ethiopian Jews to Israel, many thousands still live in the mountains surrounding Gonder and tourists are typically brought to their villages to buy carved images of Solomon and the Queen of Sheba, Lions of Zion, or other handicrafts.

The Ark of the Covenant in Ethiopia?

It seems that Ethiopia is indeed the home to at least some of the lost tribes of Israel, including some of the Danites and others. But did they bring with them the true Ark of the Covenant as claimed in the *Kebra Nagast*?

Perhaps it was just a big game between the Jews and Christians in ancient Ethiopia as to who was the true Solomonic heir to the premier kingship of Ethiopia, a large and fertile land with little strife except for occasional periods of war, often triggered by religious differences. It is interesting that the *Kebra Nagast* indicates that

249

Ethiopia fought a war with India, a curious historical "fact" that seems to be largely missing from the historical record. With the destruction of so many ancient books, it is not surprising.

We have seen the strong connection between Ethiopia and India that has not really been acknowledged by historians. We see also the connections between ancient Egypt and India—via Ethiopia—and that many facets of the Hindu world, including reincarnation, karma, masters, adepts, and all sorts of deities were known to the Egyptians, Israelites and Ethiopians.

The buildings at Axum are impressive, and like many ancient structures, one has to wonder how they were built. Like in Egypt, a very sophisticated team of engineers, stonemasons, quarrymen and architects were at work in ancient Axum designing, quarrying and erecting huge obelisks and other structures. Clearly this was not done by some inexperienced team of Ethiopians who decided to erect obelisks that weigh 520 tons so as to impress their friends and relatives. Who would dream up such a massive task and then execute it?

Maybe whoever built the obelisks in antiquity learned from the true masters of megalithic construction. On a hillside a short drive from the obelisk site are the remains of two structures that, to anyone who has seen the like before, scream out that they are the "real deal" work of the ancient race that built impossible megalithic structures all around the world with massive stones perfectly cut and fit in jigsaw patterns. The Ethiopians call these the Tombs of King Kaleb and King Gebre Meskel, although they agree that the kings were never buried there. These are kings of the 6th century AD, and there are historical records of their lives and deaths. Says Lonely Planet about these buildings:

> The Gebre Meskel (south) tomb is the most refined. The precision of the joints between its stones is at a level unseen anywhere else in Aksum. The tomb consists of one chamber and five rooms, with one boasting an exceptionally finely carved portal leading into it. Inside that room are three sarcophagi, one adorned with a cross similar to Christian crosses found on Aksumite coins. This points towards an age around the 6th century, which, as seldom happens,

corresponds with local tradition. Though the rest of the story has Meskel buried at Debre Damo.

Like Meskel's tomb, King Kaleb's is accessed via a long straight stairway. Inside you'll notice the stones are larger, more angular and less precisely joined. Of those who attribute the making of the tomb to Kaleb, few accept that he was actually buried here. The common theory is that his body lies at Abba Pentalewon Monastery, where he lived after abdicating his throne. The tomb's unfinished state fits with the theory. Local rumour has it that there's a secret tunnel leading from here to the Red Sea.

It will be no surprise to my readers that I think these structures had nothing to do with 6th century kings, and instead think they are the oldest construction in the area, probably predating even the Axumite empire. Did the Axumites or their predecessors learn from these master builders?

I think again of the curious 360-ton megalithic stone slab that covered what is called Nefas Mawcha's tomb. How old is that "tomb" and who built it? When the Great Obelisk fell it broke into pieces as it fell on the tomb's central chamber, breaking the huge roof supports.

Remember what the Lonely Planet guide said about it:

> The tomb is unusual for its large size, the sophistication of the structure and size of the stones used for its construction (the stone that roofs the central chamber measures 17.3 m by 6.4 m and weighs some 360 tons!).
>
> …Locals believe that under this tomb is a 'magic machine,' the original implement the Axumites used to melt stone in order to shape the stelae and tombs. The same type of machine was apparently also used to create some of the rock-hewn churches of Tigray.

Clearly, the Ethiopians believe that a magic machine—like the Ark of the Covenant—is beneath this huge slab of stone. So, maybe the real Ark of the Covenant was beneath this giant slab of stone, rather than in the Chapel of the Ark.

Is the Ark of the Covenant in Ethiopia?

The story of a magic machine is similar to what Graham Hancock was told in 1983 by the high priest of the church that holds the Ark. He had said that it was the power of the Ark of the Covenant that moved and lifted the great stones with "celestial fire." This priest believed that the Ark had the power to do this, and yes, special powers would be necessary for erecting such exceptional obelisks.

So, Axum is a special place and its antiquity must go back many thousands of years, to a time even before Moses. But the burning questing is: does Ethiopia have the genuine, original Ark of the Covenant or a copy?

While in Ethiopia in 2014, I read Graham Hancock's 1992 book *The Sign and the Seal*. Hancock's book remains controversial to this day, but not in Ethiopia, where it is wildly popular.

Hancock's book narrates his endeavors in searching for the Ark of the Covenant while working for Ethiopia's oppressive communist government in the mid-1980s. The communist government was overthrown in 1991 and replaced with a pro-Western government with strong ties to Europe and the United States.

In the book Hancock proposes the theory that the Ark was removed from Solomon's Temple in Jerusalem by temple priests

The small Chapel of the Tablet in Axum, said to house the Ark of the Covenant.

during the reign of the bad King Manasseh of Judah around 650 BC, and then it spent about 200 years in a purpose-built temple in Elephantine, Egypt before it was removed around 470 BC to Ethiopia via tributaries to the Nile River.

It was eventually brought to Lake Tana where it was kept on the Jewish island of Tana Kirkus for about eight hundred more years as the center of a strong Jewish community in the area. Eventually it came into the hands of the young Ethiopian Orthodox Church in the 5th century AD, and it was taken to the capital at Axum and placed in the Church of Our Lady Mary of Zion. So, in Hancock's theory, the Ark was not brought to Axum by Menelik, but it made its way there later.

Says Wikipedia:

The Ethiopian Orthodox Church claims to possess the Ark of the Covenant, or Tabot, in Axum. The object is currently kept under guard in a treasury near the Church of Our Lady Mary of Zion. Replicas of the Axum tabot are kept in every Ethiopian church, each with its own dedication to a particular saint; the most popular of these include Mary, George and Michael.

The *Kebra Nagast*, composed to legitimize the new dynasty ruling Ethiopia following its establishment in 1270, narrates how the real Ark of the Covenant was brought to Ethiopia by Menelik I with divine assistance, while a forgery was left in the Temple in Jerusalem. Although the *Kebra Nagast* is the best-known account of this belief, the belief predates the document. Abu al-Makarim, writing in the last quarter of the twelfth century, makes one early reference to this belief that they possessed the Ark. "The Abyssinians possess also the Ark of the Covenant," he wrote, and, after a description of the object, describes how the liturgy is celebrated upon the Ark four times a year, "on the feast of the great nativity, on the feast of the glorious Baptism, on the feast of the holy Resurrection, and on the feast of the illuminating Cross."

...On 25 June 2009, the patriarch of the Orthodox Church of Ethiopia, Abune Paulos, said he would announce to the world the next day the unveiling of the Ark of the Covenant, which he said had been kept safe and secure in a church in Axum, Ethiopia.

The following day, on 26 June 2009, the patriarch announced that he would not unveil the Ark after all, but that instead he could attest to its current status.

The Ethiopian Ark continues to be in the news, even fake news like that about the Ark being stolen in November of 2014. But is the sacred Ark of the Covenant really in a small church in the mountains of northern Ethiopia?

Is the Ark in Axum a Replica?

Though the fortunes of Axum have waxed and waned, it seems clear to me that the city has been important since early Egyptian times. However, the ark now kept in Axum is probably a replica, perhaps first brought by Menelik to Axum circa 920 BC. Maybe the replica was made much later. The replica—whilch is used four times a year at festivals—would seem to be the golden cherubim statue of the two angels holding a bowl between them placed on top of a wood and gold chest whose dimensions are described in Exodus. However, when brought out of the church it is draped in cloth and the ark beneath it cannot be seen by those in attendance.

As has been noted, the ark can only be seen by the monk delegated its caretaker. Says crisismagazine.com in an article from January 24, 2012:

> …be aware that while Ethiopians insist that the Ark is there, no one is actually allowed to see it. No one, that is, except the High Priest of Axum, an aged monk who is charged with protecting the Ark and is expected to spend his days doing nothing else. Indeed, he can't do anything else, for he is confined to the chapel that houses the Ark, and a small yard outside.
>
> On his deathbed he is charged with designating his own successor, who may be forgiven for taking the duty as a dubious blessing: the Ethiopians remember and take very seriously all the Old Testament prohibitions on touching

the Ark, and the accounts of its fearsome holy power. One British explorer who tried to get permission to see the Ark recounted what the monks told him, sounding as if he were reading from the script of the next Indiana Jones movie:

> If I approached the Ark I would be punished. The theory is that it would become invisible and unleash upon me its terrible power. I would be killed outright, probably incinerated.

As we have seen, the real Ark could do that, but it seems to me the one guarded in Axum has to be a replica. Perhaps this replica ark arrived, as Graham Hancock suggests, from the Jewish community at Elephantine Island of the 6th century BC. Lake Tana is an important part of the early Ark of Ethiopia story, but the *Kebra Nagast* would essentially have us believe that the early ark went first to Axum (c.920 BC) and then to Lake Tana for safekeeping during various turbulent times in Axum, and finally back to Axum at the time of King Ezana (c.321 – c.360 AD).

Perhaps the replica was made during the time of King Ezana, as many foreign scholars surmise. Indeed, when the ark is brought out every year at the festivals, it may be only a second-generation duplicate of the original Ethiopian ark — because the original Ethiopian ark (which was itself a replica) has deteriorated too much or is just too sacred and fragile to ever be brought outside of its current sanctuary at the small, protected chapel.

Nearly every church in Ethiopia, which number in the thousands, has its own replica of the Ark of the Covenant. This replica is a wooden box with gold decoration, and various fabrics placed on it. The amount of gold in the making of the elaborate chest would depend on the wealth of that particular church and no doubt many of the replica arks have no gold in them at all, or very little.

It is probably safe to say that the Ark of the Covenant is the most copied artifact ever created. The mere fact that there are thousands of copies in Ethiopia alone would give it that distinction. Other copies of the Ark may be found on eBay and other stores on the Internet. Some copies are made of cheap plastic while others are elaborate and adorned with gold. But there is only one real Ark of the Covenant.

So, our quest for the Ark of the Covenant in Ethiopia is coming to an end. While we can't say for sure, it seems likely that the Ethiopian Ark, currently residing in Axum, is probably a replica and does not possess the awesome power of the Ark as described in the Bible. Outside of Ethiopia, Jewish scholars largely doubt that the Ethiopian ark is the real Ark. The Beta Israel do not seem to regard it as the real Ark either.

What would the real Ark look like? The machine that created the death and devastation may have been removed from the chest thousands of years ago but the golden statue and the chest would remain.

This valuable relic may still exist today somewhere in Jerusalem or elsewhere in the Middle East or Europe. Statues and other things made of gold are virtually indestructible, as has been noted. If the genuine Ark of the Covenant is not in Ethiopia, then where might we possibly find it?

CHAPTER TEN

SECRET HIDING PLACES OF THE ARK

At the end-time the Ark, with the stone tablets,
will resurrect first: it will come out of the rock and
be placed on Mount Sinai. There the saints will
assemble to receive the lord.
— *The Lives of the Prophets 2:15*

Today, there is probably no more valuable or important artifact in the world than the Ark of the Covenant. Where is this sacred object? If the Ark wasn't taken to Ethiopia, then where is it now? Is it still in Jerusalem? Could it be in some other place in Africa?

The Lemba Tribe of Zimbabwe and the Ark

The Lemba Tribe of Zimbabwe and its connection to the Ark of Covenant was the subject of a 2008 book by the British researcher Tudor Parfitt[5] who maintained that the Lemba were one of the lost tribes of Israel. They had come to southern Africa from Arabia they told him, and had brought with them an object they called an ngoma which Parfitt took to be the Ark of the Covenant.

Wikipedia says of Parfitt:

His interest in marginal Jewish groups led him in the 1990s to study the Lemba tribe of southern Africa, who claimed partial male descent from ancient Jewish ancestors in present-day Yemen. He published *Journey to the Vanished City* (1992) about his six-month journey throughout Africa tracing the origins of the tribe to the ancient city of Senna in present-day Yemen. This, together with TV programs about the discoveries, and major newspaper coverage, brought him international attention (and earned him the sobriquet the British Indiana Jones). Seeking more data, he helped organize Y-DNA studies of Lemba males in 1996 and later. These found a high proportion of Semitic ancestry, DNA common to both Arabs and Jews from the Middle East. The work confirmed that the male line had descended from ancestors in southern Arabia.

The Lemba have a tradition of having brought a drum, or ngoma, which they believe they brought from the Middle East centuries ago. Parfitt noted that their description of the ngoma was similar to that of the Biblical Ark of the Covenant. Parfitt has observed that Rabbinic sources maintain that there were two Arks of the Covenant—one the ceremonial Ark, covered with gold, which was eventually placed in the Holy of Holies in the Temple; the other the Ark of War, which had been carved from wood by Moses and was a relatively simple affair.

Parfitt proposed that the Ark of War may have been taken by Jews across the Jordan River and, citing Islamic sources, proposed that they migrated south into Arabia. Southern Arabia was known as Arabia Felix in antiquity and today is called Yemen. The Lemba claim to have brought their ark/ngoma from Arabia to Zimbabwe at some point after that.

Parfitt's 2008 book *The Lost Ark of the Covenant: Solving the 2,500 Year Old Mystery of the Fabled Biblical Ark*[5] recorded his findings in Arabia and Africa. There were documentaries on Parfitt on the History Channel in America and Channel Four in Britain. In 2010 Parfitt was invited to address a symposium in Harare on the subject; attendees included the government's cabinet and vice president John Nkomo.

The Lemba claim that their 700-year-old replica is created from the core wood of the original Ark of the Covenant. It is traditionally carried on poles and contact with the sacred object is avoided. It would not seem to have any kind of electrical charge however. Since it is completely made of wood, it is clear that this is not some sort of weapon of god, but merely a wooden box meant to hold sacred artifacts similar to the ark found in the tomb of King Tut.

Parfitt's hunt for the Ark brings out the difficulty in finding the true artifact when there are so many stories and legends surrounding it. He was led hither and yon tracking down stories and leads, and finally found in rabbinic literature that there were purported to be two Arks of the Covenant! I think this reflects the confusion, even amongst the early scholars, surrounding the true Ark. They suggest that there was the Ark of War, a simple wood affair constructed by Moses to be carried in front of the troops, and the Ark of the Covenant that was the ceremonial, highly-decorated box that was to hold the sacred tablets of the Ten Commandments, the Rod of Aaron, and a cup of manna from the days in the desert (and an electrical device?).

I think this confusion stems from the many replicas of the arks in existence. We have already noted that many ancient armies paraded an ark in front of their ranks. Also, that every Ethiopian church has a replica of the Ark of the Covenant. Every Jewish synagogue also has a Holy Ark, in which is placed the congregation's copy of the Torah scrolls. Parfitt's book is actually about the many sacred chests that were used by the Jews and others, and in the end, rather than solving the mystery of the Ark, in some ways he adds to it. He was satisfied that the Lemba had a fragment of the Ark, however, and made an interesting comment on his find:

> "There can be little doubt that what I found Harare is the last thing on Earth in direct descent from the Ark of the Covenant. Now that it has been discovered, one can only hope that its influence will be benign." (*Daily Mail*, February 22, 2008)

The authors of the 1999 book *The Ark of the Covenant*, Roderick Grierson and Stuart Munro-Hay,[1] think that the Ark of the Covenant

259

may have been brought to Ethiopia through Arabia at the time of the Axumite King Kaleb, who ruled circa 520 AD. They suggest that the chest may contain a meteorite like that worshipped at the Kaaba in Mecca.

They theorize that Kaleb got this ark and meteorite from the Arab tribe called the Jurhum, who once controlled Mecca and the Kaaba. According to Arabic accounts, the tribe of Jurhum gave protection to Abraham's wife Hagar and her son Ishmael, and were involved in the worship at the Kaaba in Mecca. The Kaaba is the holy sanctuary rebuilt by Ishmael and Abraham, and was revered as a pilgrimage site, even before Islam.

The Jurhum got the Ark when the Children of Israel attacked Mecca (no time is given, but we might assume around 800 BC when Israel and Judah were still relatively strong countries). They were defeated by the Jurhum and the Ark was captured. King Kaleb then brought it to Axum after attacking Mecca circa 520 AD, over a thousand years later, say Grierson and Munro-Hay.

They discount Graham Hancock's theory of the Ark coming through Egypt, but for some reason think that the Ethiopian Ark may be the true the Ark of the Covenant. For Grierson and Munro-Hay the Ark seems to be a wooden box with a stone from the Tablets of Moses and possibly a meteorite, maybe a twin of the one still worshipped by Muslims at the Kaaba. It is now in Axum at the Chapel of the Tablet, they surmise.

That the original Ark of the Covenant was somehow lost in battle in Mecca and kept there for over a thousand years seems rather far-fetched. But, as we have seen, many of the stories concerning the Ark of the Covenant are quite fantastic. Even so, it would seem that if the Ark of the Covenant was lost by the Israelites in a battle at Mecca, some mention of this would occur in the Bible or other texts, and there is no such mention.

Most theories about the Ark of the Covenant being taken somewhere outside of Jerusalem are based on the Babylonian sacking of Jerusalem, first in 598 BC and then again in 586 BC. During this period the Ark seems to have disappeared from Solomon's Temple and the Bible essentially ceases any mention of it.

The Babylonian Conquest and the Lost Ark

Gold is indestructible and so all gold from ancient times still exists today. If it is in the form of a statue or mask, such as the gold mask of Tutankhamun, it will still exist after thousands of years with no real deterioration or oxidation. Such objects are virtually eternal.

However, a gold mask or statue, such as the cherubim statue on the lid of the Ark, could have been melted down into ingots or other items. This is one possible fate of the Ark, one accepted by many historians: that it was captured and melted down by the Babylonians. However, no record of this exists.

In 598 BC, the Babylonians attacked Jerusalem and Solomon's Temple for the first time. They were trying to establish hegemony in the region, and were attempting to quell rebellions by the Judeans. The young king Jehoiachin was taken prisoner by Nebuchadnezzar. Says 2 Kings 24:12-14:

> In the eighth year of the reign of the king of Babylon, he took Jehoiachin prisoner. As the Lord had declared, Nebuchadnezzar removed the treasures from the temple of the Lord and from the royal palace, and cut up the gold articles that Solomon king of Israel had made for the temple of the Lord. He carried all Jerusalem into exile: all the officers and fighting men, and all the skilled workers and artisans—a total of ten thousand. Only the poorest people of the land were left.

After this there is no record of what became of the Ark in the Books of Kings and Chronicles. It is not specifically mentioned that it was taken, and one would think such an important artifact would be remarked upon. Maybe Nebuchadnezzar confiscated it, or maybe it was hidden by a temple priest to save it.

After the first attack, Nebuchadnezzar set up a puppet king, Zedekiah, but he, too, rebelled against Babylonian rule. In 587 BC Nebuchadnezzar returned to Jerusalem and laid siege to the city, but had to leave to fight its Egyptian allies. Having won that skirmish, the huge Babylonian army went back to Jerusalem and finally breached the city walls in 586 BC after months of siege. This time, the city and temple were out and out destroyed, being burned to the ground by the Babylonian soldiers. Did they capture the Ark this time? This seems unlikely again, as such a venerated treasure as the Ark would have been mentioned as part of the spoils, which it was not—and there was a pretty exhaustive list of the spoils. We are told in Jeremiah 52:17-19:

> The Babylonians broke up the bronze pillars, the movable stands and the bronze Sea that were at the temple of the Lord and they carried all the bronze to Babylon. They also took away the pots, shovels, wick trimmers, sprinkling bowls, dishes and all the bronze articles used in the temple service. The commander of the imperial guard took away the basins, censers, sprinkling bowls, pots, lampstands, dishes and bowls used for drink offerings—all that were made of pure gold or silver.

But the Greek Book of Ezra (1 Esdras) hints that the Ark was still around, saying the Babylonians took away the vessels of the ark of God, but again does not mention the Ark itself being taken. 1 Esdras 1:54 states:

> And they took all the holy vessels of the Lord, both great and small, with the vessels of the ark of God, and the king's treasures, and carried them away into Babylon.

The denizens of Jerusalem were taken into captivity in Babylon at this time. The Jews were allowed to return to Jerusalem in 538 BC however, after some decades in captivity. In that year the Persian king Cyrus, who had vanquished the Babylonian empire, made a decree that granted the Jews the right to worship their God in Jerusalem. Supposedly, around 50,000 Jews returned to Jerusalem and the land of Israel, but in fact most remained in Babylon. After about 100 years there was a second return of the deportees to Judah, and together these events are known as "the return to Zion."

The Temple was rebuilt after the Israelites returned to Jerusalem from their Babylonian captivity starting in 538 BC. However, it seems that there was no Ark of the Covenant to place in the Holy of Holies. Rather, a portion of the floor was raised a little bit to indicate the place where the Ark had formerly stood. Some Christians believe however that the Ark was placed back in the Holy of Holies but then disappeared at Christ's crucifixion—and the Ark will return with the return of Christ.

Most scholars think that the Ark was missing before the Second Temple was built. In rabbinic literature, the final disposition of the Ark is disputed. Some rabbis hold that it must have been carried off to Babylon, while others hold that it must have been hidden from the invaders somehow. A late 2nd century rabbinic work known as the Tosefta documents the opinions of these rabbis as to the Ark's whereabouts.[38]

In the Tosefta, it states anonymously that during the reign of Josiah, a king of Judah, he stored away the Ark, along with the following items: a jar of manna, and a jar containing the holy anointing oil, the rod of Aaron which budded, and a chest given to Israel by the Philistines. Josiah became king of Judah at the age of eight, after the assassination of his father, King Amon, and reigned for 31 years, from about 640 BC to 609 BC. So Josiah would have done this at least 10 years before the first attack on Jerusalem.

The hiding of the Ark with the items inside it was said to have been done in order to prevent their being carried off into Babylon—however the attacks from Babylon would not actually happen during Josiah's reign. Babylon finally shed the yoke of Assyrian rule in 625 BC, however, when Nebuchadnezzar's father founded the Neo-Babylonian Empire, so maybe the threat of aggression was growing in Josiah's time. Rabbi Eliezer and Rabbi Shimon, in the same rabbinic work, purport that the Ark was, in fact, taken into Babylon. Rabbi Yehudah, dissenting, says that the Ark was stored away in its own place, meaning, somewhere on the Temple Mount.[38]

In the apocryphal book 2 Maccabees 2:4-7, we read that Jeremiah (also known as Jeremy) the prophet may have hidden the Ark on Mount Nebo:

...the prophet [Jeremiah], being warned of God, commanded the tabernacle and the ark to go with him, as he went forth into the mountain, where Moses climbed up [Mount Nebo], and saw the heritage of God. And when Jeremy came thither, he found a hollow cave, wherein he laid the tabernacle, and the ark, and the altar of incense, and so stopped the door. And some of those that followed him came to mark the way, but they could not find it. Which when Jeremy perceived, he blamed them, saying, As for that place, it shall be unknown until the time that God gather His people again together, and receive them unto mercy.

What this book is speaking about is Jeremiah removing the Ark to Mount Nebo (now in Jordan, on the northeast corner of the Dead Sea) which was the peak from which Moses had glimpsed the Promised Land before dying. Jeremiah hid the Ark in a cave, and then concealed the entrance. We will come back to Mount Nebo later in this chapter.

As noted above, some scholars think the Ark was hidden in Jerusalem in secret caves beneath the Temple Mount itself. Others believe it was removed to Egypt and then to Europe, and many Irish and Scots believe that the Jewish-Egyptian princess named Scota escaped to Ireland with the Ark just after the Babylonian siege of 586 BC.

The Ark in Ireland and Scotland

An Irish tradition says that the Ark of the Covenant was taken to Ireland by Jeremiah himself. He fled to Egypt when the Babylonians invaded Israel, and then to Ireland with Queen Tamar Tephi (known as Tea and also called Scota), who married King Eochaidh of Ireland. She died only a short time after her marriage and is buried in county Meath, at Tara, north of Dublin. Buried with her was a great chest said to contain relics from Palestine. Some believe that this chest was the Ark of the Covenant!

Tea/Tamar Tephi is known as the Maid of Destiny and is listed on ancestry.com as a Jewish-Irish princess under the name of Tea Tephi, daughter of Zedekiah, the last king of Judah. Says ancestry.com:

> Tea Tephi Queen of Ireland, daughter of Zedekiah Last King of Judah, was born in Spain and died in Odhbha, Meath, Leinster, Ireland.
>
> The Chronicles say: Tephi born of the House of the High One, Princess of Zion, loved of The Lord, Home of the House of her God, daughter of David, Shepherd in Judah, Tribe of the Lion, Queen over Bethel, and Dan where they be scattered abroad.

While this website says Tea was born in Spain, it is more likely she was born in Jerusalem and spent time in Spain later. Still, how could a princess from Jerusalem end up in Ireland? At the time of the Babylonian invasion in 586 BC, Jeremiah was put in prison because his doom-filled prophecies were causing low morale within the Judean troops. When they captured Jerusalem the Babylonians released Jeremiah from prison and showed him great kindness, allowing him to choose the place of his residence, according to a Babylonian edict.

Jeremiah went to the town of Mizpah in the nation of Benjamin, just north of Jerusalem, with a man named Gedaliah, who had been appointed the governor of Judea by the Babylonians. Jerusalem was also part of the nation of Benjamin, a small but central part of the 12 tribes-12 nations that made up a united Israel. Immediately west of Benjamin was the nation of Dan who had the important port of Jaffa. South of Benjamin and Jerusalem was the nation of Judah with the nation of Simeon below that, reaching south into the Negev Desert.

North of Jerusalem was the nation of Ephraim and east of the Jordan were the nations of Reuben, Gad and Manasseh. Manasseh was a large territory, spanning both sides of the Jordan, and it had a sizeable section along the eastern Mediterranean coast. The nations of Simeon, Judah, Benjamin, Gad and Reuben were all land-locked. North of Manasseh were also the landlocked nations of Issachar and

265

Zebulun and Naphtali. The most northern of all the 12 tribe nations was Asher, which included the important Phoenician ports of Tyre and Sidon, which were now part of Israel.

The 12 tribe nations of Israel had already begun to crumble hundreds of years before the time of Jeremiah, but its major ports survived, including the port of Jaffa, a major city inhabited by loyal Israelites who also trafficked in all shipping that was occurring in the Mediterranean at the time. This would have included ships coming from the Atlantic ports of Europe.

Jeremiah was given permission by the Babylonians to accompany the new governor, Gedaliah, who was now to rule Judea and Jerusalem, and they headed to Mizpah. However, shortly after arriving, Gedaliah was assassinated by Ishmael, a Judean prince, for working with the Babylonians. Johanan, son of Kareah, and his army officers with him went in pursuit of Ishmael, knowing he was bringing on even more trouble in the already tumultuous time. Johanan thereby became the leader of the army and the remnant of the population of the Kingdom of Judah, and he decided to lead them to Egypt for safety. Jeremiah, however, warned Johanan about going to Egypt and was completely against this plan, but Johanan and his men decided to go anyway.

So, fearing Babylonian retribution for the killing of Gedaliah, Johanan fled to Egypt, taking with him Jeremiah and the scribe Baruch, plus the king's daughters, a small army of Judean troops who had survived the devastating war with the Babylonians, and the remaining Judeans. We are told in Jeremiah 43:4-7:

> So Johanan, son of Kareah, and all the army officers and all the people disobeyed the Lord's command to stay in the land of Judah. Instead, Johanan son of Kareah and all the army officers led away all the remnant of Judah who had come back to live in the land of Judah from all the nations where they had been scattered. They also led away all those whom Nebuzaradan commander of the imperial guard had left with Gedaliah son of Ahikam, the son of Shaphan—the men, the women, the children and the king's daughters. And

they took Jeremiah the prophet and Baruch son of Neriah along with them. So they entered Egypt in disobedience to the Lord and went as far as Tahpanhes.

Except to say that there is a sizable presence of Jews around Tahpanhes in the Nile Delta, there is little else told in the Bible about Jeremiah and the Jews living in Egypt. Says Wikipedia about Jeremiah's tenure in Egypt:

> There, the prophet probably spent the remainder of his life, still seeking in vain to turn the people to God from whom they had so long revolted. There is no authentic record of his death.

So what really happened to Jeremiah after he went to Egypt? The Bible doesn't give us a clue, although he wrote some letters to the kings of foreign countries, as recorded at the end of Jeremiah. Were some of the Jews with him from the tribe of Dan? The Bible does not say how they arrived at Tahpanhes—did they arrive in ships?

Indeed, Tahpanhes was a port city. Tahpanhes (known by the ancient Greeks as Daphnae) was located on Lake Manzala on the Tanitic branch of the Nile, near the Mediterranean coast of Egypt. The archeological site, which includes brick docks and pavement, is now situated on the Suez Canal. When the site was "discovered" by Sir William Matthew Flinders Petrie in 1886 it was known to the locals as the "Castle of the Jew's Daughter."

The city of Jaffa was the main port for the tribe of Dan, whose territory was along the Mediterranean coast directly west of Jerusalem. The major city of Tel-Aviv now sits at the site of Jaffa (which is a suburb). Did Jeremiah and others leave Jaffa in ships of the tribe of Dan and make what would be a two or three day journey to the Nile-Mediterranean port of Tahpanhes? It would seem logical. Later, Jeremiah and his group of followers made the more adventurous, but ultimately successful, journey to Ireland to found a new royal family there.

Ancient Irish texts say that Jeremiah left Tahpanhes with his small fleet of ships and, guided by the tribe of Dan—the Phoenician sailors of Israel—they went west through the Mediterranean to Spain, and then proceeded to Scotland and finally the northeastern part of Ireland. The part of Spain that they stopped in was probably the Catalonia region of Barcelona, with nearby Perpignon in the Languedoc region of France. This area was a Phoenician trading port area, as was Cadiz in southwest Spain. Perpignon is near Rennes-le-Chateau, which has also been mentioned as the location of a great treasure rumored to be from King Solomon's temple. Did Jeremiah bring the Ark to Catalonia? Did he take it on to Ireland as the Irish legends claim? All of this will be examined soon.

So, many Irish legends tell us that Jeremiah traveled abroad with the Ark of the Covenant, along with a retinue of Egyptian and Jewish nobles. It is interesting to note that according to Irish legends, Jeremiah is buried on Devenish Island in Loch Erne in the southwest portion of Northern Ireland, UK. Devenish Island also contains ancient megaliths, monastic remains and one of the mysterious Irish round towers.

Irish chronicles also talk about the arrival of the Tuatha de Danann who were said to come from Egypt and Israel with the Stone of Destiny. The Irish version of this story can be found in the old Irish book, *Chronicles of Eri,* which says that sometime around 580 BC, a ship landed at Ulster, and on board were the prophet Ollamh Fodhla, the Princess Tara and a scribe named Simon Brech. These three were apparently the prophet Jeremiah, Princess Tea and the scribe Baruch.[68]

The magical items said to be possessed by the Tuatha de Danann were probably various items of machinery and electric devices that still existed in those days in Egypt and the Middle East, but were unknown in the northern lands. A simple but effective device such as a crossbow, or even a gunpowder-fireworks-type rocket, would seem like "magic spears" to people who had never seen one, and similarly an electrical device, such as the Ark of the Covenant, would seem magical to any primitive observer.

It was thought that the Tuatha de Danann—the tribe of Dan—

had brought the Ark of the Covenant to the Hill of Tara and buried it there. This belief became so strong that during the turn of the 20th century, British Israelites carried out some excavations of the Tara (Torah?) looking for the Ark of the Covenant. The Royal Society of Antiquaries of Ireland campaigned successfully to have them stopped before they destroyed the hill.[69]

A medieval manuscript called the Scotichronicon, or Chronicles of the Scots, written in AD 1435 by a monk named Walter Bower, tells the following legend about the origin of the Scots:

> In ancient times Scota, the daughter of pharaoh, left Egypt with her husband Gaythelos by name and a large following. For they had heard of the disasters which were going to come upon Egypt, and so through the instructions of the gods they fled from certain plagues that were to come. They took to the sea, entrusting themselves to the guidance of the gods. After sailing in this way for many days over the sea with troubled minds, they were finally glad to put their boats in at a certain shore because of bad weather.[18]

Bower seems to miss that this party fleeing Egypt had originally fled Judah, and the princess is the daughter of the Judean king, not the pharaoh. At any rate, the manuscript goes on to say that the Egyptians settled in what is today western Scotland but they soon moved to Northern Ireland because of conflicts with the local population (probably the Picts). This Egyptian group then merged with an Irish tribe and became known as the Scotti. They became the High Kings of Ireland, and being a seafaring group, eventually reinvaded and reconquered Scotland, which retains their name and that of the Egyptian-Jewish princess Scota. They then founded their capital at the Hill of Tara, today near the River Boyne in County Meath, Republic of Ireland.

The Hill of Tara and the Ark of the Covenant

The Hill of Tara today is a high hill covered in green pasture with sheep grazing on it. Yet, it commands a tremendous view of the countryside in four directions, and in ancient times people came from all over Ireland to Tara, for celebrations, coronations, or simply pilgrimage. Atop the hill stands a stone pillar that was the Irish Lia Fáil (Stone of Destiny, not to be confused with the Stone of Destiny called the Stone of Scone we will discuss below) on which the High Kings of Ireland were crowned; legends suggest that the stone was

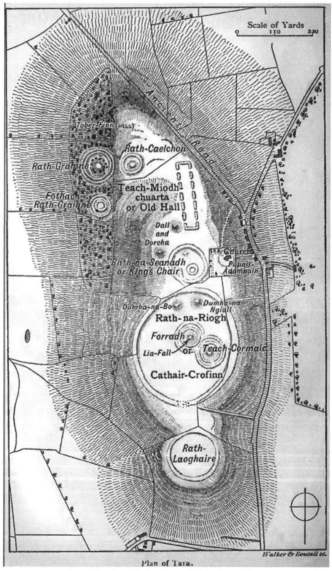

An old print of the plan of Tara in Ireland.

required to roar three times if the chosen one was a true king. This menhir-type stone is one of the last things still standing at Tara, which is basically a grassy hill today. Since the time of St. Patrick the significance of Tara has declined to the point of there being very little to see there.

Tara, two and a half thousand years ago, was a huge palace with a great wooden tower and a Druidic college. James Bonwick, in his 1894 book *Irish Druids and Old Irish Religions*,[66] says:

> The palace of Teamair, or Tara, was held by the Tuatha. The chief college of the Druids was at Tara. At Tara was held the national convention of the Teamorian Fes. It was associated with the marriage sports of the Tailtean. The foundation is attributed to the wise Ollam Fodhla.

The story of Tara goes back to Princess Tea/Tamar Tephi and her marriage to the local Irish King Eochaidh the Heremon, forming the Kingdom of the Tuatha de Danann. It didn't last long, with the Tuatha de Danann having to fight the Firbolgs for control of Ireland. The Tuatha de Danann defeated the Firbolgs, but Nuada, the first Tuatha de Danann king, lost a hand in the battle. Since kings had to be perfectly whole, in a magnificent gesture of reconciliation, he abdicated in favor of Bress, son of the Fomorian king.[66]

The Stone of Destiny

Bonwick quotes from various Irish historians and tells that the Irish *Csalacronica,* dated 1355, had this to say about the scribe of Jeremiah, Simon Brech:

> [He] brought with him a stone on which the Kings of Spain were wont to be crowned, and placed it in the most sovereign beautiful place in Ireland, called to this day the Royal Place; and Fergus, son of Ferchar, brought the Royal Stone before received, and placed it where it is now, the Abbey of Scone.

271

The Irish Stone of Destiny at Tara, about all that is left to see at the site.

Thus we have the Stone of Scone. Bonwick cites another 14th-century version from Baldred Bisset:

> The stone which had first served Jacob for his pillow, was afterwards transported to Spain, where it was used as a seat of justice by Gathalus, contemporary with Moses.

Bonwick then says that the historian Boece declared that Gathalus was the son of Cecrops of Athens, and married "Scota, daughter of Pharaoh."[66] As with all studies of history going back into the mists of time, things can get pretty confusing. If Gathalus were contemporary with Moses, it would date him to about 1200

BC. If he was the son of Cecrops, the mythical Greek king often said to have founded Athens, he would have to go back to at least 3000 BC. The other Irish tales of Scota related here place her on the shores of Eire around 580 BC, in which case she couldn't have been married to Gathalus.

But were the kings of Spain and Tartessos also crowned for a time on the Stone of Destiny? Princess Tea, or Scota, probably came to Ireland via Spain, and may have stopped in Spain for several years. It is also possible that her Irish husband-to-be may have also lived in Spain for a time. Ireland, apparently, has always had a close connection with Spain and North Africa. Spain, of course, would be a natural stopping place for any ships coming from the eastern Mediterranean to Ireland.

In a chapter on Tara, Bonwick says:

> Other stories connected with the preacher at Tara are narrated elsewhere in the present work, and relate to a period subsequent to the institution of the Ollamh Fodhla college at Tara... Heber of Heber of the Bards is to them Hebrew. Tara is named for Terah (Torah). Jeremiah fled thither after the siege of Jerusalem, carrying away the treasures of the temple; as, the ark, the scepter of David, the Urim and Thummin, and others. Some persons at this day affect to believe that in the hill of Tara might yet be found these memorials of Judaism, and hope to recover thence David's harp, carried to Ireland by Jeremiah and the Princess Scota, daughter of Pharaoh.

Bonwick also mentions the Reverend F.R.A. Glover, M.A., who says the Stone of Destiny was taken from the sanctuary in 588 BC and "brought thither by Hebrew men in a ship of Dan, circa 584."[66]

Reverend Glover goes on to say that Jacob's pillow was taken to Tara. "In Ireland, in the royal precincts of Tara, circa BC 582-3, there was a Hebrew system and a transplanted Jerusalem..."

The idea of ancient Ireland and Scotland being a land of Egyptian refugees and sailors from the tribe of Dan is a fascinating thought.

273

Perhaps the tribe of Dan were also the inheritors of an ancient route through the Orkney and Shetland Islands to North America and the St. Lawrence seaway.

Ireland, Scotland, Wales and the Isle of Man may have had connections with Egypt going back to 1500 BC and before. Egyptian and Phoenician ships were continually plying the naval routes from the eastern Mediterranean to the Iberian Peninsula and ports in northern Europe. That these green lands on the far edge of Europe—reachable only by boat—would have been safe havens for Egyptian and Jewish royalty (who were often aligned), is not surprising. That a great treasure (plus princesses and priests) was loaded onto a small fleet of ships and taken out of the eastern Mediterranean to a remote colony or trading post seems only natural.

But, was the Ark of the Covenant actually brought to Scotland and then Ireland? If so, this Ark has deteriorated to the point of nonexistence, and its golden statue lost; all that is left is the Stone of Scone, the coronation stone of the kings of the United Kingdom. Today it is kept in Edinburgh Castle and is on display for tourists to view and photograph. Was this stone once inside the Ark of the Covenant?

The Ark in France?

There are other stories of the Ark of the Covenant being taken to Phoenician-Jewish enclaves in Spain and southern France that would appear to be related to the stories about the Ark in Ireland and Scotland. Perhaps a copy of the original Ark was created in Catalonia and then taken on to Ireland.

The theory is that the Ark of the Covenant was taken to Catalonia where Phoenician and later Essene enclaves existed in the Pyrenees Mountains between France and Spain. In this area, not far from several Mediterranean ports, is the small village of Rennes-le-Château that has a church dedicated to Saint Mary Magdalene, which is the reputed location of a legendary treasure which might have contained the Ark of the Covenant.

Rennes-le-Château is a small French hilltop village that receives tens of thousands of visitors per year. It is at the center of

274

various theories that include (1) Mary Magdalene being married to Jesus and having his children in the vicinity, and (2) it being the location of a buried treasure discovered by a 19th-century priest named Bérenger Saunière.

The village church dedicated to Saint Mary Magdalene was rebuilt several times by Saunière, and it is reputed that he found a fantastic treasure in vaults deep beneath the church that were thousands of years old. Indeed, it seemed that the church had been built over a natural cavern system that had also been worked by

Bérenger Sauniére.

man. Although no one in recent times has seen these caverns, one legend says that the Ark of the Covenant is being kept there.

The earliest church of which there is any evidence on the site may date to the 8th century AD. This church was probably in ruins by the 11th century, when another church was built upon the site. This church survived until the 19th century, when it desperately needed restoration.

This restoration was being done by the local priest, Bérenger Saunière, when he allegedly stumbled upon the treasure. He began going to Paris and selling items of gold, and ultimately had a very large bank account with which he paid for lavish restorations of the small church. Surviving receipts and existing account books belonging to Saunière reveal that the renovations of the church, including works on the presbytery and cemetery, cost 11,605 francs over a ten-year period between 1887 and 1897.

Saunière added the Latin inscription *Terribilis est locus iste* above the front doors: "This is a place of awe," while the rest of the dedication on church arches reads "this is God's house, the gate of heaven, and it shall be called the royal court of God." Following Sauniere's renovations and redecorations, the church was re-dedicated in 1897 by his bishop, Monsignor Billiard.

275

Other account books belonging to Saunière reveal that the construction of his estate, including a tower and villa, plus the purchase of local land between 1898 and 1905 cost the priest 26,417 francs. He also lived a rather lavish life, dining and drinking with opera stars in Paris and such.

Bérenger Sauniére's villa in Rennes-le-Chateau.

In 1910–1911 Bérenger Saunière was summoned by the bishopric to appear before an ecclesiastical trial to face charges of "trafficking in masses"; the Catholic church lets priests collect money for saying private masses dedicated to the contributor's loved one, but it was determined that Sauniere was advertising and collecting money for more masses than he could possibly carry out. He was found guilty and suspended from the priesthood. When asked to produce his account books he refused to attend his trial. He died in 1917.

Books began appearing in France about the strange church of Mary Magdalene and its mysterious treasure, and also about the idea that Mary Magdalene had been the wife of Jesus and bore his children. This bloodline from Jesus was the real secret behind the "Holy Grail." In the 1970s and 80s the story formed the basis of several documentaries in the UK, and books such as *Holy Blood, Holy Grail* by Michael Baigent, Richard Leigh, and Henry Lincoln.[25] Many elements of these theories were later used by Dan Brown in his best-selling 2003 novel *The Da Vinci Code*, in which the fictional character Jacques Saunière is named after the priest.

Says Wikipedia about Rennes:

> The entire area around Rennes-le-Château became the focus of sensational claims during the 1950s and 1960s involving Blanche of Castile, the Merovingians, the Knights Templar, the Cathars, the treasures of the Temple of Solomon that was the booty of the Visigoths that included the Ark of the Covenant and the Menorah (the seven-branched candlestick from the Temple of Jerusalem). From the 1970s onwards claims have extended to the Priory of Sion, the Rex Deus, the Holy Grail, ley lines, sacred geometry alignments, the remains of Jesus Christ, alleged references to Mary Magdalene settling in the south of France, and even flying saucers. Well-known French authors like Jules Verne and Maurice Leblanc are suspected of leaving clues in their novels about their knowledge of the "mystery" of Rennes-le-Château.

Though it remains only a legend, there is a strong belief—included in dozens of books—that the Ark of the Covenant is amongst a fabulous treasure beneath the church in Rennes-le-Château. Saunière may have turned some of this treasure into French francs in his bank accounts, but most of it must still be there in the vaults beneath the church. Does this treasure include the Ark of Covenant? If it is at this small village in France, it probably came via Jeremiah circa 580 BC, who may have hidden it in the natural caves.

Nearby, on the Spanish side of the Pyrenees Mountains, is the monastery of Montserrat located a short distance outside of Barcelona. There is an obscure tradition that the Ark of Covenant is kept there in a secret cave. Indeed, the symbol for the monastery is three mountain peaks with a box on the top of the center peak. Is this the Ark of the Covenant? Montserrat, a popular tourist spot to this day, is also associated with the Holy Grail and is mentioned in the grail quest poem Parsival written in the early 1200s.

Stories of the Ark of the Covenant being in southern France or Catalonia are intriguing. There is also the theory by French author Louis Charpentier, who claimed in his book *The Mysteries of Chartres Cathedral*[70] that the Ark of the Covenant was removed from a secret chamber beneath Solomon's Temple by the Knights Templar. The Templars then returned to France with the Ark where it was put in a secret room beneath Chartres Cathedral located to the west of Paris.

In a similar tale, British author Graham Phillips says in his book *The Templars and the Ark of the Covenant: The Discovery of the Treasure of Solomon*[71] that the Templars discovered a treasure, including the Ark, on a mountain at Petra, Jordan. Phillips hypothesizes that the Ark was taken to Jebel al-Madhbah above Petra in the Valley of Edom by the Maccabees circa 134 BC. Phillips claims it remained there until about 1180 AD, when Ralph de Sudeley, a leader of the Templars at that time, discovered the treasure on Jebel al-Madhbah while camped at Petra. Phillips, and others, believe that Jebel al-Madhbah is the real Mount Sinai of the Bible.

De Sudeley returned home to his estate at Herdewyke in

Warwickshire, England, and Phillips thinks that he brought the treasure with him. De Sudeley died in 1192 AD and later his Templar properties were seized by the English crown. Phillips says that if de Sudeley did have the Ark, then he is the last person known to have possessed the relic.

Similarly, there is a legend that a small room beneath Rosslyn Chapel in Scotland was built to hold the Ark of the Covenant. If de Sudeley had the Ark of the Covenant in England, perhaps it was sent to Rosslyn Chapel.

If we follow such a Templar connection to the Ark of the Covenant, we could even theorize that the Ark was brought across the Atlantic by Sir Henry Sinclair of Rosslyn. A noted sailor who had a fleet based in the Orkney Islands, he allegedly built a small castle on Oak Island in Nova Scotia and then constructed the famous Money Pit on the island to hide the Ark. The Sinclair family with their Templar friends believed that they would be building the New Jerusalem in this New World that they were attempting to colonize, and the Ark of the Covenant would be safe in this faraway land. The strange shaft dug deep into Oak Island continues to enthrall people to this day, and it is a fantastic thought that the Ark of the Covenant might be at the bottom of this pit.

The Ark Hidden Beneath the Temple Mount

Historically, the search for the Ark of the Covenant largely centered on the object being located in a secret room somewhere beneath the Temple Mount or nearby. This secret room would have been reached through a secret tunnel or series of tunnels. Later the tunnels and entrances were sealed up, either on purpose, or accidently.

The Moorish writer Maimonides, also called Rambam, a Jewish Torah scholar who lived in Cordoba, Spain from 1135 to 1204 during the period of Moorish rule, quotes an earlier Jewish scholar named Abaraita as saying:

> …when Solomon built the temple he foresaw its destruction and built a deep secret cave where Josiah ordered the Ark to be hidden.[38]

The Knights Templar were the first group to gain access to the site of Solomon's Temple (in 1120) and it is known that they did do some excavating there. Louis Charpentier suggests that the Templars did indeed find the Ark of the Covenant at this time and brought it back to Europe.

However, since the Ark never actually surfaced, many an Ark hunter has sought to find the Ark where others have failed. The most famous of these often ill-conceived quests was the infamous Parker Expedition of 1909.

The Parker Expedition to Find the Ark

The so-called Parker Expedition began at the Topkapi Museum/ Library in Istanbul in 1908 where a certain Swedish biblical scholar named Valter H. Juvelius accidentally stumbled on a sacred code in the book of Ezekiel while studying it in ancient manuscript form. This code, he claimed, described the exact location of the long-lost treasures hidden within a tunnel system underneath the temple mount.

Juvelius teamed up with Captain Montague Parker, who got the Duchess of Marlborough, among other backers, to put up $125,000 to search for the elusive treasure. They bribed their way through the red tape of the Ottoman Empire and worked beneath the city of Jerusalem starting in 1909. They tunneled beneath the city and indeed uncovered hidden passageways, but their search came to a sudden halt on April 17, 1911, when Captain Parker and his men attempted to enter a natural cavern that they had discovered beneath the surface of the Sacred Rock on the Temple Mount itself.

The Sacred Rock is where Abraham was supposed to have offered his son Isaac to God, and where Mohammed is said to have ascended to heaven on his horse Buraq. Local tradition said that evil spirits in this cavern guarded an ancient treasure vault.[38]

Captain Parker and his crew lowered themselves down into the cavern and began to break the stones that closed off the entrance to an ancient tunnel. But, unfortunately, one of the temple attendants had chosen to spend the night on the Temple Mount, and heard the sounds of the expedition. He followed the noises to the sacred stone, one the holiest places in all of Islam, and, to his utter horror, found the sacred shrine occupied by a group of strangely clothed foreigners!

With mad shrieks, he fled into the city, spreading cries of how the temple was being desecrated. Within the hour, the entire city was in a tumult. There were riots in the streets as the rumors spread that Englishmen had discovered and stolen the crown and magical ring of Solomon, the Ark of the Covenant, and the sword of Mohammed! For this they must pay with their lives! Parker and his men fled the city and headed for Jaffa Harbor on the Mediterranean Coast where Parker's yacht allowed them an escape. He was banned from ever entering Jerusalem again, and the local Turkish governor and commissioners were replaced.[38]

Antonia Futterer and the Ark on Mount Nebo

It was a close call for those lucky "Ark Raiders," but the exploration did not stop there, though it took a different turn. In the 1920s an American explorer named Antonia Frederick Futterer searched for the Ark on Mount Nebo in Jordan (then Trans-Jordan) where it was said that Jeremiah had hid it more than 2,500 years before. Futterer published a pamphlet in 1927 entitled *Search is on for Lost Ark of the Covenant* (Los Angeles, 1927). In it, he claimed that while either on Mount Nebo or somewhere nearby in the Pisgah Range, he squeezed into a cave leading to a long vault or corridor with "hieroglyphics" on the walls. At the end of the corridor he found two locked doors. Futterer made sketches of the hieroglyphs and when he returned to Jerusalem, "a Hebrew scholar" deciphered his signs "numerically." The numerical value of the signs totaled 1927, claimed Futterer. If there is any truth to this, it would seem that the signs were ancient Hebrew (which do indeed have numerical values, as well as phonetic meanings) rather than being hieroglyphs in the Egyptian sense.

Futterer interpreted this to mean that he would discover the Ark of the Covenant in 1927. After uncovering the Ark he planned "to build a Tourist Resort here out of these already prepared stones of old ruins." His pamphlet solicited funds for the project, asking,

"What will you give to see the lost Ark restored to Jerusalem? Will you help us materially?"[39]

What became of the funds Futterer collected, we do not know. That the tourist resort was never built can be considered fact.

Yet, to his credit, Futterer never claimed to have actually discovered the Ark, though in his second book entitled *Palestine Speaks*, published in 1931, he stated that he still believed that the Ark was to be found there.

A close friend of Futterer's, a minister named Clinton Locy, fell heir to Futterer's papers. In 1981, a Kansas resident named Tom Crotser visited the aging Reverend Locy and obtained a copy of the inscription that Futterer had taken from the wall on Mount Nebo. According to Crotser, the inscription read, "Herein lies the Ark of the Covenant."

From Reverend Locy, Crotser also obtained a sketch that Futterer had made showing where the cave was located.

Tom Crotser and the Ark

Crotser and three associates proceeded to Jordan to discover for themselves the Ark of the Covenant, perhaps the most precious relic in the world. The full story is told in an article published by the *Biblical Archeology Review* (*BAR*) which took a rather dim view of the whole affair. The article relates that in October of 1981, Crotser and his companions spent four days in the Mount Nebo area, sleeping in sleeping bags. On Mount Pisgah, they found a depression, or crevice, which they believed to be the cave opening identified in Futterer's sketch. Without any permits from the Jordanian government, the "Ark Raiders" removed a tin sheet covering the opening and proceeded into a passageway at 2:00 a.m. on October 31, 1981, the third night of their stay.

Crotser estimates that the initial passageway was 600 feet long, four to six feet wide and about seven feet high. It led through several room-like enlargements with numerous tomb openings on both sides containing two or three levels of tombs. In the course of their exploration, Crotser and his associates illegally broke though two walls. The walls were made of mud and rock mixed together, sort of like cement, according to Crotser. He believed that someone had been there not long before, and had plugged up the passageways.

At the end of these passageways, Crotser and his friends encountered a third wall, more substantial than the ones they had already broken through. They found no inscriptions, as Futterer had described, but they broke through the wall anyway with hand picks. They cut a four feet by four feet opening in the wall, which led them into a rock-hewn chamber measuring about seven feet by seven feet. Crotser estimated that this chamber was directly beneath an old Byzantine church that stands on the very summit of the mountain, and was connected to the church by a vertical shaft.

It was here in this chamber that Crotser claims to have seen the Ark of the Covenant. He described it as a gold-covered, rectangular box measuring 62 inches long, 37 inches wide, and 37 inches high. Wisely, they did not touch the box, though they took photographs, measured it and took notes.

The golden cherubim were not on the lid, as often depicted. In the corner were some gauze-covered packages that Crotser took to be the golden statues of the angels. He did not touch the packages, so he was unable to confirm his suspicion. He also noticed that poles to carry the Ark lay beside it, and that gold rings for holding the poles were fastened to the sides.[39]

Crotser and his companions then departed for Amman, where they unsuccessfully attempted to interest the Jordanian authorities in their important discovery. They then flew back to Kansas and reported their find.

The UPI bureau in Kansas was quite interested in Crotser's unusual announcement that he had discovered the Ark of the Covenant, and released it to the world's newspapers the next day, creating something of an instant scandal. Crotser showed his photos to reporters, but refused to allow them to be printed or broadcast for reasons we will visit shortly. However, he later published them in a book entitled *Elijah, Rothschilds and the Ark of the Covenant.*[40] They are also reprinted in this book.

One person to view Crotser's photos of the supposed Ark of the Covenant is the well-known archaeologist Siegfried H. Horn, who was asked to check into Crotser's claims by a number of interested groups. Only one of the slides was clear enough to give Horn a good view of the box.

From memory, Horn drew a description of the box from the slide, and noted a few telltale details. Horn decided that the box in Crotser's slides was quite modern, noting such details as the heads of nails and the regularity of machine-produced decorative strips. Said Mr. Horn, "I became convinced that the object he had found is a comparatively modern box covered with metal sheets and strips."[39]

The ramifications of Crotser's wild expedition in search of the Ark of the Covenant were quite far-reaching. For one thing, the Jordanian government canceled all archaeological expeditions to that country as a direct result of Crotser's claim. Then, a staff member of *Biblical Archaeological Review* resigned because of the article run in that magazine, which the member stated exhibited poor journalism and had slandered Jordan because of Jordan's refusal to allow any more archaeological expeditions.

More importantly, what of Crotser's claims, and what did he really find? It is quite possible that Crotser fabricated the entire story as well as the "modern ark" of which he took photos. This possibility is not even addressed in the *Biblical Archaeological Review (BAR)* article, perhaps out of respect and politeness to Crotser. The *BAR* article simply asks, what was it that Crotser and friends photographed in the sealed room they illegally entered on

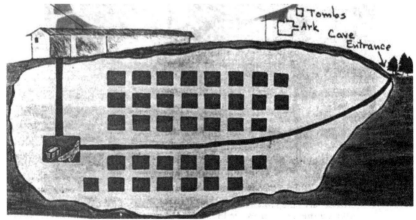

Tom Crotser's map of the cavern system beneath the monastery on Mount Pisgah.

Tom Crotser's picture of the ark that he photographed in a cave in Jordan.

that night of October 31, 1981?

No one has an answer, but one suspects that whatever it was, it was known to the Byzantine Church directly above it. Was it a copy of the Ark, or a box containing some other sacred relics? We may never know. If there really was something of great importance in that chamber, you can probably bet that the Jordanian government has it now. It may have been more than embarrassment that made them cancel all archaeological expeditions to the country.

If the Jordanian government had the Ark of the Covenant, would they acknowledge the fact? Probably not, for political reasons. The Israelis would gain a great boost by its discovery, one would think. And the general instability of the Middle East might be a reason to keep it a secret, if by a remote chance the Jordanian government now had the Ark.

Crotser's story gets even more bizarre when we discover his claims that God told him to only release the photos of the Ark to London banker David Rothschild. Crotser claims that Rothschild is a direct descendant of Jesus and is to rebuild Solomon's Temple.[39, 40] The Ark would then be put in Rothschild's restored temple.

Rothschild, part of the dynastic French- British- Jewish banking family that has controlled Europe's monetary wealth for hundreds of years, will have nothing to do with Crotser.[39] It is interesting to note here that the Rothschilds are a key element in nearly every banking conspiracy book ever written, and have strong links to the so-called Illuminati.

It is also worth noting that according to the New Testament book of Revelations, the final world battle of Armageddon is to occur after the Third Temple is built, which is exactly what Crotser claimed Rothschild should do. As time has marched on from Crotser's early claims clearly the Ark has not surfaced, nor did the Rothchilds fund the building of the Third Temple. Most believe Crotsers claims to be a hoax, probably to raise funds for his self-styled church and expeditions.

A similar Ark hunter was Ron Wyatt (1933-1999) who was originally drawn to another ark—in this case Noah's ark—which he believed was a large boat-shaped structure he identified at the Durupinar site near Mount Ararat in northeastern Turkey.

Having "discovered" that ark, Wyatt turned to looking for the Ark of the Covenant, which he believed was in sealed chambers near the Temple Mount.

Wyatt was a devout Seventh Day Adventist and he won a devoted following among some fundamentalist Christians, but he was not considered a professional archaeologist, and biblical scholars largely disparaged his various expeditions and claims. In addition to Noah's ark, Wyatt claimed to have found the graves of Noah and his wife, the site of the Tower of Babel, the location of Sodom and Gomorrah and brimstone balls from their destruction, and the site of Jesus' crucifixion.

Eventually Wyatt began digging a pit in the Garden Tomb in Jerusalem because he believed that it would connect to a maze of tunnels beneath the Temple Mount which contained a number of treasures from Solomon's Temple, including the Ark of the Covenant. According to Wikipedia, the Garden Tomb Association of Jerusalem state in a letter they issue to visitors on request:

> The Council of the Garden Tomb Association (London) totally refute the claim of Mr. Wyatt to have discovered the

original Ark of the Covenant or any other biblical artifacts within the boundaries of the area known as the Garden Tomb Jerusalem. Though Mr. Wyatt was allowed to dig within this privately owned garden on a number of occasions (the last occasion being the summer of 1991) staff members of the Association observed his progress and entered his excavated shaft. As far as we are aware nothing was ever discovered to support his claims nor have we seen any evidence of biblical artifacts or temple treasures.

Wyatt's efforts did not yield an entrance to his theorized tunnel system beneath the Temple Mount, and he died in 1999 in Memphis, Tennessee of cancer without proving any of his major theories.

More Tales of Discovering the Ark of the Covenant

Larry Blaser, a Seventh Day Adventist from Englewood, Colorado, also believed that he had discovered the resting place of the Ark of the Covenant. Blaser decided that the book of Maccabees, in the Apocrypha, which tells of Jeremiah hiding the Ark on Mount Nebo, is not accurate. Blaser concluded that the Ark could not have been hidden on Mount Nebo because Mount Nebo was too far from Jerusalem, being beyond the borders of Judah, across the Jordan River. He came to believe that the Ark was hidden near the Dead Sea in "David's Cave" where David had hidden from King Saul and his army with his own six hundred soldiers.

Near En-Gedi, the ancient Essene retreat on the Dead Sea, is a cave locally called "David's Cave," but Blaser believed that this cave could not be the actual cavern that David and his army hid in; it was far too small and afforded little in the way of protection or shelter. Therefore, the real cave was still to be found somewhere in the hills, and inside it, Blaser reasoned, lay the Ark of the Covenant.[38, 42]

After a preliminary scouting trip in 1976, Blaser returned in 1977 with Frank Ruskey, a geophysical engineer, and Richard Budick, an engineering geology technician, in order to conduct a thorough geophysical investigation to find a hidden cave on the En-Gedi nature reserve. From the resistivity work and the seismic survey, combined with visual observations of the area, the scientists concluded that there was indeed a cave-like void, possibly twenty feet high, fifteen to twenty feet wide, and several hundred feet deep, with tunnels branching out like a two-pronged fork. Further visual investigation confirmed the initial impression that the cave had two possible entrances–both blocked–about ten to fifteen meters (30 to 45 feet) apart.[38]

This was a large cave indeed. At it was found what appeared to be a man-made wall. Man-made works around the cave included a system designed to divert seasonal runoff water over the entrance of the cave, thereby concealing it and calcifying the entrance at the same time. Blaser, Ruskey and Burdick returned in 1979 with the author Rene Noorbergen and scholarly archaeologists, like Dr. James F. Strange of the University of South Florida, to attempt to open the cave. Dr. Strange did not believe that the Ark would be found in the cave, but felt that any cave in the area was worth exploring, especially given the important discoveries of the Essene "Dead Sea Scrolls" in caves nearby between 1947 and 1956.

Unfortunately, it proved impossible to enter the cave. A huge boulder blocked the entrance to the cave system. Without the use of dynamite, expressly forbidden by Israeli authorities as the area is a nature reserve, there was no way to enter the cave system, which further soundings indicated was genuinely there.[38,42] The expedition returned to the United States empty-handed, and another group of "Ark Raiders" became history.

What is interesting in reading the stories of those who would be "Raiders of the Lost Ark" in the scholarly journal *Biblical Archaeology Review* (which published several such articles) is the obvious disdain that the academic scholars seem to have for such pursuits. Admittedly, Crotser's quest for the Ark led Jordan to cancel all foreign archaeological research in the country, yet for what specific reason? *BAR* itself states:

> It is well known, however, that the Jordanians do not want any Biblical discoveries made in Jordan.

They also point out that no mention of discovering the Ark was given to the Israeli authorities by Blaser when his group sought permission to enter the En-Gedi cave. What is obvious here, as *BAR* alludes, is that anyone seeking permission to excavate for the Ark of the Covenant would never get a permit either from the Israeli government, or the Jordanian. Therefore, only "Raiders" would be able to search for the Ark. A legitimate attempt would be doomed by red tape.

Is the Ark of the Covenant inside the strange cave system near En-Gedi? We may never know. Perhaps there is another entrance, still cleverly concealed. *BAR* says that no person, not even animals, ever entered those caves. How do they know?

A Strange Story from WWII

Rene Noorbergen, who accompanied Blaser on his 1979 caving expedition, relates a fascinating story in his book *Treasures of the Lost Races*.[38] In 1944, says Noorbergen, part of Rommel's North Afrika Corps split away from Rommel's army as it disintegrated. They stabbed northeast and attempted to reach the Balkan states by going around Jerusalem to the east and into Syria and Turkey. Aware of their plans, the Allied High Command dispatched roving armored units to the area east of Jerusalem to intercept them.

On one night, a small American unit was camped in a narrow valley east of Jerusalem when it was strafed and bombed by a German dive bomber. When one of the explosives hit the side of a cliff, it opened a small hole in the rock, exposing a cave. Scrambling for shelter, several men clawed their way through the opening and into the cave. As their eyes grew accustomed to the darkness, they saw "a coffin with what looked like two angels with outstretched wings on top. It had been covered with cloth which had disintegrated and was now hanging down like torn cobwebs..."[38]

Investigating the story, Noorbergen discovered that an army chaplain by the name of Captain Diefenbach had told this same story; he had been assigned to the 28th Field Hospital in Palestine in 1944. Noorbergen attempted to find Diefenbach during his research into the Ark in the 1970s, but unfortunately learned that Captain Diefenbach had died on June 10, 1957. No other information was to be found about him, not even a list of relatives. Even his army records were accidentally destroyed in a fire. Noorbergen's quest for the Ark via Diefenbach came to a sudden end.

The Ark of the Covenant and the Rebuilding of the Temple

Most of the self-styled Ark Raiders are fundamentalist Christians who believe that the Ark of the Covenant is still in the Middle East somewhere, probably hidden inside tunnels beneath the Temple Mount and Wailing Wall, at which many orthodox Jews pray.

One quest along these lines was featured in a book entitled *In Search of Temple Treasures*.[23] The author, Randall Price, is a minister from Austin, Texas, who is clearly fascinated with end-times prophecy, the rebuilding of Solomon's Temple and the Ark of the Covenant.

Like a similar Baptist minister, Vendyl Jones (1930-2010), Price believed that the Old Testament predicted that the Ark of the Covenant would be rediscovered, and then the Jews would rebuild the temple and place the Ark of the Covenant in a new specially-built chamber called, as in antiquity, the Holy of Holies. The Messiah and the prophet Elijah would then enter the temple through the eastern gateway, the ruins of which are now walled up. Price points out that a Muslim graveyard is now in front of this walled-up eastern gate, and this is to prevent Elijah from entering the gate; crossing a cemetery would defile him since he is a priest.

Price and Jones get part of this belief from a brief paragraph in a pseudepigraphal book called *The Lives of the Prophets*.[31] This is an ancient text puporting to be contemporaneous with the people it describes, but was actually written later. In chaper 2, verse 15, we read:

> At the end-time the Ark, with the stone tablets, will resurrect first: it will come out of the rock and be placed on Mount Sinai. There the saints will assemble to receive the lord.

Vendyl Jones.

According to his Wikipedia page, Price has served as Director of Excavations on the Qumran Plateau in Israel (site of the community that preserved the Dead Sea Scrolls) since 2002, and has excavated at other sites in Israel since 1990. He is the author of over 20 books and DVDs and *In Search of Temple Treasures* was published in 1994.

He says in his book that he thinks that the Ark was originally stored in the Qumran caves by Jeremiah just prior to the Babylonian destruction of the temple. He and a Dr. Gary Collett, who was doing excavations at Qumran in the early 1990s, believe that the Ark was then removed from the caves and placed in a secret chamber beneath the Temple Mount.

Price describes himself as a Christian Zionist and is the president of World of the Bible Ministries, Inc., in Texas. This is a "non-profit organization doing research in the biblical lands and educating the public on archaeological, biblical issues and the Middle East conflict through books, media, and conferences."

Since writing his 1994 book, Price continued archeological work at Qumran and according to his Wikipedia post (apparently written by himself), in 2009, he drew media attention because of an expedition to Turkey to find Noah's ark. He returned to Turkey in 2010 where he accused a competing search team—who claimed to have discovered Noah's ark—of fraud and fabricating evidence.

The other team accused Price of fraud, and the verbal sparring has yet to come to an end.

The fact that he has not found the Ark of the Covenant yet does not seem to have dampened Price's Christian-Zionist beliefs, though perhaps he does not think that the Messiah's return is as imminent as he did in the 1990s.

Like Price, Vendyl Jones spent decades in Israel and Jordan searching for the temple treasures listed in the Copper Scroll that was one of the Dead Sea Scrolls discovered at Qumran in 1952. The obituary for Jones in the *Bible News Daily* (April 18, 2011) said:

> Vendyl Jones, a Baptist minister turned amateur archaeologist who spent a career in Israel searching for the Ark of the Covenant, passed away in December. He was 80 years old.
>
> Often rumored to be the inspiration for Indiana Jones, "Vendy" Jones spent more than four decades scouring the Judean desert for the Ark as well as the priceless treasures listed on the famous Copper Scroll, thought by many to record the locations of the hidden treasures of the Jerusalem Temple.
>
> While Jones found neither the Ark nor any of the tons of gold and silver mentioned in the Copper Scroll, he did manage to find more than 600 pounds of a unique reddish powder in a Judean desert cave, a substance that he said might have been the *qetoret* (or incense) used during Temple rituals and observances. During another expedition, his volunteers helped archaeologists Joseph Patrich and Benny Arubas uncover a small first-century CE juglet containing an oily liquid that some, including Jones, speculated was the oil used to anoint the priests and kings of ancient Jerusalem.
>
> Despite his Baptist background, Jones eventually became a Noahide, a follower of the Jewish tradition that all non-Jews (i.e., all mankind), as descendants of Noah, are obligated to obey the seven laws given by God to Noah after the flood. The seven laws, most of which are similar to the Ten Commandments, are found in the Talmud.

According to Wikipedia, Jones conducted eight excavations at the Dead Sea Scrolls location of Qumran. Also:

> Jones believed his archaeology to have eschatological significance, and that when he found the ancient religious items he was looking for, God would be revealed to the world, all Jews will return to Israel, and there would be peace in the Middle East. Also, Israeli democracy will be replaced by a Sanhedrin, not unlike the group that was formed by various Israeli rabbis in 2004, and with which Jones was closely associated. In May 2005, it was reported that he had consulted with Kabbalists and that he believed he would find the Ark of the Covenant by August 14, 2005, the anniversary of the destruction of the Jerusalem Temple. However, as the date approached and passed he claimed that this was a misquote. He then hoped that a drill-hole bore would reveal the Ark's location in September, but was prevented from proceeding due to lack of funds and the need for another environmental study required by the government.

Jones died in 2011 and his dream of finding the Ark never came true. As seen above, it has been surmised by some that Vendyl Jones was the inspiration for the movie character of Indiana Jones, but according to Wikipedia, George Lucas came up with the name as a combination of his Alaskan malamut's name, Indiana, and the Steve McQueen character in the movie *Nevada Smith*. Steven Spielberg changed the name from Indiana Smith to Indiana Jones.

The Final Quest

Tales of the lost Ark of the Covenant are many and contradictory. As we know, in the film *Raiders of the Lost Ark*, the Ark is taken by the Egyptians and placed in the city of Tanis, which is then buried in a sandstorm, until uncovered by the Nazis and Indiana Jones. This is mere fanciful storytelling. However, there is some truth to the story, as the Nazis were indeed after quite a few ancient, mystical relics, and the Ark of the Covenant was probably one of them.

It is known to historians (though rarely related by them in more mundane histories of the Third Reich) that the Nazis sought the Spear of Destiny (which they actually obtained, it now being in the National Museum in Vienna), the Chintamani Stone taken to Tibet by Nicholas Roerich (see my book, *Lost Cities of China, Central Asia & India*[73]) and other sacred relics reputed to have magical powers. Hitler's quest to actually harness the power of the supernatural in a bid for world domination is a little over the top, but is emblematic of all of mankind's eternal search for the eternal, our quest to know the power and magic of the divine.

Could the Ark of the Covenant have survived until today? It seems unlikely that such a beautiful gold statue would be melted into ingots. Unless lost in some cavern or sealed chamber, it could be in the secret possession of some government or secret society. Could it be in a government warehouse or in some fabulous private collection? Perhaps locked away in a remote monastic church? Is it still in the vicinity of Jerusalem? Or was it taken in antiquity to Ethiopia, France, Ireland or Scotand?

Many Arks—One Ark of God

There were many arks, which were boxes used by the Egyptians, Hittites, Babylonians and others to hold gods or deities with which to go into battle with a large army. The chosen god, in one of his aspects, would be personified in a golden statue that would rally the soldiers on to victory, knowing the power of this god was with them and they should not fail. Egyptian armies were well known to march an ark of their god, typically Amun or Horus, into battle as an insignia and focus point. Modern day mascots are the last relic of this ancient practice.

Every year at the Timkat Festival in Ethiopia, which is the Ethiopian Orthodox celebration of Jesus' baptism, thousands of arks are brought out of churches. It is celebrated on January 19 every year, which corresponds to the 10th day of Terr on the Ethiopian calendar. During the ceremonies of Timkat, the Tabot, a model of the Ark of the Covenant, which is present in every Ethiopian church, is wrapped in rich cloth and brought forth in procession and then returned to the church.

But there was only one Ark of God—a powerful electrical device that was feared by friend and foe alike. With today's sophisticated weapons we are capable of electrocuting people from great distances, and electronic warfare is at the cutting edge of military spending. This Ark of the Covenant, which seems to have had similar powers, was not an object to be taken lightly, and it would seem that a secret priesthood was entrusted with the object many thousands of years ago and may be still keeping watch over it today. But where would that special place of residence be? It is interesting to see how the obsession with the Ark of the Covenant spans not just centuries, but millennia and continues to this day.

The New Testament, in Hebrews, describes a time when the need for the tabernacle and its physical wonders, including the Ark of the Covenant and the need for a human priesthood, will cease to exist. Under a "new covenant" people will come to know for themselves the truth of spiritual matters without outward inspiration and the use of "miraculous" signs. Says Hebrews 8:8-12:

> See, the days are coming—it is the Lord who speaks— when I will establish a new covenant with the House of Israel and the House of Judah, but not a covenant like the one I made with their ancestors on the day I took them by the hand to bring them out of the land of Egypt. They abandoned that covenant of mine, and so I on my side deserted them. No, this is the covenant I will make with the House of Israel when those days arrive. I will put my laws into their minds and write them on their hearts. Then I will be their God and they shall be my people. There will be no further need for neighbor to try to teach neighbor, or brother to say to brother, "Learn to know the Lord." No, they will all know me, the least no less than the greatest, since I will forgive their iniquities and never call their sins to mind.

FOOTNOTES &
BIBLIOGRAPHY

1. *The Ark of the Covenant*, Roderick Grierson and Stuart Munro-Hay, 1999, Weidenfield and Nicholson, London.
2. *Kingdoms of Asia, the Middle East & Africa*, Gene Gurney, 1986, Crown Publishers. NYC.
3. *Secrets of the Lost Races*, Rene Noorbergen, 1977, Harper & Row, NY.
4. *The Sign and the Seal*, Graham Hancock, 1992, Crown Publishers, NY.
5. *The Lost Ark of the Covenant*, Tudor Parfitt, 2008, Harper Collins, NY.
6. *Petra*, E. Raymond Capt, 1987, Artisan Sales, Thousand Oaks, CA.
7. *Vanished Cities*, Hermann & Georg Schreiber, 1957, Alfred A. Knopf, NYC.
8. *Explorers Extraordinary*, John Keay, 1986, Jeremy Tarcher Inc, LosAngeles.
9. *Legends of the Jews*, Louis Ginzberg, 1911, Vol. 3, Jewish Publication Society of America, Philadelphia.
10. *The Search For Lost Cities*, James Wellard, 1980, Constable & Co. London.
11. *The Gold of Exodus*, Howard Blum, 1998, Simon & Schuster, NYC.
12. *Atlas of Ancient History*, Michael Grant, 1971, Dorset Press, Dorset, England.
13. *Kebra Nagast*, translated by Sir E. A. Wallis Budge, 1932, Dover, London.
14. *Atlas of the Ancient World,* edited by Frances Clapham, 1979, Crescent Books, NYC.
15. *Lost Cities of China, Central Asia & India*, David Hatcher Childress, 1985, AUP, Kempton, IL.

297

Bibliography and Footnotes

16. *The Phoenicians*, Gerhard Herm, 1975, William Morrow & Co. NYC.

17. *Peoples of the Sea*, Immanuel Velikovsky, 1977, Doubleday & Co. Garden City, NY.

18. *Kingdom of the Ark*, Lorraine Evans, 2000, Simon and Schuster, London.

19. *Ethiopia, Djibouti & Somaliland*, 2013, Lonely Planet Books Ltd, London.

20. *The Disappearance of the Ark*, M. Haran, IEJ 13 (1963), p.46-58.

21. *Saga America*, Barry Fell, 1983, Times Books, NYC.

22. *The Enigma of Cranial Deformation,* David Childress and Brien Foerster, 2012, AUP, Kempton, IL.

23. *In Search of Temple Treasures*, Randall Price, 1994, Harvest House, Eugene, OR.

24. *We Are Not the First*, Andrew Tomas, 1971, Souvenir Press, London.

25. *Holy Blood, Holy Grail*, Michael Baigent, Richard Leigh, and Henry Lincoln, 1982, Random House, London and New York.

26. *Ancient Ethiopia*, David W. Phillipson, 1998, British Museum Press, London.

27. *The Bible As History*, Werner Keller, 1956, William Morrow & Co. NYC.

28. *Wonders of Ancient Chinese Science*, Robert Silverburg, 1969, Ballantine Books, NYC.

29. *Anti-Gravity & the World Grid*, David Hatcher Childress, 1987, AUP, Kempton, IL.

30. *Technology of the Gods*, David Hatcher Childress, 1999, AUP, Kempton, IL.

31. *The Lives of the Prophets*, from *The Old Testament Pseudepigraph*, translated by D.R.A. Hare, 1985, Doubleday Co., NY.

32. *Remarkable Luminous Phenomena in Nature*, William Corliss, 2001, Sourcebook Project, Glen Arm, MD.

33. *Ancient Man: A Handbook of Puzzling Artifacts*, William Corliss, 1978, Sourcebook Project, Glen Arm, MD.

34. *Ball Lightning Explanation Leading to Clean Energy*, Clint Seward, 2011, Amazon.com

35. *Lost Cities of Ancient Lemuria & the Pacific*, David Hatcher Childress, 1988, AUP, Kempton, IL.

36. *Electric UFOs*, Albert Budden, 1998, Blandford Books, London.

37. *Vimana: Flying Machines of the Ancients*, David Hatcher Childress, 2013, AUP, Kempton, IL.

38. *Treasures of the Lost Races*, Rene Noorbergen, 1982, Bobbs-Merrill Co. NYC

39. *Biblical Archaeological Review*, May-June 1983

40. *Elijah, Rothschilds and the Ark of the Covenant*, Tom Crotser and Jeremiah Patrick, 1983, Restoration Press, Frankston, TX.

41. *Altai Himalaya*, Nicholas Roerich, 1929, Roerich Museum, New York.

42. *Biblical Archaeological Review*, July-August, 1983.

43. *What the Bible Really Says*, Manfred Barthel, 1982, Souvenir Press, London.

44. *The Treasure of the Copper Scroll*, John Allegro, 1960, Doubleday, NYC.

45. *6000 Years of Seafaring*, Orville Hope, 1983, Hope Associates, Gastonia, NC.

46. *Ships and Seamanship in the Ancient World*, Lionel Casson, 1971, Princeton University Press, Princeton, NJ.47. The Bible As History, Werner Keller, 1956, William Morrow, NYC.

48. *Secrets of the Bible Seas*, Alexander Flinder, 1985, Severn House, London.

49. *The Maldive* Mystery, Thor Heyerdahl, 1986, Adler and Adler, Bethesda, MD.

50. *War in Ancient India*, Ramachandra Dikshitar, 1944, Motilal Banarsidass, Delhi.

51. *Investigating the Unexplained*, Ivan T. Sanderson, 1972, Prentice Hall, Englewood Cliffs, NJ.
52. *The Ancient Secret: Fire from the Sun*, Flavia Anderson, 1953, R.I.L.K.O. Books, Orpington, Kent, England.
53. *The Yahweh Encounters*, Ann Madden Jones 1995, Sandbird Publishing, Chapel Hill, NC.
54. *Laserbeams from Star Cities*, Robyn Collins, 1971, Sphere Books, London.
55. *Secret Cities of Old South America*, Harold Wilkins, 1952, London, reprinted 1998, Adventures Unlimited Press, Kempton, Illinois.
56. *The Classic Tales: 4.000 Years of Jewish Lore*, Ellen Frankel, 1996, Jason Aronson, NYC.
57. *Ark of the Covenant, Holy Grail*, Henrietta Bernstein, 1998, DeVorss Publications, Marina del Rey, CA.
58. *The Riddle of the Pyramids*, Kurt Mendelssohn, Thames & Hudson, London.
59. *Nefertiti*, Philipp Vandenberg, 1978, Hodder and Stoughton, London.
60. *Lost Cities of Ancient Lemuria & the Pacific*, David Hatcher Childress, 1988, AUP, Kempton, IL.
61. *Investigating the Unexplained*, Ivan T. Sanderson, 1972, Prentice Hall, Englewood Cliffs, NJ.
62. *The Magic of Obelisks*, Peter Tompkins, 1981, Harper & Row, NYC\.
63. *Secrets of the Great Pyramid*, Peter Tompkins, 1971, Harper & Row, NYC\.
64. *Egypt Before the Pharaohs*, Michael A. Hoffman, 1979, Alfred Knopf, NYC\.
65. *Magi: The Quest for a Secret Tradition*, Adrian Gilbert, 1996, Bloomsbury, London.
66. *Irish Druids and Old Irish Religions*, James Bonwick, 1894, reprinted by Dorset Press, 1986.
67. *Irish Symbols of 3500 B.C.*, N.L. Thomas, 1988, Mercier Press, Dublin.

68. *The Search for the Stone of Destiny*, Pat Gerber, 1992, Cannongate Press, Edinburgh.
69. *Tara and the Ark of the Covenant: A Search for the Ark of the Covenant by British Israelites on the Hill of Tara, 1899-1902*, Mairead Carew, Royal Irish Academy, 2003.
70. *The Mysteries of Chartres Cathedral*, Louis Charpentier, 1980, Avon Books, NYC.
71. *The Templars and the Ark of the Covenant: The Discovery of the Treasure of Solomon*, Graham Phillips, 2003, Bear & Company, Rochester, VT.
72. *Egyptian Myth and Legend*, Donald Mackenzie, 1907, Bell Publishers, NYC.
73. *Lost Cities of China, Central Asia & India*, David Hatcher Childress, 1985, AUP, Kempton, IL.
74. *Nazca: Journey to the Sun*, Jim Woodman, 1977, Simon and Schuster, NYC.
75. *Where Moses Stood*, Robert Feather, 2014, Copper Scroll, London.
76. *Mystery of the Ancient Seafarers*, Robert D. Ballard, 2004, National Geographic Society, Washington DC.
77. *The Lost Cities of Africa*, Basil Davidson, 1959, Atlantic-Little, Brown Co., Boston.
78. *In Quest of Lost Worlds*, Count Byron de Prorok, 1935, E.P. Dutton & Co, `NYC.
79. *The Taste of Conquest*, Michael Krondl, 2007, Random House, New York.
80. *The World's Last Mysteries,* Nigel Blundell, 1980, Octopus Books, London.
81. *Citta Perdute nel Deserto*, Cino Boccazzi, 1977, SugarCo Edizioni, Milan, Italy.
82. *YHWH*, Jerry Ziegler, 1985, Star Publishers, Morton, Illinois.
83. *The Bible Came from Arabia*, Kamal Salibi, 1985, Pan Books, London.
84. *Arabia*, Jonathan Raban, 1979, Picador, London.
85. *Arabian Sands*, Wilfred Thesiger, 1959, Penguin Books, NYC.

86. *Oman*, John Whelan, 1981, MEED Books, London.
87. *Qataban and Sheba*, Wendell Phillips, 1955, Harcourt, Brace & Co., NYC.
88. *The Queen of Sheba*, H. St. John Philby, 1981, Quartet Books, London.
89. *Indra Girt by Maruts*, Jerry Ziegler, 1994, Next Millennium Publishers, Stamford, CT.
90. *Ka: A Handbook of Mythology, Sacred Practices, Electrical Phenomena, and their Linguistic Connections in the Ancient World*, H. Crosthwaite, 1992, Metron Publlications, Princeton, NJ.
91. *Lost Technologies of Ancient Egypt*, Christopher Dunn, 2010, Bear & Company, Rochester, VT.
92. *The Giza Power Plant*, Christopher Dunn, 1998, Bear & Company, Rochester, VT.
93. *Picture-Writing of the American Indians*, Garrick Mallory, 1889, Smithsonian Institute, Reprinted by Dover Books.
94. *The Cosmic Serpent*, Meremy Narby, 1998, Jeremy Tarcher, New York.
95. *The Ark, the Shroud, and Mary*, Philip Gardiner, 2007, New Page Books, Franklin Lakes, NJ.
96. *Travels in Ethiopia*, David Buxton, 1949, Ernest Benn Ltd. London.
97. *Phoencians*, Glen Markoe, 2000, University of California Press, Berkeley.

Get these fascinating books from your nearest bookstore or directly from: Adventures Unlimited Press

www.adventuresunlimitedpress.com

DEATH ON MARS
The Discovery of a Planetary Nuclear Massacre
By John E. Brandenburg, Ph.D.

New proof of a nuclear catastrophe on Mars! In an epic story of discovery, strong evidence is presented for a dead civilization on Mars and the shocking reason for its demise: an ancient planetary-scale nuclear massacre leaving isotopic traces of vast explosions that endure to our present age. The story told by a wide range of Mars data is now clear. Mars was once Earth-like in climate, with an ocean and rivers, and for a long period became home to both plant and animal life, including a humanoid civilization. Then, for unfathomable reasons, a massive thermo-nuclear explosion ravaged the centers of the Martian civilization and destroyed the biosphere of the planet. But the story does not end there. This tragedy may explain Fermi's Paradox, the fact that the cosmos, seemingly so fertile and with so many planets suitable for life, is as silent as a graveyard.

278 Pages. 6x9 Paperback. Illustrated. Bibliography. Color Section. $19.95. Code: DOM

BEYOND EINSTEIN'S UNIFIED FIELD
Gravity and Electro-Magnetism Redefined
By John Brandenburg, Ph.D.

Brandenburg reveals the GEM Unification Theory that proves the mathematical and physical interrelation of the forces of gravity and electromagnetism! Brandenburg describes control of space-time geometry through electromagnetism, and states that faster-than-light travel will be possible in the future. Anti-gravity through electromagnetism is possible, which upholds the basic "flying saucer" design utilizing "The Tesla Vortex." Chapters include: Squaring the Circle, Einstein's Final Triumph; A Book of Numbers and Forms; Kepler, Newton and the Sun King; Magnus and Electra; Atoms of Light; Einstein's Glory, Relativity; The Aurora; Tesla's Vortex and the Cliffs of Zeno; The Hidden 5th Dimension; The GEM Unification Theory; Anti-Gravity and Human Flight; The New GEM Cosmos; more. Includes an 8-page color section.

312 Pages. 6x9 Paperback. Illustrated. $18.95. Code: BEUF

VIMANA:
Flying Machines of the Ancients
by David Hatcher Childress

According to early Sanskrit texts the ancients had several types of airships called vimanas. Like aircraft of today, vimanas were used to fly through the air from city to city; to conduct aerial surveys of uncharted lands; and as delivery vehicles for awesome weapons. David Hatcher Childress, popular *Lost Cities* author and star of the History Channel's long-running show Ancient Aliens, takes us on an astounding investigation into tales of ancient flying machines. In his new book, packed with photos and diagrams, he consults ancient texts and modern stories and presents astonishing evidence that aircraft, similar to the ones we use today, were used thousands of years ago in India, Sumeria, China and other countries. Includes a 24-page color section.

408 Pages. 6x9 Paperback. Illustrated. $22.95. Code: VMA

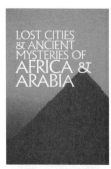

LOST CITIES & ANCIENT MYSTERIES OF AFRICA & ARABIA
by David Hatcher Childress

Childress continues his world-wide quest for lost cities and ancient mysteries. Join him as he discovers forbidden cities in the Empty Quarter of Arabia; "Atlantean" ruins in Egypt and the Kalahari desert; a mysterious, ancient empire in the Sahara; and more. This is the tale of an extraordinary life on the road: across war-torn countries, Childress searches for King Solomon's Mines, living dinosaurs, the Ark of the Covenant and the solutions to some of the fantastic mysteries of the past.
423 PAGES. 6x9 PAPERBACK. ILLUSTRATED. $14.95. CODE: AFA

LOST CITIES OF ATLANTIS, ANCIENT EUROPE & THE MEDITERRANEAN
by David Hatcher Childress

Childress takes the reader in search of sunken cities in the Mediterranean; across the Atlas Mountains in search of Atlantean ruins; to remote islands in search of megalithic ruins; to meet living legends and secret societies. From Ireland to Turkey, Morocco to Eastern Europe, and around the remote islands of the Mediterranean and Atlantic, Childress takes the reader on an astonishing quest for mankind's past. Ancient technology, cataclysms, megalithic construction, lost civilizations and devastating wars of the past are all explored in this book.
524 PAGES. 6x9 PAPERBACK. ILLUSTRATED. $16.95. CODE: MED

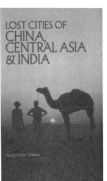

LOST CITIES OF CHINA, CENTRAL ASIA & INDIA
by David Hatcher Childress

Like a real life "Indiana Jones," maverick archaeologist David Childress takes the reader on an incredible adventure across some of the world's oldest and most remote countries in search of lost cities and ancient mysteries. Discover ancient cities in the Gobi Desert; hear fantastic tales of lost continents, vanished civilizations and secret societies bent on ruling the world; visit forgotten monasteries in forbidding snow-capped mountains with strange tunnels to mysterious subterranean cities! A unique combination of far-out exploration and practical travel advice, it will astound and delight the experienced traveler or the armchair voyager.
429 PAGES. 6x9 PAPERBACK. ILLUSTRATED. FOOTNOTES & BIBLIOGRAPHY. $14.95. CODE: CHI

LOST CITIES OF ANCIENT LEMURIA & THE PACIFIC
by David Hatcher Childress

Was there once a continent in the Pacific? Called Lemuria or Pacifica by geologists, Mu or Pan by the mystics, there is now ample mythological, geological and archaeological evidence to "prove" that an advanced and ancient civilization once lived in the central Pacific. Maverick archaeologist and explorer David Hatcher Childress combs the Indian Ocean, Australia and the Pacific in search of the surprising truth about mankind's past. Contains photos of the underwater city on Pohnpei; explanations on how the statues were levitated around Easter Island in a clockwise vortex movement; tales of disappearing islands; Egyptians in Australia; and more.
379 PAGES. 6x9 PAPERBACK. ILLUSTRATED. FOOTNOTES & BIBLIOGRAPHY. $14.95. CODE: LEM

THE COSMIC WAR
Interplanetary Warfare, Modern Physics, and Ancient Texts
By Joseph P. Farrell

There is ample evidence across our solar system of catastrophic events. The asteroid belt may be the remains of an exploded planet! The known planets are scarred from incredible impacts, and teeter in their orbits due to causes heretofore inadequately explained. Included: The history of the Exploded Planet hypothesis, and what mechanism can actually explode a planet. The role of plasma cosmology, plasma physics and scalar physics. The ancient texts telling of such destructions: from Sumeria (Tiamat's destruction by Marduk), Egypt (Edfu and the Mars connections), Greece (Saturn's role in the War of the Titans) and the ancient Americas.

436 Pages. 6x9 Paperback. Illustrated. Bibliography. $18.95. Code: COSW

TECHNOLOGY OF THE GODS
The Incredible Sciences of the Ancients
by David Hatcher Childress

Childress looks at the technology that was allegedly used in Atlantis and the theory that the Great Pyramid of Egypt was originally a gigantic power station. He examines tales of ancient flight and the technology that it involved; how the ancients used electricity; megalithic building techniques; the use of crystal lenses and the fire from the gods; evidence of various high tech weapons in the past, including atomic weapons; ancient metallurgy and heavy machinery; the role of modern inventors such as Nikola Tesla in bringing ancient technology back into modern use; impossible artifacts; and more.

356 PAGES. 6x9 PAPERBACK. ILLUSTRATED. BIBLIOGRAPHY. $16.95. CODE: TGOD

VIMANA AIRCRAFT OF ANCIENT INDIA & ATLANTIS
by David Hatcher Childress, introduction by Ivan T. Sanderson

In this incredible volume on ancient India, authentic Indian texts such as the *Ramayana* and the *Mahabharata* are used to prove that ancient aircraft were in use more than four thousand years ago. Included in this book is the entire Fourth Century BC manuscript *Vimaanika Shastra* by the ancient author Maharishi Bharadwaaja. Also included are chapters on Atlantean technology, the incredible Rama Empire of India and the devastating wars that destroyed it.

334 PAGES. 6x9 PAPERBACK. ILLUSTRATED. $15.95. CODE: VAA

LOST CONTINENTS & THE HOLLOW EARTH
I Remember Lemuria and the Shaver Mystery
by David Hatcher Childress & Richard Shaver

Shaver's rare 1948 book *I Remember Lemuria* is reprinted in its entirety, and the book is packed with illustrations from Ray Palmer's *Amazing Stories* magazine of the 1940s. Palmer and Shaver told of tunnels running through the earth—tunnels inhabited by the Deros and Teros, humanoids from an ancient spacefaring race that had inhabited the earth, eventually going underground, hundreds of thousands of years ago. Childress discusses the famous hollow earth books and delves deep into whatever reality may be behind the stories of tunnels in the earth. Operation High Jump to Antarctica in 1947 and Admiral Byrd's bizarre statements, tunnel systems in South America and Tibet, the underground world of Agartha, the belief of UFOs coming from the South Pole, more.

344 PAGES. 6x9 PAPERBACK. ILLUSTRATED. $16.95. CODE: LCHE

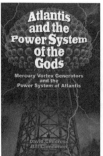

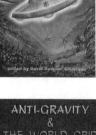

MAPS OF THE ANCIENT SEA KINGS
Evidence of Advanced Civilization in the Ice Age
by Charles H. Hapgood

Charles Hapgood has found the evidence in the Piri Reis Map that shows Antarctica, the Hadji Ahmed map, the Oronteus Finaeus and other amazing maps. Hapgood concluded that these maps were made from more ancient maps from the various ancient archives around the world, now lost. Not only were these unknown people more advanced in mapmaking than any people prior to the 18th century, it appears they mapped all the continents. The Americas were mapped thousands of years before Columbus. Antarctica was mapped when its coasts were free of ice!

316 PAGES. 7x10 PAPERBACK. ILLUSTRATED. BIBLIOGRAPHY & INDEX. $19.95. CODE: MASK

PATH OF THE POLE
Cataclysmic Pole Shift Geology
by Charles H. Hapgood

Maps of the Ancient Sea Kings author Hapgood's classic book *Path of the Pole* is back in print! Hapgood researched Antarctica, ancient maps and the geological record to conclude that the Earth's crust has slipped on the inner core many times in the past, changing the position of the pole. *Path of the Pole* discusses the various "pole shifts" in Earth's past, giving evidence for each one, and moves on to possible future pole shifts.

356 PAGES. 6x9 PAPERBACK. ILLUSTRATED. $16.95. CODE: POP

SECRETS OF THE HOLY LANCE
The Spear of Destiny in History & Legend
by Jerry E. Smith

Secrets of the Holy Lance traces the Spear from its possession by Constantine, Rome's first Christian Caesar, to Charlemagne's claim that with it he ruled the Holy Roman Empire by Divine Right, and on through two thousand years of kings and emperors, until it came within Hitler's grasp—and beyond! Did it rest for a while in Antarctic ice? Is it now hidden in Europe, awaiting the next person to claim its awesome power? Neither debunking nor worshiping, *Secrets of the Holy Lance* seeks to pierce the veil of myth and mystery around the Spear. Mere belief that it was infused with magic by virtue of its shedding the Savior's blood has made men kings. But what if it's more? What are "the powers it serves"?

312 PAGES. 6x9 PAPERBACK. ILLUSTRATED. BIBLIOGRAPHY. $16.95. CODE: SOHL

THE FANTASTIC INVENTIONS OF NIKOLA TESLA
by Nikola Tesla with additional material by
David Hatcher Childress

This book is a readable compendium of patents, diagrams, photos and explanations of the many incredible inventions of the originator of the modern era of electrification. In Tesla's own words are such topics as wireless transmission of power, death rays, and radio-controlled airships. In addition, rare material on a secret city built at a remote jungle site in South America by one of Tesla's students, Guglielmo Marconi. Marconi's secret group claims to have built flying saucers in the 1940s and to have gone to Mars in the early 1950s! Incredible photos of these Tesla craft are included. •His plan to transmit free electricity into the atmosphere. •How electrical devices would work using only small antennas. •Why unlimited power could be utilized anywhere on earth. •How radio and radar technology can be used as death-ray weapons in Star Wars.

342 PAGES. 6x9 PAPERBACK. ILLUSTRATED. $16.95. CODE: FINT

ANCIENT ALIENS ON THE MOON
By Mike Bara
What did NASA find in their explorations of the solar system that they may have kept from the general public? How ancient really are these ruins on the Moon? Using official NASA and Russian photos of the Moon, Bara looks at vast cityscapes and domes in the Sinus Medii region as well as glass domes in the Crisium region. Bara also takes a detailed look at the mission of Apollo 17 and the case that this was a salvage mission, primarily concerned with investigating an opening into a massive hexagonal ruin near the landing site. Chapters include: The History of Lunar Anomalies; The Early 20th Century; Sinus Medii; To the Moon Alice!; Mare Crisium; Yes, Virginia, We Really Went to the Moon; Apollo 17; more. Tons of photos of the Moon examined for possible structures and other anomalies.
248 Pages. 6x9 Paperback. Illustrated.. $19.95. Code: AAOM

ANCIENT ALIENS ON MARS
By Mike Bara
Bara brings us this lavishly illustrated volume on alien structures on Mars. Was there once a vast, technologically advanced civilization on Mars, and did it leave evidence of its existence behind for humans to find eons later? Did these advanced extraterrestrial visitors vanish in a solar system wide cataclysm of their own making, only to make their way to Earth and start anew? Was Mars once as lush and green as the Earth, and teeming with life? Chapters include: War of the Worlds; The Mars Tidal Model; The Death of Mars; Cydonia and the Face on Mars; The Monuments of Mars; The Search for Life on Mars; The True Colors of Mars and The Pathfinder Sphinx; more. Color section.
252 Pages. 6x9 Paperback. Illustrated. $19.95. Code: AMAR

ANCIENT ALIENS ON MARS II
By Mike Bara
Using data acquired from sophisticated new scientific instruments like the Mars Odyssey THEMIS infrared imager, Bara shows that the region of Cydonia overlays a vast underground city full of enormous structures and devices that may still be operating. He peels back the layers of mystery to show images of tunnel systems, temples and ruins, and exposes the sophisticated NASA conspiracy designed to hide them. Bara also tackles the enigma of Mars' hollowed out moon Phobos, and exposes evidence that it is artificial. Long-held myths about Mars, including claims that it is protected by a sophisticated UFO defense system, are examined. Data from the Mars rovers Spirit, Opportunity and Curiosity are examined; everything from fossilized plants to mechanical debris is exposed in images taken directly from NASA's own archives.
294 Pages. 6x9 Paperback. Illustrated. $19.95. Code: AAM2

ANCIENT TECHNOLOGY IN PERU & BOLIVIA
By David Hatcher Childress
Childress speculates on the existence of a sunken city in Lake Titicaca and reveals new evidence that the Sumerians may have arrived in South America 4,000 years ago. He demonstrates that the use of "keystone cuts" with metal clamps poured into them to secure megalithic construction was an advanced technology used all over the world, from the Andes to Egypt, Greece and Southeast Asia. He maintains that only power tools could have made the intricate articulation and drill holes found in extremely hard granite and basalt blocks in Bolivia and Peru, and that the megalith builders had to have had advanced methods for moving and stacking gigantic blocks of stone, some weighing over 100 tons.
340 Pages. 6x9 Paperback. Illustrated.. $19.95 Code: ATP

PIRATES & THE LOST TEMPLAR FLEET
The Secret Naval War Between the Templars & the Vatican
by David Hatcher Childress

Childress takes us into the fascinating world of maverick sea captains who were Knights Templar (and later Scottish Rite Free Masons) who battled the ships that sailed for the Pope. The lost Templar fleet was originally based at La Rochelle in southern France, but fled to the deep fiords of Scotland upon the dissolution of the Order by King Phillip. This banned fleet of ships was later commanded by the St. Clair family of Rosslyn Chapel (birthplace of Free Masonry). St. Clair and his Templars made a voyage to Canada in the year 1298 AD, nearly 100 years before Columbus! Later, this fleet of ships and new ones to come, flew the Skull and Crossbones, the symbol of the Knights Templar.

320 PAGES. 6x9 PAPERBACK. ILLUSTRATED. BIBLIOGRAPHY. $16.95. CODE: PLTF

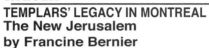

TEMPLARS' LEGACY IN MONTREAL
The New Jerusalem
by Francine Bernier

The book reveals the links between Montreal and: John the Baptist as patron saint; Melchizedek, the first king-priest and a father figure to the Templars and the Essenes; Stella Maris, the Star of the Sea from Mount Carmel; the Phrygian goddess Cybele as the androgynous Mother of the Church; St. Blaise, the Armenian healer or "Therapeut"- the patron saint of the stonemasons and a major figure to the Benedictine Order and the Templars; the presence of two Black Virgins; an intriguing family coat of arms with twelve blue apples; and more.

352 PAGES. 6x9 PAPERBACK. ILLUSTRATED. BIBLIOGRAPHY. $21.95. CODE: TLIM

THE HISTORY OF THE KNIGHTS TEMPLARS
by Charles G. Addison, introduction by David Hatcher Childress

Chapters on the origin of the Templars, their popularity in Europe and their rivalry with the Knights of St. John, later to be known as the Knights of Malta. Detailed information on the activities of the Templars in the Holy Land, and the 1312 AD suppression of the Templars in France and other countries, which culminated in the execution of Jacques de Molay and the continuation of the Knights Templars in England and Scotland; the formation of the society of Knights Templars in London; and the rebuilding of the Temple in 1816. Plus a lengthy intro about the lost Templar fleet and its North American sea routes.

395 PAGES. 6x9 PAPERBACK. ILLUSTRATED. $16.95. CODE: HKT

OTTO RAHN AND THE QUEST FOR THE HOLY GRAIL
The Amazing Life of the Real "Indiana Jones"
by Nigel Graddon

Otto Rahn led a life of incredible adventure in southern France in the early 1930s. The Hessian language scholar is said to have found runic Grail tablets in the Pyrenean grottoes, and decoded hidden messages within the medieval Grail masterwork *Parsifal*. The fabulous artifacts identified by Rahn were believed by Himmler to include the Grail Cup, the Spear of Destiny, the Tablets of Moses, the Ark of the Covenant, the Sword and Harp of David, the Sacred Candelabra and the Golden Urn of Manna. Some believe that Rahn was a Nazi guru who wielded immense influence on his elders and "betters" within the Hitler regime, persuading them that the Grail was the Sacred Book of the Aryans, which, once obtained, would justify their extreme political theories and revivify the ancient Germanic myths. But things are never as they seem, and as new facts emerge about Otto Rahn a far more extraordinary story unfolds.

450 pages. 6x9 Paperback. Illustrated. Appendix. Index. $18.95. Code: ORQG

THE MYSTERY OF THE OLMECS
by David Hatcher Childress

The Olmecs were not acknowledged to have existed as a civilization until an international archeological meeting in Mexico City in 1942. Now, the Olmecs are slowly being recognized as the Mother Culture of Mesoamerica, having invented writing, the ball game and the "Mayan" Calendar. But who were the Olmecs? Where did they come from? What happened to them? How sophisticated was their culture? Why are many Olmec statues and figurines seemingly of foreign peoples such as Africans, Europeans and Chinese? Is there a link with Atlantis? In this heavily illustrated book, join Childress in search of the lost cities of the Olmecs! Chapters include: The Mystery of Quizuo; The Mystery of Transoceanic Trade; The Mystery of Cranial Deformation; more.

296 PAGES. 6x9 PAPERBACK. ILLUSTRATED. BIBLIOGRAPHY. COLOR SECTION. $20.00. CODE: MOLM

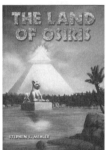

THE LAND OF OSIRIS
An Introduction to Khemitology
by Stephen S. Mehler

Was there an advanced prehistoric civilization in ancient Egypt who built the great pyramids and carved the Great Sphinx? Did the pyramids serve as energy devices and not as tombs for kings? Mehler has uncovered an indigenous oral tradition that still exists in Egypt, and has been fortunate to have studied with a living master of this tradition, Abd'El Hakim Awyan. Mehler has also been given permission to present these teachings to the Western world, teachings that unfold a whole new understanding of ancient Egypt . Chapters include: Egyptology and Its Paradigms; Asgat Nefer—The Harmony of Water; Khemit and the Myth of Atlantis; The Extraterrestrial Question; more.

272 PAGES. 6x9 PAPERBACK. ILLUSTRATED. COLOR SECTION. BIBLIOGRAPHY. $18.00 CODE: LOOS

ABOMINABLE SNOWMEN:
LEGEND COME TO LIFE
The Story of Sub-Humans on Six Continents from the Early Ice Age Until Today
by Ivan T. Sanderson

Do "Abominable Snowmen" exist? Prepare yourself for a shock. In the opinion of one of the world's leading naturalists, not one, but possibly four kinds, still walk the earth! Do they really live on the fringes of the towering Himalayas and the edge of myth-haunted Tibet? From how many areas in the world have factual reports of wild, strange, hairy men emanated? Reports of strange apemen have come in from every continent, except Antarctica.

525 PAGES. 6x9 PAPERBACK. ILLUSTRATED. BIBLIOGRAPHY. INDEX. $16.95. CODE: ABML

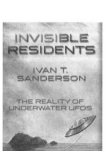

INVISIBLE RESIDENTS
The Reality of Underwater UFOS
by Ivan T. Sanderson

In this book, Sanderson, a renowned zoologist with a keen interest in the paranormal, puts forward the curious theory that "OINTS"—Other Intelligences—live under the Earth's oceans. This underwater, parallel, civilization may be twice as old as Homo sapiens, he proposes, and may have "developed what we call space flight." Sanderson postulates that the OINTS are behind many UFO sightings as well as the mysterious disappearances of aircraft and ships in the Bermuda Triangle. What better place to have an impenetrable base than deep within the oceans of the planet? Sanderson offers here an exhaustive study of USOs (Unidentified Submarine Objects) observed in nearly every part of the world.

298 PAGES. 6x9 PAPERBACK. ILLUSTRATED. BIBLIOGRAPHY. INDEX. $16.95. CODE: INVS

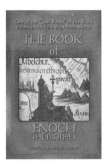

THE BOOK OF ENOCH
translated by Richard Laurence
This is a reprint of the Apocryphal *Book of Enoch the Prophet* which was first discovered in Abyssinia in the year 1773 by a Scottish explorer named James Bruce. One of the main influences from the book is its explanation of evil coming into the world with the arrival of the "fallen angels." Enoch acts as a scribe, writing up a petition on behalf of these fallen angels, or fallen ones, to be given to a higher power for ultimate judgment. Christianity adopted some ideas from Enoch, including the Final Judgment, the concept of demons, the origins of evil and the fallen angels, and the coming of a Messiah and ultimately, a Messianic kingdom.
224 PAGES. 6x9 PAPERBACK. ILLUSTRATED. INDEX. $16.95. CODE: BOE

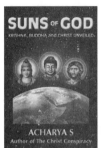

SUNS OF GOD
Krishna, Buddha and Christ Unveiled
by Acharya S
Over the past several centuries, the Big Three spiritual leaders have been the Lords Christ, Krishna and Buddha, whose stories and teachings are so remarkably similar as to confound and amaze those who encounter them. As classically educated archaeologist, historian, mythologist and linguist Acharya S thoroughly reveals, these striking parallels exist not because these godmen were "historical" personages who "walked the earth" but because they are personifications of the central focus of the famous and scandalous "mysteries." These mysteries date back thousands of years and are found globally, reflecting an ancient tradition steeped in awe and intrigue.
428 PAGES. 6x9 PAPERBACK. ILLUSTRATED. BIBLIOGRAPHY. INDEX. $18.95. CODE: SUNG

EDEN IN EGYPT
by Ralph Ellis
The story of Adam and Eve from the Book of Genesis is perhaps one of the best-known stories in circulation, even today, and yet nobody really knows where this tale came from or what it means. But even a cursory glance at the text will demonstrate the origins of this tale, for the river of Eden is described as having four branches. There is only one river in this part of the world that fits this description, and that is the Nile, with the four branches forming the Nile Delta. According to Ellis, Judaism was based upon the reign of the pharaoh Akhenaton, because the solitary Judaic god was known as Adhon while this pharaoh's solitary god was called Aton or Adjon. But what of the identities of Adam and Eve? Includes 16 page color section.
320 PAGES. 6x9 PAPERBACK. ILLUSTRATED. BIBLIOGRAPHY. INDEX. $20.00. CODE: EIE

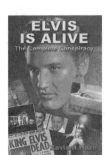

ELVIS IS ALIVE
The Complete Conspiracy
By Xaviant Haze
Haze blows the Elvis conspiracies vault wide open with the first book dedicated to the mysteries surrounding the King of Rock n' Roll. His was a tale of screaming fans, untold riches and a spectacular free fall into obliteration. It was also a tale of UFO encounters, zany fake funerals, studies in metaphysics, numerology, occult theology—and a strange connection with Michael Jackson. An infamous pill addiction led the King to an early "death" and in the aftermath a pop culture phenomenon was born, enabling Elvis to sustain a famous afterlife thanks to over three decades of conspiracy theories. Includes the complete comic strip "Elvis Presley: His Story in Pictures." Contents include: Pills and Cheeseburgers; Elvis Dies!; Elvis Lives!; Elvis versus the Mafia; Elvis the Esoteric; The Michael Jackson Connection; Long Live the King; more. Eight-page color section.
204 Pages. 6x9 Paperback. Illustrated. $19.95 Code: ELVA

ORDER FORM

10% Discount When You Order 3 or More Items!

One Adventure Place
P.O. Box 74
Kempton, Illinois 60946
United States of America
Tel.: 815-253-6390 • Fax: 815-253-6300
Email: auphq@frontiernet.net
http://www.adventuresunlimitedpress.com

ORDERING INSTRUCTIONS

✓ Remit by USD$ Check, Money Order or Credit Card

✓ Visa, Master Card, Discover & AmEx Accepted

✓ Paypal Payments Can Be Made To:

　info@wexclub.com

✓ Prices May Change Without Notice

✓ 10% Discount for 3 or More Items

SHIPPING CHARGES

United States

✓ Postal Book Rate { $4.50 First Item
50¢ Each Additional Item

✓ POSTAL BOOK RATE Cannot Be Tracked!
Not responsible for non-delivery.

✓ Priority Mail { $6.00 First Item
$2.00 Each Additional Item

✓ UPS { $7.00 First Item
$1.50 Each Additional Item

NOTE: UPS Delivery Available to Mainland USA Only

Canada

✓ Postal Air Mail { $15.00 First Item
$3.00 Each Additional Item

✓ Personal Checks or Bank Drafts MUST BE
US$ and Drawn on a US Bank

✓ Canadian Postal Money Orders OK

✓ Payment MUST BE US$

All Other Countries

✓ Sorry, No Surface Delivery!

✓ Postal Air Mail { $19.00 First Item
$7.00 Each Additional Item

✓ Checks and Money Orders MUST BE US$
and Drawn on a US Bank or branch.

✓ Paypal Payments Can Be Made in US$ To:
info@wexclub.com

SPECIAL NOTES

✓ RETAILERS: Standard Discounts Available

✓ BACKORDERS: We Backorder all Out-of-
Stock Items Unless Otherwise Requested

✓ PRO FORMA INVOICES: Available on Request

✓ DVD Return Policy: Replace defective DVDs only

ORDER ONLINE AT: www.adventuresunlimitedpress.com

**10% Discount When You Order
3 or More Items!**

Please check: ☑

☐ This is my first order　　☐ I have ordered before

Name	
Address	
City	
State/Province	Postal Code
Country	
Phone: Day	Evening
Fax	Email

Item Code	Item Description	Qty	Total

Please check: ☑

☐ Postal-Surface

☐ Postal-Air Mail
(Priority in USA)

☐ UPS
(Mainland USA only)

☐ Visa/MasterCard/Discover/American Express

Subtotal ▶	
Less Discount-10% for 3 or more items ▶	
Balance ▶	
Illinois Residents 6.25% Sales Tax ▶	
Previous Credit ▶	
Shipping ▶	
Total (check/MO in USD$ only) ▶	

Card Number:

Expiration Date:　　　　　　　　Security Code:

✓ SEND A CATALOG TO A FRIEND: